D1566897

MARVELS, MONSTERS, AND MIRACLES

Marvels, Monsters, and Miracles

Studies in the Medieval and Early Modern Imaginations

Edited by

Timothy S. Jones

and

David A. Sprunger

2002
Studies in Medieval Culture XLII
Medieval Institute Publications

WESTERN MICHIGAN UNIVERSITY

Kalamazoo, Michigan, USA 49008-5432

© 2002 by the Board of the Medieval Institute
Kalamazoo, Michigan, USA 49008-5432

Library of Congress Cataloging-in-Publication Data

Cataloging-in-Publication data applied for. Cataloging data for this publication can be retrieved at the Library of Congress web site: <http://lcweb.loc.gov/z3950/gateway.html>

Cover design by Linda K. Judy

Printed in the United States of America

For
John Block Friedman

"… a man of gret auctorite"

CONTENTS

ACKNOWLEDGMENTS

THE EDITORS EXTEND SPECIAL THANKS to all the contributors for their patience, perseverance, and enthusiasm for the monstrous and marvelous.

We are also grateful to the libraries and museums who have allowed us to reproduce items from their collections: Bibliothèque Nationale de France, Paris; Bodleian Library, Oxford; British Library, London; Catherijnconventmuseum, Utrecht; Hermitage Museum, St. Petersburg; Houghton Library of Harvard University, Cambridge, Mass.; Österreichische Nationalbibliothek, Vienna; Patrimonio Nacional, Madrid; Pierpont Morgan Library, New York; Society of Antiquaries, London; Universitäts- and Landesbibliothek, Bonn; Rare Book and Special Collections Library, University of Illinois at Urbana-Champaign; and Württembergische Landesbibliothek, Stuttgart.

The editors would like to thank Nona Flores, who helped to organize sessions in honor of John Block Friedman at the 1996 International Congress on Medieval Studies in Kalamazoo, Michigan; Paul Szarmach, director of the Medieval Institute at Western Michigan University; Hayley Humpal, Amy Olson, and Stephanie Johnson, who helped to prepare the manuscript; Art Olson, Michael Mullin, Mark Van Wienen, and Jeffrey Miller, members of the Augustana College faculty who were willing to talk about monsters and marvels; and our families, who have supported us patiently throughout this project.

INTRODUCTION:
THE MARVELOUS IMAGINATION

MARVELS ARREST OUR ATTENTION. Read through the *Anglo-Saxon Chronicle* and the marvels stand out: in this year there was a great mortality of birds (671); in this year the moon appeared covered with blood (734); in this year dragons were seen in the sky (793).[1] Historians might be just as thrilled to see some more commonplace information recorded: in September of this year Wulfnoth of Newton took three cows to Newmarket and sold them. But in general, people are more attracted to the striking and anomalous. The History Book Club offers dozens of titles on the Holocaust, few—if any—on changing crop distribution on the Great Plains in the nineteenth century. The latter is mundane, while the former shakes us by the collar and demands that we confront its monstrosity. But when changing agricultural practices allow the Red River of the North to overflow its banks and inundate the valley, then the network anchors arrive and raise questions about the everyday business of flood plain drainage and levee construction. The mundane becomes monstrous.

This collection of essays examines the perceptions of the marvelous and monstrous by the people of medieval and early modern Europe. The essays investigate the nature of those phenomena which people of

---

[1] All three events are recorded in the Peterborough manuscript of the *Chronicle* (Oxford, Bodleian Library MS Laud 636). The first two also occur in the Winchester manuscript (Cambridge, Corpus Christi College MS 173) and the latter two in the Worcester manuscript (British Library MS Cotton Tiberius B.iv). The marvelous sights of 793 are implicitly interpreted as portents of the Viking raids on Lindisfarne.

these periods experienced as marvels. They explore how these people interpreted their experience of astonishment and how they re-created it for others. They trace the development of representations of marvels and explicate individual incarnations of monsters and miracles. They analyze the importance of marvelous difference in defining ethnic, racial, religious, class, and gender identities. Finally, these essays ask what legacy the medieval confrontations with marvels have left for the modern world and how the modern fascination with medieval marvels has defined the difference between the two periods.

When creating a substantive like "the marvelous," one is in danger of promoting the illusion of a unified set of phenomena that are recognized universally. The very nature of marvels, however, insists on their subjectivity: they are defined by the experience of their viewer. To *marvel*, from the Latin *mirari* via French, or to *wonder*, from the Germanic *wundar*, is to be filled with awe, surprise, admiration, or astonishment. Clearly the phenomena that will stimulate such responses will vary from age to age, region to region, and person to person. Just as a modern invention such as the telephone, which seems mundane to us, would have astonished medieval people, so the stimuli of wonder varied chronologically and geographically within medieval Europe. Consider Gregory the Great's famous encounter with the Angle slaves recorded in Bede's *Ecclesiastical History*. Observing slave boys from Britain in the Roman marketplace and commenting on their beautiful appearance, Gregory complained when told of their paganism: "Alas, it is a piteous case, that the author of darkness possesseth such bright beautied people and that men of such a gracious outward shew do bear a mind void of inward grace."[2] Would a Celt, Frank, or Saxon used to fair hair and skin have responded with the same surprise as the Roman pontiff?

---

[2] Bede, *Historia Ecclesiastica Gentis Anglorum*, II.1; trans. J. E. King, *Opera Historica*, 2 vols. (London: Heinemann, 1930), 1:200 (Latin), 201 (English): "'Heu, proh dolor!' inquit, 'quod tam lucidi vultus homines tenebrarum auctor possidet, tantaque gratia frontispicii mentem ab interna gratia vacuam gestat!'"

Marvels unsettle established certainties. The seemingly angelic pagans upset Gregory's sense of divine order and the necessary connection among language, appearance, and nature that undergirded medieval theories of etymology and physiognomy. Indeed, much of the scholarship and criticism on the marvelous has focused on its ability to disturb. Mikhail Bakhtin, in his influential analysis of the carnivalesque in Rabelais, reads the grotesque, monstrous body as a challenge to both the aesthetics of classical form and the politics of institutional oppression.[3] The same claim is extended to the marvels of Renaissance epic by Douglas Biouw, who contends that they "symbolically define the normative boundaries of a cultural system, either by being excluded from that system or by existing on, or just within, its margins."[4] Thus the marvelous is "symbolically impure," as Mary Douglas observes, "the by-product of a systematic ordering and classification of matter, in so far as ordering involves rejecting inappropriate elements."[5] Indeed, as an experience of difference, marvels and the experience of wonder are at the root of many attempts to order and classify Nature and human experience.[6]

It is perhaps no surprise then that when we try to generalize about the meaning of marvels and the uses of wonder we are confronted with multiplicity. The meaning and value of marvels long have perplexed readers: can they be read in earnest, or only appreciated as play? Aristotle chose to comment on the latter when he observed, "That which excites wonder and surprise is pleasant to people, as may be seen from the fact that everyone, when relating [such incidents] makes

---

[3] Mikhail Bakhtin, *Rabelais and His World*, trans. Hélène Iswolsky (Bloomington: Indiana University Press, 1984).

[4] Douglas Biouw, *Mirabile Dictu: Representations of the Marvelous in Medieval and Renaissance Epic* (Ann Arbor: University of Michigan Press, 1996), 6.

[5] Mary Douglas, *Purity and Danger: An Analysis of the Concepts of Pollution and Taboo* (New York: Praeger, 1966), 35. Cited in Biouw, *Mirabile Dictu*, 6.

[6] See, for instance, Lorraine Daston and Katherine Park, *Wonders and the Order of Nature 1150–1750* (New York: Zone Books, 1998).

additions because he thinks they are pleasing."[7] Likewise, the grotesque illuminations in manuscript margins may be merely playful. But *merely* suggests that they have no other meaning, whereas even playful, pleasurable figures represent ideas, individually or commonly held, about order and difference and, hence, the creator's definition of self and Other. And as observers who co-create the experience of wonder, we readers also uncover our constructions of ourselves. Thus the essays here represent a variety of approaches to reading the marvelous. Some attempt to read in the light of medieval thought, while others apply modern and postmodern paradigms. Some examine specific marvelous phenomena in particular cultural or textual contexts, while others construct broader histories or theories of marvels. Some investigate the seriousness and others the playfulness of marvels, miracles, and monsters.

One of the most useful critical tools for discussing the nature of difference that is central to the experience of the marvelous is the idea of the Other, which offers both psychological and political means of analyzing the experience of wonder. On the psychological level, every self defines itself by engaging an Other, some one or thing that is both attractive and repulsive, similar and different. On a larger scale, whole social groups define themselves through the same dialectical process. Asia, Africa, and the Americas all serve as Others for Europe: Jews, Muslims, Viking "heathen," and various heretics all serve as Others for Christendom.[8] Over the past quarter century, this concept of the Other has become one of the most commonly used tools for analyzing

---

[7] Aristotle, *The Poetics of Aristotle*, trans. Preston H. Epps (Chapel Hill: University of North Carolina Press, 1942), 53.

[8] For a survey of both geographical points of encounter and the European attitudes that informed those encounters see Seymour Phillips, "The Outer World of the European Middle Ages," in *Implicit Understandings: Observing, Reporting, and Reflecting on the Encounters Between European and Other Peoples in the Early Modern Era*, ed. Stuart B. Schwartz (Cambridge: Cambridge University Press, 1994).

experiences with foreign phenomena.

The investigation of the interaction between European colonial power and Asian, African, and American peoples has produced a volume of historical, political, critical, and theoretical writing that employs the concept of Otherness as an interpretive tool. Perhaps most influentially, Edward Said has described the particular European fixation with Asia as "orientalism," a simultaneous attraction and revulsion that facilitates a politics of imperialism.[9] But while this is an attractive model for categorizing European representations of encounters with other peoples, Paul Freedman points out that the colonial power dynamic that defines this relationship was absent during the Middle Ages. Without the technologies that in later centuries would facilitate both confidence and domination, medieval encounters with foreign cultures necessarily took on a different character. The character of these encounters is the subject of the first five essays in this collection.

In the opening essay, Paul Freedman begins his investigation of the utility of the concept of Otherness for the study of medieval culture by noting two poles of medieval thought regarding monstrous races. First, these mysterious and distant peoples could be taken as a sign of the universality of the Christian gospel: though perhaps lacking the outward appearance of humanity, they were capable of belief, salvation, and incorporation into the body of Christ. This is the position put forward by Augustine of Hippo and one that Greta Austin finds in the organization of the Anglo-Saxon *Wonders of the East*. Alternately, monsters and monstrous races were read as indications of divine anger. This reading has its roots in the etymology of *monster*: monsters were admonishments, prodigies that might be read as predictions of the future. The modern version of this interpretation may be found in Andrea Rossi-Reder's reading of the abjection of the marvels of the East as indicators of a proto-colonialist discourse. Now, however, the monsters do not warn of divine disfavor with the monsters themselves

---

[9] Edward Said, *Orientalism* (New York: Random House, 1978).

but, rather, point a finger of admonishment at European ethnocentrism, racism, and imperialism.

The two approaches to monstrous races embody the very dichotomy that defines the concept of the Other: human and sub-human, civilized and savage, blessed and cursed, curiosity and fear. In many ways the monstrous races seem to anticipate the features of orientalism as described by Said, but Freedman notes that the medieval version lacked the component of power that dictated modern European attitudes. Moreover, by comparing the characterization of various marginal groups during the Middle Ages—especially the very real Jews, heretics, lepers, and Saracens—with the imagined monstrous races, Freedman becomes skeptical of the utility of the concept of the Other because of its inability to handle either different degrees of marginalization or chronological and geographical difference within the European Middle Ages.

Freedman's observation that recent scholarship has turned toward recovering the grotesque, irrational, and intolerant Middle Ages, as opposed to the foundational and modern version sought by scholars earlier in this century, describes much of the work in this volume.[10] It is notably true of Rossi-Reder's article, which analyzes classical and medieval descriptions of India in the light of postcolonialist theory. Rossi-Reder argues that the differences embodied by many of the marvelous peoples in Ktesias' *Indika* and the Anglo-Saxon *Wonders of the East* are characterized by abjection and hybridization, two principles of defining difference that Homi Bhabha has identified with colonialist discourse.[11] Because these medieval and classical texts conditioned the expectations of later explorers and colonists, Rossi-Reder concludes that they exacerbated European xenophobia and the

---

[10] See also Paul Freedman and Gabrielle Spiegel, "Medievalisms Old and New: The Rediscovery of Alterity in North American Medieval Studies," *American Historical Review* 103 (1998), 677–704.

[11] Homi K. Bhabha, *The Location of Culture* (London and New York: Routledge, 1994), 112.

imposition of subalternity on non-Western peoples.

Reading the same texts, however, Greta Austin and Joyce Tally Lionarons come to a quite different conclusion. Austin argues against translating the words *genus* and *kyn* in the *Wonders of the East* as *race* and thereby introducing modern connotations unknown to the medieval text. Instead, she observes that rather than distinguishing the marvelous peoples on the basis of physical appearance, the *Wonders of the East* attempts to create a scale of relative humanity based on ethical behavior and social organization. Rather than scientific categorization, the interest of the text, Austin claims, is soteriological—who is human and thus may receive Christian salvation?

Lionarons pursues the same problem by focusing on the tradition that St. Christopher was a *cynocephalus*, a creature with the body of a man and the head of a dog. Although Augustine had dictated that the marvelous races were human and could be saved, Lionarons argues that the *Wonders* and the *Letter of Alexander to Aristotle* emphasize the animal nature of the *cynocephali*. As a result, she claims that the story of Christopher never fully reconciles the differences but, instead, "opens for its readers the disturbing possibility that we too could fail to distinguish properly between categories, that we too could become monstrous."

The geography, as well as the inhabitants, of the East can be marvelous. In his essay, Martin Camargo examines the geography of *Mandeville's Travels* and finds that it serves a rhetorical function rather than the pragmatic one of modern cartography. In contrast to guidebooks for pilgrims, *Mandeville's Travels* does not provide a realistic and efficient route to Jerusalem. Rather, Mandeville follows a route akin to the rhetorical practice of *praeteritio* and emphasizes "the alienation of actual Christians from their true home." Likewise, as Mandeville moves away from Jerusalem, his erratic path leads to encounters with exotic Others who both flout and affirm Christian values, embodying the fragmentation of Christianity. Thus the entire work, Camargo contends, defines Christendom and challenges European readers to reconsider and recover their identity as Christians.

Working with the same issue of identity and geography on a different border, Kristen M. Figg studies Jean Froissart's representation of the travel experience in Scotland. Although Froissart was unable to apply many of the marvelous conventions of the Eastern traveler's tale to the account of his journey in the known world of Western Europe, Figg claims that he recognized the importance of wonder in the genre of travel writing and so applied the same sensibility to the different customs of class and ethnicity that he encountered, as well as to the talking animal conceit that he employed. By reading Froissart's *Le Debat dou Cheval et dou Levrier* against his account of the war between England and Scotland in the first book of his *Chroniques*, Figg shows how Froissart used the marvelous perspective of the dog and horse to surprise and delight by revealing the wonders of the familiar.

If the marvelous symbolizes what is left out, what about the miraculous? In his essay, "The Marvelous in the Medieval West," Jacques Le Goff contends that while the marvelous "played no essential role in Christian thought . . . the supernatural and the miraculous are central concepts of Christianity." However, while Le Goff asserts that miracle and marvel differ in "both nature and function," in fact, the difference lies not in the phenomena themselves but in the framework that the viewer employs to comprehend them.[12] Without changing in their nature, the marvelous Plinian races became miracles for St. Augustine, revealing the creative power of God over nature.[13] What changed was Augustine's interpretation of the marvels. Rather than products of disorder, they became products of a divine order. The same is true of miracles: by disturbing the perceived natural order they

---

[12] Jacques Le Goff, "The Marvelous in the Medieval West," in *The Medieval Imagination*, trans. Arthur Goldhammer (Chicago: University of Chicago Press, 1988), 28.

[13] See John Block Friedman, *The Monstrous Races in Medieval Art and Thought* (Cambridge, Mass.: Harvard University Press, 1981), 119–20; and Augustine, *The City of God*, 21.5–8, 22.8–10.

remind the believer of a transcendent order.[14]

In their essays, Thomas N. Hall and Michael W. Twomey both investigate medieval Christian traditions of representing and reading miracles. Hall traces the motif of the miraculous augmentation of various building materials in medieval religious literature. He locates the roots of this motif in a series of miracles credited to the boy Jesus in the *Infancy Gospel of Thomas* and follows its dissemination throughout Europe during the Middle Ages. He shows that this miracle proved to be remarkably flexible and was adapted to fit a variety of saints and situations. Hall concludes by noting the evidence that this motif provides for collusion between oral folklore and written tradition in creating the corpus of medieval hagiography and, thus, suggests how easily secular wonder and humor could become miraculous and be read as a sign of Christian doctrine.

On a related note, Michael W. Twomey investigates the use of two marvelous items in the Middle English poem *Cleanness*. Like medieval hagiography, *Cleanness* sets out to establish a Christian conception of a divine order operating in the world, in this case God's moral judgment operating in history. Twomey argues that the poet adopts the same principles of exegesis and elaboration used by Peter Comestor in his *Historia scholastica*, employing the examples of the antediluvian giants and the marvelous features of the Dead Sea. These curiosities introduced from Jewish legend and *Mandeville's Travels* use the transgressiveness inherent in the marvelous to amplify the poem's moral theme of the importance of purity.

Joyce Tally Lionarons notes that one lesson of the St. Christopher story is the realization "of how easy it would be, in the absence of

---

[14] For a discussion of the patristic understanding of miracles, particularly in the writing of Augustine and Gregory the Great, see William D. McCready, *Signs of Sanctity: Miracles in the Thought of Gregory the Great*, Studies and Texts 91 (Toronto: Pontifical Institute of Mediaeval Studies, 1989), esp. chaps. 1 and 8.

direct textual pointers to the contrary, to mistake the saint for the monster, the monster for the saint." Three essays in this volume investigate some of the "pointers" to monstrosity found in medieval texts and the problems of reading and representation that they raise. As Jeffrey Jerome Cohen recently has asserted, "the monster exists only to be read."[15] This is so, he argues, because the monster is "pure culture," always and only a projection of something else. Long before the advent of postmodern sensibilities, however, the earliest sense of the Latin word *monstrum* was 'portent,' and it was used to translate the Greek τέρας, from which derives *teratology*, the practice of interpreting portents or prodigies.[16] In the second century, Marcus Cornelius Fronto wrote that "*monstrum* is something against nature, as for example the Minotaur," distinguishing it from *ostentum*, a deviation from the customary, and *portentum* and *prodigum*, which are prophetic signs.[17] All, of course, demand attention and interpretation. For the Romans, anomalous births were termed *monstra* and commonly were read as warnings of divine anger. By the time of Isidore of Seville, the range of the term had extended to include races of abnormal beings, including giants and pygmies, yet the older sense continued to inform responses to monsters. In Christian hands, marvels came to signify the power of God and were read morally and allegorically in texts like the Bestiary as special revelations of spiritual truths.

The classical and Christian traditions, however, provide only one potential approach to reading monsters. What does one do with the

---

[15] Jeffrey Jerome Cohen, "Monster Culture (Seven Theses)," in his *Monster Theory: Reading Culture* (Minneapolis: University of Minnesota Press, 1996), 4. See also Lesley Kordecki, "Losing the Monster and Recovering the Non-Human in Fable(d) Subjectivity," in *Animals and the Symbolic in Medieval Art and Literature*, ed. L. A. J. R. Houwen, Mediaevalia Groningana 20 (Groningen: Egbert Forsten, 1997), 25–37.

[16] On the meaning of *monster* see Jean Céard, *La Nature et les prodiges*, Travaux d'Humanisme et Renaissance 158 (Geneva, 1977); and Friedman, *Monstrous Races*, 108–30.

[17] *De Differentiis Vocabulorum*, ed. Heinrich Keil, in *Grammatici Latini*, vol. 7 (Hildesheim, 1961), 520; trans. Friedman, *Monstrous Races*, 111.

monsters and marvels of the pagan peoples of Europe? A reading of the Old Testament may provide a context for understanding giants or even dragons, but what about *berserkir* or *draugar* of Old Norse culture? Demons, the medieval Christian would undoubtedly respond. But such an answer only replaces one embodied fear with another. As demons are the Other for the Christian, *berserkir*, *draugar*, giants, elves, and trolls are the Others for the various social, religious, and ethnic groups that made up medieval Europe. By reading the monster, we read the culture.[18]

The fight between the hero and the monster is a staple of medieval literature. But in the *Gesta Herewardi*, we are asked to accept as heroic a young man who picks fights, steals his long suffering father's property, and eventually is outlawed for his recreant behavior. In his essay, Timothy S. Jones shows how this twelfth-century English story of out-lawry adopts principles of structure and characterization from related Icelandic literature in order to comprehend narratively the actions of the outlawed hero. In particular, the *Gesta* employs monsters repre-sentative of irrational rage, absolute lawlessness, and transgressive sexuality as obstacles in a rite of passage that confirms the character of the hero.

Monstrous sexuality is the subject of Malcolm Jones's essay as well. The grotesque pair Bigorne and Chicheface embody an admoni-tion against inappropriate gender roles: the corpulent Bigorne feasts on docile husbands, while the gaunt Chicheface starves for want of obe-dient wives. By examining pictorial representations and reading texts that he edits here for the first time, Jones explicates the iconography of these misogynistic monsters and shows how they draw together features of other grotesque and carnivalesque creatures and popular satire on gendered behavior. Jones's evidence suggests that this

---

[18] For additional discussion and an explication of monsters as various elements of Otherness see Albrecht Classen, "Monsters, Devils, Giants, and Other Creatures: 'The Other' in Medieval Narratives and Epics, with Special Emphasis on Middle High German Literature," in *Canon and Canon Transgression in Medieval German Liter-ature*, ed. Classen (Göppingen: Kümmerle Verlag, 1993), 83–121.

iconography must have been familiar to English readers earlier than previously thought.

Insanity can be imagined as a monstrosity of the mind rather than the body, yet the medieval imagination invented a distinct set of visual techniques for representing madness. In his essay, David A. Sprunger catalogs these various strategies of representation in both literature and visual art, analyzes them with respect to medieval medical and religious thought, and employs them to explicate two illustrations from a thirteenth-century manuscript of the *Prose Lancelot*.

While the unfamiliarity of marvels provokes a desire to find meaning in them, to read them as *monstra*, they serve as well simply to engage the imagination of the reader. Certainly we know this from the last twenty years of Hollywood movies: special effects rather than plot, character, or theme create a blockbuster. Likewise, the non-ecclesiastical audience for the *Life* of St. Margaret probably would have delighted more in the details of the dragon's eyes, teeth, and breath than in its figuring of patristic commentary on the devil. Marvels are thus a salient example of story as integument, the outer covering of the seed of knowledge.

It is a short step from here to the metafictional use of the marvelous as a comment on the act of literary creation. In his essay, Paul Battles examines such figurative connections between the marvelous illusions of magic and those of literature in Chaucer's The Franklin's Tale. Combining a careful reading of the tale with attention to the practices of illusion and entertainment in medieval England, Battles reads the Clerk of Orléans as the Franklin's self representation. By inserting a likeness of himself into the story as a master illusionist, the Franklin, Battles contends, extends a dialog with the Squire that exposes the complexity of the Franklin's social ideals and aspirations.

Monsters inhabit the Middle Ages, and the Middle Ages are monstrous. This might be the assessment of the student who has read *Beowulf* and *Sir Gawain and the Green Knight* in a survey of English

Literature. It was also the assessment of European historians for three hundred years and, after a fifty-year hiatus, is becoming the fashionable position once again.[19] In 1981, Katherine Park and Lorraine Daston suggested that from the medieval to the modern age monsters followed a linear (and progressive) history from prodigies to wonders to naturalized objects.[20] More recently, however, they have replaced this model with "one of sensibilities that overlapped and recurred like waves."[21] More radically, Jeffrey Jerome Cohen has argued that "monstrosity challenges a coherent or totalizing concept of history"[22] and repudiates any form of diachronic organization for the essays in his book. The issue is complex and perplexing. As historians have expanded the questions and interests of history to include issues of gender, class, and ethnicity, to include the unorthodox, the marginalized, the hidden, and the silenced, they have found not one history but many. The narrative of the monstrous that Park and Daston proposed in 1981 is not wrong, merely incomplete. It approximates the change in attitudes in the minds of a set of Europeans who shared certain educational, religious, social, and economic experiences. The final two essays in this collection are concerned with that same set of people and with their interpretive and taxonomic practices.

---

[19] See Freedman and Spiegel, "Medievalisms"; John M. Ganim, "Medieval Literature as Monster: The Grotesque before and after Bakhtin," *Exemplaria* 7 (1995), 27–40; Stephen G. Nichols, "Modernism and the Politics of Medieval Studies," in *Medievalism and the Modernist Temper*, ed. R. Howard Bloch and Nichols (Baltimore: Johns Hopkins University Press, 1996); Lee Patterson, *Negotiating the Past: The Historical Understanding of Medieval Literature* (Madison: University of Wisconsin Press, 1987); and Lee Patterson, "Critical Historicism and Medieval Studies," in *Literary Practice and Social Change in Britain, 1380–1530*, ed. Patterson (Berkeley and Los Angeles: University of California Press, 1990).

[20] Katherine Park and Lorraine Daston, "Unnatural Conceptions: The Study of Monsters in Sixteenth- and Seventeenth-Century France and England," *Past and Present* 92 (1981), 20–54.

[21] Daston and Park, *Wonders and the Order of Nature*, 11, 176.

[22] Cohen, *Monster Theory*, x.

Norman R. Smith observes in his essay that the monsters of greatest interest during the sixteenth century were those close to home, prodigious events, rather than those reputed to live in distant lands. Following largely in the Roman tradition of reading signs and wonders, the early modern teratologists took a particular interest in the interpretation of monsters. By examining the catalogs and treatises of Jakob Mennel, Konradus Lykosthenes, and others, Smith demonstrates the range of interpretations applied to monsters, uncovers the religious and political uses of monsters, and reads the profusion of sixteenth-century monsters in light of the development of print and Marshall McLuhan's "hypertrophy of the unconscious."[23]

Confronting some of the same issues in reading a sixteenth-century costume book, Mary Baine Campbell discovers a depiction of a cyclops that is an amalgam of the medieval monstrous races and other traditional monsters. In the Otherness of this creature, which is both familiar in the individual elements of its body and different in its combination of those elements, Campbell sees also an early modern representation of the alterity of the medieval imagination. Reading this monster in the context of the costume book and its proto-anthropological classification of phenomena, Campbell concludes that the cyclops represents and defines that which is excluded from the new modern, scientific comprehension of nature. The costume book cyclops is ironically playful, and Campbell sees its creation as a moment when the medieval conception of the monstrous was "banished to the purely festive realm of the comic, of excess and transgression."

This, then, is the life of the modern monster. Monsters may continue to populate gothic novels, summer blockbusters, and science fiction, but they are gone from our geography and biology books. Among the descendants of medieval Christianity, miracles are still a prominent part of Pentecostalism, Evangelicalism, and elements of

---

[23] Marshall McLuhan, *The Gutenberg Galaxy* (Toronto: University of Toronto Press, 1962; New York: New American Library, 1969), 304.

Roman Catholicism, but they largely are ignored by the mainstream Protestant denominations and virtually nonexistent to the secular world. Marvels happen every day, but they are explicable in terms of modern science and technology: as editors of this volume, we have been able to send copies of these essays back and forth over hundreds of miles of prairie in fractions of a second. Even our fictional monsters are embodied psychoses, environmental disasters, political threats, and social anxieties. And yet we must continue to read these marvels: by engaging our sense of wonder and our curiosity, they urge us to look into them and see ourselves.

This collection of essays owes direct and indirect debts to John Block Friedman, whose *Monstrous Races in Medieval Art and Thought* surveyed this area and established an interdisciplinary model for investigating such materials. His work on medieval iconography, geographical and cosmological texts and manuscripts, travel literature, and religious and philosophical thought has influenced all of the essays collected here as well as a significant body of other medieval scholarship. Several of the present essays were read at the 1996 International Medieval Congress in sessions honoring Professor Friedman's retirement from the English Department at the University of Illinois. Five of the contributors are former students of Professor Friedman, and others have benefitted from his exhaustive knowledge of medieval literature and culture, his generosity, and both his advice and dissent. These essays are a tribute both to John Friedman and his scholarship.

THE MEDIEVAL OTHER:
THE MIDDLE AGES AS OTHER

PAUL FREEDMAN

Worlds of Difference

IN HIS ABSORBING AND PATH-BREAKING BOOK on the "monstrous races," John Block Friedman showed how lavish and exuberant were medieval ideas of geography and anthropology that peopled the world with so many forms of imagined humanity.[1] However fanciful or strange, the Apple-Smellers, *Blemmyae*, and Giants were usually regarded as human, not extraneous creatures of an animal or supernatural sort, but their very humanity posed certain problems in relation to Divine intentions. They demonstrated the variety of God's creation but were at the same time puzzling. The existence of peoples bordering on the non-human provoked questions about why they were created and whether or not they had souls, were rational, or might be converted to Christianity. Their ambiguous role within a Christian scheme of salvation and their relation to the ultimate purpose of the secular order differentiated the medieval monstrous races from their classical antecedents. It is not that medieval scholars were necessarily more

---

[1] John Block Friedman, *The Monstrous Races in Medieval Art and Thought* (Cambridge, Mass.: Harvard University Press, 1981).

1

elaborate or fanciful than their sources (such as Pliny or Solinus) but, rather, that discussion of distant peoples in the Middle Ages tended to go beyond exoticism to treat perceived moral implications of difference and likeness. The monstrous races were more than peripheral fancies of an imagined geography: they were disturbing because they required a non-naturalistic reason to explain their existence.

An optimistic rendering of the purpose of such creatures might consider them objects of divine solicitude, capable of receiving the Christian message. Indeed, some nations thought of as mysterious and distant by the medieval West (such as Armenia or Ethiopia) *had* become Christian. The legend of Prester John acknowledged the potential reach and universality of the faith in addition to serving as anti-Muslim wish-fulfillment.[2] That even stranger and more distant inhabitants of the earth were human, even rational—that they could be converted—was a message communicated by depictions of Pentecost and the mission of the apostles as in the Vézelay tympanum with its pygmies, its noseless, big-eared, and dog-headed peoples marked off from civilized space but, nonetheless, capable of embracing the Gospel.[3]

Opposed to this ecumenism was the depiction of the monstrous races as cursed, or at least descendants of cursed progenitors, notably Cain, whose notorious mark was interpreted as some deformity trans-mitted with subsequent variations to his progeny.[4] Here the higher pur-pose of the bizarre peoples of the earth was not to demonstrate a benign

---

[2] Friedman, *Monstrous Races*, 60, quoting the "Letter of Prester John," in which the putative ruler says that among the exemplary Christians of his realm are men with hoofed legs and claws and pygmies who ride horses no bigger than sheep. There is a substantial literature concerning the Prester John legend. See especially the recent article by Hilário Franco, "La construction d'une utopie: l'Empire de Prêtre Jean," *Journal of Medieval History* 23 (1997), 211–25.

[3] Friedman, *Monstrous Races*, 59–86, esp. 77–82. See also Ofelia Manzi, "Formes de reconocimiento y representación del otro. Un ejemplo medieval," *Estudios e investi-gaciones Instituto de Teoria e Historia del Arte Julio Payró* 5 (1994), 9–16.

[4] Friedman, *Monstrous Races*, 87–107.

universality but, rather, to provide a grim lesson in the consequences of sin and defiance of God visited upon succeeding generations.

In this tension between fully human (i.e., rational and either Christian or potentially Christian) and hapless savage (naked, ignorant, subsisting on raw food), the monstrous races exemplify the image of "the medieval other." They form a collection of literally marginalized peoples, inhabiting the most remote spaces of medieval maps. They are alternatively (or even simultaneously) human and sub-human; saved and cursed; rational and savage.

In a recent article in a volume on European encounters with other continents, Friedman outlines the utility of the concepts of "the Other" and marginalization for the study of medieval cartography.[5] He shows, with characteristic élan, how maps in the Middle Ages were active texts that expressed ideas of difference and similitude, not simply the products of antiquarian credulity. The strange peoples of the East most graphically exemplify the process of "orientalism" described by Edward Said and invoked in this article by Friedman: the act of pushing eastward so as to render a group negatively; exotic, curious, but in a sinister, inferior, even sub-human fashion.[6] Medieval maps marginalized a perceived cultural Other, placing the monstrous nations in inaccessible or at least remote space, cut off from Europe by the ocean, the torrid zones, walls (Gog and Magog), or simply by virtue of distance.

At the same time, the East was the site of Jerusalem, of the terrestrial paradise, of the kingdoms of the magi, the source of treasure, spices, wisdom, and enlightenment (*ex oriente lux*). The medieval Other differs from that of the modern period described by Said in that

---

[5] John Friedman, "Cultural Conflicts in Medieval World Maps," in *Implicit Understandings: Observing, Reporting, and Reflecting on the Encounters between Europeans and Other Peoples in the Early Modern Era*, ed. Stuart B. Schwartz (Cambridge: Cambridge University Press, 1994), 64–95.

[6] Edward Said, *Orientalism* (New York: Pantheon, 1978). See a group of articles on Edward Said, orientalism, and the Middle Ages in the journal *Medieval Encounters* 5 (1999).

neither the westward course of history, nor occidental technological superiority, nor a global empire were as yet conceived of, let alone confidently maintained. The East was alluring in accord with modern exoticism (the harem, hashish, languor, cruelty); more awe-inspiring and immediately threatening than in modern times, yet united cosmo-logically and eschatologically (despite its strangeness) with the rest of the world.[7] The Middle Ages certainly created a panoply of mistrusted and persecuted enemies—Saracens, Jews, lepers, heretics, apocalyptic peoples. But the very heterogeneity and proliferation of such despised peoples calls into question how "the Other" is to be used as a theo-rizing tool. Is it merely a general term for the marginal or outcast?[8] Or does it imply a more actively sinister process whereby a formerly tolerant (or at least not savagely intolerant) society became obsessed with pollution, danger, and subversion?

The medieval monstrous races certainly form a quintessential Other: they were distant and physically different, but above all they were a mental construct in a more obvious sense than Jews, Muslims, or other aliens. That there were traces of real far-off peoples (pygmies, brahmins) in the lore of the monstrous races hardly affects the fanciful nature of that material. Whole nations were invented and endowed with characteristics that placed them at the boundaries of the human. This process of constructing the Other was especially gratuitous because unlike Saracens, Jews, lepers, or any of those whom Western Christen-dom needed to classify according to their perceived difference, the

---

[7] The feared peoples of the East were both real and fantastic. Turks and Mongols were regarded as dangerous, but so too were the imagined hordes of Jews enclosed by mountains (combining the biblical Gog and Magog with legends of Alexander the Great), whose terrible release into civilization would presage the apocalypse. See Andrew Colin Gow, *The Red Jews: Antisemitism in an Apocalyptic Age, 1200–1600* (Leiden: E. J. Brill, 1995).

[8] See, for example, the recent collection *Other Middle Ages: Witnesses at the Margins of Medieval Society*, ed. Michael Goodich (Philadelphia: University of Pennsylvania Press, 1998).

monstrous races literally were invented rather than shaped to answer some pre-existing need for taxonomy itself.

Although they seem perfect examples of a single relentless process of "othering," even the monstrous races were depicted in a variety of ways not all unfavorable. They might be rational or irrational, capable of salvation or irremediably cursed, but most important, they oscillated in the Western imagination between Other and not-Other. In *Mandeville's Travels*, commonly regarded as an imaginative farrago of received and newly minted fancy, the Plinian races adhere scrupulously (and with comic literalism) to familiar biblical examples and prescriptions. Thus the inhabitants of Damoria are nude because Adam and Eve were created in this state. They eschew monogamy in order to obey God's instructions to increase, multiply, and fill the earth.[9] This is not to say that thereby such peoples became accepted or familiar, but that Mandeville, in a manner anticipating Montaigne, played with cultural relativism and the question of who is following acceptable human behavior and who is deviant.

Those dwelling within Europe, or at its immediate margins, who were regarded as alien constituted an even more imperfect or at least inconsistent Other in comparison to the monstrous races. Jews living in European cities, for example, could hardly be seen as unfamiliar in the same way as distant nations. To the extent that they *were* regarded as appropriate targets for persecution, however, they were victims of

---

[9] Christiane Deluz, "'Et y a en ces ylles moult le diverses gens': La vision de l'Autre dans le Livre Jehan de Mandeville," in *L'image de l'autre: Étrangers–Minoritaires–Marginaux*, vol. 1, ed. Hélène Ahrweiler (Paris: CISH, 1985), 194–202; and Benjamin Braude, "The Sons of Noah and the Constitution of Ethno-Geographical Identity in the Medieval and Early Modern Periods," *William and Mary Quarterly* 54 (1997), 103–42. Similarly, Odorico da Pordenone (whose voyage to the East lasted from 1318 to 1330) reported that the inhabitants of *Lamori* (northern Sumatra) mocked him for wearing clothes against God's will as, after all, he had created Adam naked (*Descriptio orientalium partium*, Liber XX, in *Cathay and the Way Thither, Being a Collection of Medieval Notices of China*, trans. and ed. Henry Yule, Hakluyt Society 37, vol. 2 [London, 1866], appendix 1, xvi–xvii).

a process of imaginative construction of the Other similar to that affecting the monstrous races, although a construction of considerably more tragic consequences.[10] They could be categorized as similar or as alien, as witnesses to a divine plan, as rational beings capable of teaching wisdom to Christians, as despised outsiders, as dangerous and unclean enemies, or as some combination of these. Malleable images and classifications that demonized Jews and at the same time regarded them as targets for rational persuasion or coercion accompanied the degradation of their status in High Medieval Europe. That the situation of the Jews deteriorated hardly can be questioned. What is worth exploring is whether or not this produced (or was produced by) a particular set of new negative images, or if a free-floating hostility affected in a similar fashion other outcasts such as lepers or heretics.[11]

Muslims also appear as a dangerous enemy, usually external to Europe rather than (as with the Jews) internal. *The Song of Roland* is a well-known example of the image of Islam as rich, teeming, and savage. At the same time, however, the "pagan" enemy in the poem at times imitates Christian standards of chivalry sufficiently to provoke the author to rhapsodize that certain Muslim warriors would have made marvelous knights were they only of the Christian faith.[12]

The process of becoming more familiar with the tenets of Islam promoted by Christian expansion in Spain and Outremer did not produce

---

[10] Among many works on the adverse changes in the image of Jews, a recent article of Robert Chazan's should be singled out: "The Deteriorating Image of the Jews—Twelfth and Thirteenth Centuries," in *Christendom and its Discontents: Exclusion, Persecution, and Rebellion, 1000–1500*, ed. Scott L. Waugh and Patrick D. Diehl (Cambridge: Cambridge University Press, 1996), 220–33.

[11] The thesis of R. I. Moore, *The Formation of a Persecuting Society: Power and Deviance in Western Europe, 950–1250* (Oxford: Basil Blackwell, 1987). This is not to argue that there was no crossover from images associated with the monstrous races or apocalyptic peoples to the Jews (for which see Gow, *The Red Jews*), but that a storehouse of negative typologies was not applied indiscriminately to all despised groups.

[12] *La Chanson de Roland*, ed. Cesare Segre, vol. 1 (Geneva: Droz, 1989), iii–iv, vv. 24–61, pp. 94–95; lxxii, vv. 894–899, p. 138.

greater toleration. In fact, it has been argued, quite the contrary resulted. Greater knowledge increased fear of Muslim strength and of the
resources and diversity of the infidel.[13] Here again, the image of the
Other is not related directly to unfamiliarity but is produced by fears
and desires read onto a mistrusted alien group.

The European concept of a world inhabited by hostile and semi-
human forces was the result of both success and anxiety. The High
Middle Ages was a time of an aggressive European expansion. Robert
Bartlett has underscored the mentality of conquest manifested by the
Norman expeditions, German settlement in the East, the colonization
of Ireland, and the Crusades.[14] This mentality reinforced a political and
economic demonstration of power and, in turn, encouraged a discourse
about the conquered populations that rendered them inferior, savage,
and deserving of subjugation. Bartlett and others refer to this as "racism,"
drawing parallels to modern justifications for overseas exploitation.[15]
The term *racism* also has been applied to the treatment of internal
lower-class groups who were not on the frontier or members of another
faith. Douglas Moffat refers to "racial disharmony" between Normans
and Anglo-Saxons in discussing the laments of fourteenth-century
chroniclers over the legacy of 1066.[16]

---

[13] R. W. Southern, *Western Views of Islam in the Middle Ages* (Cambridge: Cambridge
University Press, 1962); and Norman Daniel, *Islam and the West: The Making of an
Image* (Edinburgh: Edinburgh University Press, 1960), and *Islam, Europe and Empire*
(Edinburgh: Edinburgh University Press, 1966).

[14] Robert Bartlett, *The Making of Europe: Conquest, Colonization and Cultural Change,
950–1350* (Princeton: Princeton University Press, 1993), 85–105, 197–242.

[15] Richard C. Hoffmann, "Outsiders by Birth and Blood: Racist Ideologies and Realities
around the Periphery of Medieval European Culture," *Studies in Medieval and
Renaissance History*, n.s. 6 (1983), 3–34.

[16] Douglas Moffat, "Sin, Conquest, Servitude: English Self-Image in the Chronicles of
the Early Fourteenth Century," in *The Work of Work: Servitude, Slavery, and Labor
in Medieval England*, ed. Allen J. Frantzen and Douglas Moffat (Glasgow: Cruithne
Press, 1994), 146–68.

The most useful aspect of the concept of the Other is to emphasize the arbitrary way in which groups are defined as alien, independent from actual degrees of familiarity. "Othering" or marginalization is an active process but one that is related problematically to historical circumstances and the different images of minorities or despised communities. There is no doubt that the Middle Ages witnessed a growing intolerance, perceptible both in popular disturbances and officially sanctioned persecution. Why this seemingly obvious point is supposed to come as a surprise and its putative foundational significance are discussed further on in this essay. Historians offer two basic explanations for the increased climate of intolerance, one focusing on irrational fears and the second, in a more Foucauldian fashion, on rationalism and the growth of an official apparatus of taxonomy and control (especially in the Church). Norman Cohn's *Europe's Inner Demons* exemplifies the irrationalist theory, but more nuanced recent versions point to anxiety over social change or the perception of a wider more alien world rather than fanatical upheaval.[17] R. I. Moore has argued the rationalist or bureaucratic theory most effectively: that institutions such as the papal curia or the seigneurial regime carried with them a tendency to organize populations, define dogma, create a taxonomy of outsiders, and to suppress them.[18]

That a mood and means to enforce a more repressive order existed does not quite lead logically to the conclusion that outcasts were categorized uniformly as Other and so excluded in an interchangeable or undifferentiated manner. There are, it seems to me, three interrelated dangers in applying the concept of the Other to medieval studies. The

---

[17] Norman Cohn, *Europe's Inner Demons: An Enquiry Inspired by the Great Witch-Hunt* (New York: Basic Books, 1975). See also the introduction by Scott Waugh to *Christendom and its Discontents*, ed. Waugh and Diehl, 1–13, and, in the same volume, Chazan, "The Deteriorating Image of the Jews," 220–32.

[18] Moore, *Formation of a Persecuting Society*, and "Heresy, Repression, and Social Change in the Age of Gregorian Reform," in *Christendom and its Discontents*, ed. Waugh and Diehl, 19–42.

first is that of totalizing all unfavorable descriptions as if they fit into a single model of the alien, a tendency that has been described as "the fetishization of alterity."[19] Jews, Saracens, monstrous races, women, homosexuals, heretics, and peasants thus are placed in a single classification as outsiders, without regard for the differences among them both intrinsically and in their representation. This tendency reaches something of an extreme in Jeffrey Richards, *Sex, Dissidence and Damnation*, a book intended for both a scholarly and popular audience, in which medieval intolerance is a general phenomenon affecting heretics, witches, Jews, lepers, prostitutes, homosexuals, and others guilty of what was perceived as illicit sexual behavior.[20] These all are considered "minority groups" who suffered from the growth of orthodoxy and a persecutorial mentality.

It is true that signs of disparagement, the iconography of Otherness, could move from one despised group to another. Kinky or red hair, physical deformity, or odd clothes served in medieval art to mark various outcasts, including blacks, Jews, fools, and rustics.[21] Jews and lepers could be regarded as similarly cursed by pollution traceable to the effluvia of Judas' body.[22] But an indiscriminate identification of all forms of otherness as constituting a universal set of signs and assumptions tends to place these groups narrowly in terms of their relation to

---

[19] Nicholas Thomas, *Colonialism's Culture: Anthropology, Travel and Government* (Princeton: Princeton University Press, 1994), 159. Homi Bhabha criticizes Edward Said for "the fixation/fetishization of stereotypical knowledge as power"; see his "Difference, Discrimination and the Discourse of Colonialism," in *The Politics of Theory: Proceedings of the Essex Conference on the Sociology of Literature, July 1982*, ed. Francis Barker et al. (Colchester: Essex University Press, 1988), 198.

[20] Jeffrey Richards, *Sex, Dissidence and Damnation: Minority Groups in the Middle Ages* (London and New York: Routledge, 1991).

[21] Ruth Mellinkoff, *Outcasts: Signs of Otherness in Northern European Art of the Late Middle Ages*, 2 vols. (Berkeley and Los Angeles: University of California Press, 1993).

[22] David Nirenberg, *Communities of Violence: Persecution of Minorities in the Middle Ages* (Princeton: Princeton University Press, 1996), 62–63. For the modern era see also Sander Gilman, *The Jew's Body* (New York: Routledge, 1991).

the dominant forces in society, thus ironically reproducing the viewpoint of the dominant culture. This obscures not only the differences among marginal groups but also their interrelation apart from the governing classes. Muslims and Jews in Christian Spain thus tend to be lumped together, as both were subjugated by royal authority when, in fact, they were quite different and had a complex and often mutually suspicious interaction.[23]

A second problem is the tendency to treat *alien* or *Other* as if they were stable terms denoting complete and consistent rejection when in fact there were degrees of marginality, so much so, that seemingly contradictory positions could be held simultaneously. Peasants might be regarded as descendants of Ham, as unclean and boorish, and yet as close to God by reason of their oppression and humility.[24] Lepers were objects of charity whose prayers obtained God's mercy for sinful almsgivers, and yet they were punished justly for supposed sexual sins.[25]

Various attempts have been made to deal with the variety and degrees of "othering" discourses. One might posit a "proximate other" to describe those (such as women or peasants) who, despite a tradition of hostile depiction, obviously were necessary and central as opposed to the distant and economically or emotionally irrelevant strangers such as the monstrous races.[26] In a discussion of similarities between medieval marginalization of Jews and homosexuals, John Boswell identified three sorts of difference: *distinguishable insiders* (those who stand out

---

[23] Nirenberg's *Communities of Violence*, 166–99 (discussing the relations between Jews and Muslims in the Crown of Aragon), is a notable exception to this tendency.

[24] Paul Freedman, "Sainteté et sauvagerie: deux images du paysan au moyen âge," *Annales: E.-S.-C.* 47 (1992), 539–60, and, more extensively, in *Images of the Medieval Peasant* (Stanford: Stanford University Press, 1999).

[25] Moore, *Formation of a Persecuting Society*, 50–65; and Nirenberg, *Communities of Violence*, 52–63; 121–24.

[26] The term *proximate other* is used by Jonathan Dollimore, *Sexual Dissidence: Augustine to Wilde, Freud to Foucault* (Oxford: Clarendon Press, 1991), 135, cited in Kathleen Biddick, "Genders, Bodies, Borders: Technologies of the Visible," *Speculum* 68 (1993), 409, n. 43.

in an acceptable or even laudable fashion—heroes, for example); *inferior insiders* (tolerated but distinctly lowly, such as Jews before the thirteenth century or members of unclean professions); and *outsiders* (dangerous aliens).[27] Nilda Guglielmi has pointed to the difference between groups regarded as "marginal," who were at the edges of society but nevertheless formed part of it as useful or once-useful members, and those regarded as "aliens," who were excluded more completely. Examples of the first would include prostitutes and members of the urban underclass, while the monstrous races or Muslims would be considered more or less completely alien.[28]

These schemes allow for differences over time and among various groups but appear to mimic the desire for taxonomy that is supposed to mark the process of othering itself. If everyone is not consigned to the same degree of Otherness, then the process at work in representing difference is more complicated than the formation of a unified persecutorial mentality, a point to which we shall return.

Finally, a third difficulty with an oversimplified idea of the medieval Other is that elite society is presented as unanimously and unquestioningly determined to push a variety of feared or despised peoples to the margins of the human. One can point to cracks within the unity of the dominant classes. Particularly with regard to "proximate others," such as peasants or the urban poor, there was some recognition that they might be virtuous, in fact exemplary. Contempt and fear coincided with a current of opinion that extolled these large but outcast groups as closer to God's care than the comfortable classes.[29] The treatment of

---

[27] John Eastburne Boswell, "Jews, Bicycle Riders and Gay People: The Determination of Social Consensus and its Impact on Minorities," *Yale Journal of Law and the Humanities* 1 (1989), 209.

[28] Nilda Guglielmi, "Reflexiones sobre marginalidad," *Anuario de estudios medievales* 20 (1990), 317–48.

[29] Freedman, "Sainteté et sauvagerie"; and Michel Mollat, *The Poor in the Middle Ages: An Essay in Social History*, trans. Arthur Goldhammer (1978; New Haven: Yale University Press, 1986).

women's religious movements also exhibits a hesitation between repression and acceptance despite the asymmetrical power relations between the Church hierarchy and such movements.[30]

Such oscillation between likeness and difference, between humanity and alterity, might become an obsessive reiteration. Homi Bhabha describes the necessity experienced by the dominant colonial power for a continual and repetitive chain of various stereotypes in order to reinforce unstable, fragile concepts of difference.[31] Contesting Edward Said's hegemonic notion of Occidental conceptual power, Bhabha emphasizes the ambivalence of discourse concerning Otherness to the point of stressing a closeness, even unity, of colonizer and colonized in forming a "colonial subject."[32] In disputing this, Abdul R. JanMohamed frankly describes colonialist discourse, powered by an ideology of domination, as constructing a "Manichean allegory" whereby the native, the exotic, the Other, is clearly bad.[33] It is this Manichean view—that within the Western tradition the Other (or all groups constructed as Other) is despised in a virtually undifferentiated fashion—that I would like to question.

---

[30] Ann L. Clark, "Repression or Collaboration? The Case of Elisabeth and Ekbert of Schönau," in *Christendom and its Discontents*, 151–67; and E. Ann Matter, "Prophetic Patronage and Repression: Lucia Brocadelli da Narni and Ercole d'Este," in the same collection, 168–76.

[31] Bhabha, "Difference, Discrimination and the Discourse of Colonialism," 204–05. See also his articles "The Other Question—The Stereotype and Colonial Discourse," *Screen* 24 (Nov.–Dec. 1983), 18–36; "Of Mimicry and Man: The Ambivalence of Colonial Discourse," *October* 28 (1984), 317–25; and "Signs Taken for Wonders: Questions of Ambivalence and Authority under a Tree Outside Delhi, May 1817," *Critical Inquiry* 12 (Autumn, 1985), 144–65. These have been reprinted in Bhabha, *The Location of Culture* (London and New York: Routledge, 1994), 66–84, 85–92, and 102–22, respectively.

[32] Bhabha, "Difference, Discrimination." On Said, Bhabha, and orientalism see Robert Young, *White Mythologies: Writing History and the West* (London and New York: Routledge, 1990), 119–56.

[33] Abdul R. JanMohamed, "The Economy of Manichean Allegory: The Function of Racial Difference in Colonialist Literature," *Critical Inquiry* 12 (1985), 59–87.

The Progressive and the Persecutorial Middle Ages

Specific to the Middle Ages in any discussion of marginalization is the aura of irrationality that has accompanied the period for centuries. After all, in some sense it should not be astonishing that medieval people tended to be intolerant. Has this not been among the chief characteristics of the Middle Ages not only in popular culture but, rather consistently, for the Enlightenment, in a more alluring sense for Romanticism, and today as well? The historiography of medieval obscurantism goes back in this country to the studies of Henry Charles Lea and in the European literary imagination to the anti-scholastic denunciations of Petrarch and Erasmus.

Unlike such canonical periods of Western rationalism as the Renaissance or the nineteenth century, the Middle Ages usually has evoked images of irrationality, particularly a proclivity to religious fanaticism and persecution. Despite the best efforts of decades of medievalists to correct the impression of an age of darkness and ignorance, the Middle Ages has been marginalized within the academic disciplines and easily is regarded as an historiographic Other.[34]

The recent rediscovery of medieval intolerance and marginated groups does not destabilize a seemingly authoritative and foundational era in the history of progress in the manner of New Historicist investigations of the Elizabethan period. Rather, it indirectly revives the eighteenth- and nineteenth-century image of the Middle Ages as Gothic, strange, and grotesque.[35] Subjects such as voluntary starvation, the *droit de seigneur*, Pope Joan, grotesque and scatological art, medieval

---

[34] Lee Patterson, "On the Margin: Postmodernism, Ironic History and Medieval Studies," *Speculum* 65 (1990), 87–108.

[35] I have discussed this in "The Return of the Grotesque in Medieval Historiography," in *Historia a debate: Medieval*, ed. Carlos Barros (Santiago de Compostella: Historia a debate, 1995), 9–19. See also Paul Freedman and Gabrielle M. Spiegel, "Medievalisms Old and New: The Rediscovery of Alterity in North American Medieval Studies," *American Historical Review* 103 (1998), 677–704.

speculations about the body after death, and the persecutorial mentality of the Middle Ages revive an idea of the medieval that historians, especially in the United States and Britain, spent much of the twentieth century trying to combat.[36]

A considerable amount of medieval historiography until recently was predicated on the desire to demonstrate the modernity, rationality, and innovation of what was too easily dismissed as an age of picturesque backwardness. It was only a short time ago, after all, that medieval historians emphasized their period as the point of origin for prized attributes of modernity such as the rational and effective nation-state or the importance and significance of the individual. Qualities that, thanks to Burckhardt, had been claimed by the Italian Renaissance were put further back chronologically and moved to France. Charles Homer Haskins in 1927 described the medieval revival of classical learning and philosophical rationality as "the Renaissance of the twelfth century."[37] His student at Harvard, Joseph Strayer, devoted a long and influential career to demonstrating the constitutional realism and sophistication of the French and Norman state apparatus, summarized in a brief volume with the title *On the Medieval Origins of the Modern State*.[38]

Among the chief subjects of research during the 1970s was the medieval "discovery of the individual," which again located further in

---

[36] Some examples: Caroline W. Bynum, *Holy Feast and Holy Fast: The Religious Significance of Food to Medieval Women* (Berkeley and Los Angeles: University of California Press, 1987); Bynum, *The Resurrection of the Body in Western Christianity, 200–1336* (New York: Columbia University Press, 1995); Michael Camille, *Image on the Edge: The Margins of Medieval Art* (Cambridge, Mass.: Harvard University Press, 1992); Alain Boureau, *La Papesse Jean* (Paris: Aubier, 1988); and Boureau, *The Lord's First Night: The Myth of the Droit de Cuissage*, trans. Lydia G. Cochrane (Chicago: University of Chicago Press, 1998).

[37] Charles Homer Haskins, *The Renaissance of the Twelfth Century* (Cambridge, Mass.: Harvard University Press, 1927).

[38] Joseph Strayer, *On the Medieval Origins of the Modern State* (Princeton: Princeton University Press, 1970).

the past what had been considered an attribute of the Renaissance.[39] Individuality was a form of progress arising out of not only religious or philosophical speculation but also a sense of the world as ordered, a system that the mind was capable of analyzing logically, even scientifically.[40] As was the case for the state, the medievalization of individuality gave to the twelfth century in particular the status of a period of origin. This was not just a primitive origin or stumbling first steps but a foundational era in the history of Western modernity.

In the United States, with a relatively vivid memory of westward expansion (in both popular culture and historiography), the medieval frontier also has been regarded favorably as a locus of dynamism, experimentation, and cultural cross-fertilization. This is especially the case in studies of medieval Spain. James Powers, for example, writes of the "frontier creativity" of the Peninsula, while Charles Julian Bishko and Lawrence McCrank have compared Castilian and American frontier expansion and settlement.[41] In Iberian history an era of openness and

---

[39] Colin Morris, *The Discovery of the Individual: 1050–1200* (New York: Harper and Row, 1973); John F. Benton, "Consciousness of Self and Perceptions of Individuality," in *Renaissance and Renewal in the Twelfth Century*, ed. Robert L. Benson and Giles Constable (Cambridge, Mass.: Harvard University Press, 1982), 263–95; and Charles Radding, "Evolution of Medieval Mentalities: A Cognitive-Structural Approach," *American Historical Review* 84 (1979), 945–69.

[40] Lynn White, "Science and the Sense of Self," *Daedalus* 107 (Spring 1978), 47–59; and Charles Radding, "Superstition to Science: Nature, Fortune and the Medieval Ordeal," *American Historical Review* 83 (1978), 577–97.

[41] James F. Powers, "Frontier Competition and Legal Creativity: A Castilian-Aragonese Case Study Based on Twelfth-Century Municipal Military Law," *Speculum* 52 (1977), 465–76; Charles Julian Bishko, "The Castilian as Plainsman: The Medieval Ranching Frontier in La Mancha and Extremadura," in *The New World Looks at its History: Proceedings of the Second International Congress of Historians of the United States and Mexico*, ed. Archibald R. Lewis and Thomas F. McGann (Austin: University of Texas Press, 1963), 457–69; and Lawrence J. McCrank, "The Cistercians of Poblet as Medieval Frontiersmen: An Historiographic Essay and Case Study," in *Estudios en homenaje a Don Claudio Sánchez Albornoz en sus 90 años*, vol. 2 (Buenos Aires: Instituto de Historia de España, 1983), 313–60. See also the essay on the appeal of the frontier to American historians of the Middle Ages by Robert I. Burns, "The

cross-cultural borrowing has been contrasted with late medieval intolerance, with the effective closing of the frontier by means of the Christian triumph over Islam.[42]

If the medieval centuries were to be regarded as progressive, rational, and "modern" from the standpoint of origins, an excessive preoccupation with outcasts, intolerance, or strangeness had to be avoided. This gave a rather bland character to medieval history writing at mid-century and accounts for its tendency to put what now seems a surprisingly favorable construction on sinister or at least unlikable figures such as Philip the Fair or Saint Bernard of Clairvaux.[43]

If this modernizing, rational Middle Ages has ceased to be fashionable, its mental force is still implicit in the sense of shock that informs recent work on medieval intolerance. R. I. Moore's indictment of the medieval persecutorial mentality or Kathryn Gravdal's emphasis on the callous sexual violence of medieval literature react against attempts to minimize or normalize the violent and unedifying side of the Middle Ages.[44] Rather than the innovative and tolerant frontier of the Hispanists, we now have the violent expansion of Christian Europe, the origins of colonialism and racism.[45]

Innovations of the Middle Ages once seen as the point of departure for a favorably conceived modernity now are regarded as rather more

---

Significance of the Frontier in the Middle Ages," in *Medieval Frontier Societies*, ed. Robert Bartlett and Angus McKay (Oxford: Clarendon Press, 1989), 307–30.

[42] See below, note 55.

[43] E.g., Joseph Strayer, "Philip the Fair—a 'Constitutional' King," *American Historical Review* 62 (1956), 18–32. For a correction of attempts to see St. Bernard as an exemplar of medieval humanism see Glenn Olson, "Twelfth-Century Humanism Reconsidered: The Case of St. Bernard," *Studi Medievali*, 3a serie 31 (1990), 27–53.

[44] Moore, *Formation of a Persecuting Society*; and Kathryn Gravdal, *Ravishing Maidens: Writing Rape in Medieval French Literature and Law* (Philadelphia: University of Pennsylvania Press, 1991). On rape as a newly discovered literary theme see also Peter Meister, "A Little Acknowledged Theme in the Courtly Romance: Rape," and a reply by Lynn Dittman, *Quondam et Futurus* 1 (1991), 23–38.

[45] Bartlett, *The Making of Europe*.

ominous. The growth of law, administrative structures, and state and ecclesiastical power are now examples not of the progress of rationality but of repression: the desire to remake a heterogenous world into a conformist order excluding (and in many cases simply defining as excluded) perceived dissent or difference.[46] Changes in the direction of a more human-centered Christianity (the emphasis on Christ's sufferings, or dialectical theology, for example), once lauded as the beginning of a more optimistic notion of the relation between God and humanity, are seen now as encouraging the growth of anti-Semitic blood libel.[47] Even movements of female piety, usually thought of as creative and unrelated to a teleological modern, have been denounced for their eucharistic obsessions and, thus, as precursors of modern anti-Semitism.[48]

The emphasis on medieval aggression and persecution of marginated groups is similar to the desire to see the period as progressive in that both agree on regarding the Middle Ages as foundational, the point of origin for the modern and contemporary Western outlook. One opinion sees the Middle Ages as the origin of a "good" modern (reason, individuality, political and social institutions from the state to the university); the other the beginning of a "bad" modern (racism, romantic misogyny, colonialism). This is particularly the case when different sorts of marginal groups or of "othering" discourses are put together to form a global indictment of a generalized growth of oppression that affected all regarded as aliens or minorities.[49]

If the Middle Ages saw the beginnings of modern evils such as colonial expansion and the deployment of state power and popular

---

[46] Moore, *Formation of a Persecuting Society*.

[47] See, for example, Chazan, "The Deteriorating Image of the Jews," 224–28; and Gavin I. Langmuir, "The Tortures of the Body of Christ," in *Christendom and its Discontents*, ed. Waugh and Diehl, 287–309.

[48] Biddick, "Genders, Bodies, Borders," 401–12.

[49] Moore, *Formation of a Persecuting Society*; Richards, *Sex, Dissidence and Damnation*; and Boswell, "Jews, Bicycle Riders and Gay People," 205–28.

prejudice against despised internal minorities, the search for reasons and the chronological placement of the change become important. It is, of course, possible to see the Middle Ages as simply the era in which irrational intolerance, what Norman Cohn refers to as "Europe's inner demons," took shape without positing an earlier golden age. Cohn describes the way in which heretics, the Templars, and, particularly, witches were demonized in the thirteenth and, especially, fourteenth centuries. Antiquity and the early Middle Ages are not rendered as admirable, merely as less obsessively intolerant. The key change—the advent of a deep-seated belief in both popular and elite culture in a series of dark fantasies of perversion and conspiracy—takes place during the High Middle Ages.[50]

Other historians have started with the concern to demonstrate a progressive and open strain in medieval history that was obscured by the dogmatism, bureaucratization, or simply hardening of attitudes after a period of creativity. Friedrich Heer's *Mittelalter* (translated into English as *The Medieval World: Europe 1100–1350*) contrasted the open, flexible, creative twelfth century with the "closed" world of the thirteenth century and after.[51] An adverse change was brought about by the Crusades, the rise of the papacy, and consequent definition of orthodox versus heretical and mobilization of power to crush deviation. Without quite so clearly condemning the scholastic mentality or the other forms of thirteenth-century system building, the exaltation of the twelfth-century Renaissance and the discovery of the individual identified a beneficial and creative period against a background of a disappointing sequel. R. W. Southern's extremely influential *The Making of the Middle Ages*, with its eloquent evocation of self-discovery and religious humanism, breaks off at 1204 with the seeming triumph of cynicism and the breakdown of cultural pluralism.

---

[50] Cohn, *Europe's Inner Demons*.

[51] Friedrich Heer, *The Medieval World: Europe 1100–1350*, trans. Janet Sondheimer (London: Weidenfeld and Nicolson, 1962).

Another important study, John Boswell's *Christianity, Social Tolerance, and Homosexuality*, identifies the thirteenth century as the point at which ideas of natural law and a more rigidly governed Church led to a break with an earlier tolerance for regard to gay sexuality.[52] Boswell, of course, does not argue for a completely open and accepting Christian opinion before 1200 but points to spiritualized erotic ideas of male companionship, a theme further developed, although for a more distant early medieval world (chronologically and geographically), in his last book on same-sex unions.[53] Elsewhere, comparing the treatment of Jews to that accorded to homosexuals, Boswell distinguishes an era of grudging tolerance of "inferior insiders" from one in which both groups were more aggressively constructed as dangerous "outsiders." The change comes between 1150 and 1250.[54]

In the historiography of the Spanish Middle Ages, an open "frontier" period of mutual coexistence (*convivencia*) among Jewish, Christian, and Muslim communities has been identified in opposition to the later intolerance that would lead to the expulsion of the Jews and Moriscos and

---

[52] John Boswell, *Christianity, Social Tolerance, and Homosexuality: Gay People in Western Europe from the Beginning of the Christian Era to the Fourteenth Century* (Chicago: University of Chicago Press, 1980).

[53] John Boswell, *Same Sex Unions in Pre-Modern Europe* (New York: Villard Books, 1994).

[54] Boswell, "Jews, Bicycle Riders, and Gay People," 208: "Whereas in 1150 they had been respected or at least left in peace in most of Europe, from 1250 to 1350 nearly every civil state in Europe restricts their freedom, enacts laws against them, or exiles them." "They" and "them" refers to both Jews and gay people. The "bicycle riders" of the title symbolically encapsulates irrational hatred, specifically referring to the grim Viennese joke of the 1930s in which one man patiently listens to another who has launched into an anti-Semitic harangue, blaming the Jews for all of society's misfortunes. At last the reasonable man observes "You're right. It's all the fault of the Jews—and the bicycle riders." The anti-Semite quite naturally asks, "why the bicycle riders?" to which the response is "why the Jews?"

An open (although threatened) twelfth century is contrasted with the triumphant intolerance of the thirteenth-century ecclesiastical authorities in Richards, *Sex, Dissidence and Damnation*, 1–13.

the pervasive authority of the Spanish Inquisition.[55] This has been understood within Spain as part of the once-burning issue of Spain's backwardness in relation to the rest of Europe and the failure of its imperial
reach. Outside of Spain, and in our era in which the Peninsula effectively has closed the economic and cultural gaps between itself and the
rest of the continent, the problem of the origins of intolerance is seen
from the perspective of European hegemony and overseas expansion.[56]

Scholars who have studied medieval anti-Jewish sentiment are
divided on whether or not there was a "good" earlier medieval era of
tolerance. This is related to the controversies over *convivencia* in Spain.
Americo Castro, who coined the term, and more recently the historian
of Judaism Norman Roth, have identified and exalted an era of com-
munal harmony, mutual respect, and cultural interchange.[57] Yitzhak
Baer and his school, advocates of what sometimes is criticized as the
"Lachrymose School," deny that there ever was a period of beneficent
treatment of the Jews of Spain.[58] Others, such as Robert Chazan, identify the controversies of the thirteenth century and the atmosphere of
hatred engendered by mendicant preaching as responsible for a marked
deterioration in the status of the Jews.[59] For Europe as a whole, Jeremy

---

[55] Americo Castro, *España en su historia: cristianos, moros, y judíos*, 2nd ed. (Barcelona: Editorial Crítica, 1983).

[56] See, for example, James H. Sweet, "The Iberian Roots of Racist Thought," in *William & Mary Quarterly* 54 (1997), 143–66.

[57] Castro, *España en su historia*. Norman Roth believes the entire history of the Jews in Spain up to the expulsion was happy and so eschews identifying a particular golden age: *Jews, Visigoths, and Muslims in Medieval Spain: Cooperation and Conflict* (Leiden: E. J. Brill, 1994), and "The Jews of Spain and the Expulsion of 1492," *The Historian* 55, no. 1 (Fall 1992), 17–30.

[58] Yitzhak Baer, *History of the Jews in Christian Spain*, 2 vols. (Philadelphia: Jewish Publication Society of America, 1978).

[59] Robert Chazan, *Daggers of Faith: Thirteenth-Century Missionizing and Jewish Response* (Berkeley: University of California Press, 1989), and *Barcelona and Beyond: The Disputation of 1263 and its Aftermath* (Berkeley: University of California Press, 1992).

Cohen ascribes to the Franciscans and Dominicans responsibility for changing the image of Jews from tolerated minority to sufficiently alien to warrant expulsion.[60] In the course of elaborating a not completely convincing theory of anti-Semitism, Gavin Langmuir identifies the sharpened, irrational hostility to Jews as beginning with accusations of ritual murder in the twelfth century and ritual cannibalism in the thirteenth century.[61]

All of these works share an implicit or explicit contrast between an actively tolerant, or at least benignly disorganized, period and a dogmatic, aggressive, and well-organized campaign of marginalization carried out at least by the thirteenth century. In recent years, with the fading belief in the progressive Middle Ages and in the "open" twelfth century, the beginnings of the persecutorial mentality have tended to move back into the eleventh and twelfth centuries, as in the work of R. I. Moore. Recent studies also partake of an implicit or explicit teleological view of medieval intolerance, seeing it in terms of modern violence against both internal European minorities and external colonized peoples.

The Medieval as Foundational

I would not want to argue that the Middle Ages was especially tolerant, or deny that the organization and expansion of Christian Europe produced by the thirteenth century a mentality of domination and irrational fear of dissent or perceived subversion. Moreover, even if one points to favorable descriptions of groups such as peasants or Muslims, the very existence of a category "the peasant" or "the Moor"

---

[60] Jeremy Cohen, *The Friars and the Jews: The Evolution of Medieval Anti-Judaism* (Ithaca: Cornell University Press, 1982).

[61] Gavin I. Langmuir, *Toward a Definition of Antisemitism* (Berkeley and Los Angeles: University of California Press, 1990), esp. the essays "Thomas of Monmouth: Detector of Ritual Murder" (209–36) and "Ritual Cannibalism" (263–81).

constructs him as alien, as a "problem" to be "solved" by those making the judgment.[62]

What I would contest is the pathologizing of medieval history as the origin of a climate and enforcement mechanism of intolerance culminating in the state-sponsored persecutions of the twentieth century. Or, more broadly, whether modern European colonialism, and internal repression—accompanied by the cultural process of "othering"—have direct medieval antecedents. For Moore, Langmuir, Cohn, and Boswell a fateful turn was taken at some point in the eleventh to fourteenth centuries, down a path that leads to various forms of repression and paranoid European fantasies directed against a multifarious and arbitrarily constructed Other. These scholars, as I have argued, have reacted against an optimistic view of medieval society as the beginning of rationality, order, and individualism—hallmarks of a favorably regarded modernity. Moore, in his introduction to *The Formation of a Persecuting Society*, explicitly takes issue with the tendency to minimize or explain away medieval persecution or to exonerate the secular and ecclesiastical authorities.[63]

A renewed emphasis on the unpleasant aspects of the Middle Ages is salutary. Attention to the medieval Other moves away from the bland, modernized Middle Ages but runs the risk of reproducing in a new key the supposed foundational aspect of the period. To what degree is the Middle Ages itself, as an historical era, conceived of as different, as Other?

Whether the medieval period is perceived as having a particular penchant for irrational persecution (the view of those emphasizing human progress) or as originating undesirable characteristics of modernity (the beginnings of colonialism, aggressive expansion, or intolerance), there is a temptation to look at the Middle Ages through

---

[62] Gayatri Chakravorty Spivak, "Can the Subaltern Speak?" in *Marxism and the Interpretation of Culture*, ed. Cary Nelson and Lawrence Grossberg (Urbana: University of Illinois Press, 1988), 271–313.

[63] Moore, *Formation of a Persecuting Society*, 1–5.

the lens of contemporary concerns, through a certain hermeneutic of suspicion. While we cannot escape our own time and certain of its assumptions, there is more to be gained by looking at a period such as the Middle Ages as much as possible in terms of its own realities, not as a negative example or foundational model.

Several recent observers surveying the situation of medievalists within universities have bemoaned the supposedly narrow erudition of the field and its unwillingness to engage itself with contemporary questions. Medievalists are chastised for walling themselves off from other disciplines and historical periods with a deliberate obscurantism.[64] The desire to apprehend medieval mentalities in their own terms has been dismissed by Kathleen Biddick as a species of "pastism," the inclination to exaggerate the difference between periods in order to lament or escape a perceived contemporary impoverishment.[65] Engagement with current political and cultural concerns, according to Biddick, is to be rejected not as naive "presentism" but, rather, as a way of troubling the image of a safely distant Middle Ages. Juxtaposing the Venerable Bede with a hypothetical Chicana feminist chair of a humanities curriculum committee, Biddick advocates a more fluid frontier between past and present.[66]

Lamentation over medievalists' alleged unwillingness to engage present concerns seems to me to amount to an impassioned critique of a non-problem. All along topics such as the medieval state and twelfth-century individualism had clear contemporary implications. The Middle

---

[64] Kathleen Biddick, "Bede's Blush: Postcards from Bali, Bombay, and Palo Alto," in *The Past and Future of Medieval Studies*, ed. John Van Engen (Notre Dame: University of Notre Dame Press, 1994), 16–44 (reprinted in Biddick's recent collection, *The Shock of Medievalism* [Durham, N.C.: Duke University Press, 1998]); Judith M. Bennett, "Our Colleagues, Ourselves," in the same volume, 245–58, esp. 246–47; and Bennett, "Medievalism and Feminism," *Speculum* 68 (1993), 309–31.

[65] Biddick, "Bede's Blush," 16–18.

[66] On problems raised by Biddick's approach to the Middle Ages in relation to contemporary concerns and theories see Gabrielle Spiegel's review of *The Shock of Medievalism* in *History and Theory* 39 (2000), 243–50.

Ages has been used for quite some time both as a point of origin and to refine a modernist aesthetic, as the recent collection *Medievalism and the Modernist Temper* makes clear.[67] We need to appreciate the way in which the medieval both is quite firmly different from the present and yet escapes efforts to cordon it off in our own minds. Even (or especially) a deliberate attempt to isolate oneself from present cataclysm such as Ernst Robert Curtius' intellectual project in wartime Germany (his *Europäische Literatur und lateinisches Mittelalter*) describes a rather German Middle Ages, reflected through a sense of culture not bounded at all by the medieval centuries but, rather, culminating with Goethe.[68]

The Middle Ages itself is placed in a subordinate subject-position with reference to the modern, by being described as if it were a single stream with a dominant tendency. Its alterity needs to be re-emphasized, but so does its heterogeneity. Intolerant as it was, the Middle Ages, with its numerous (if sometimes dangerous) varieties of Christianity, its minorities, and its acknowledgment of an often fantastic marginality reveals what Scott Waugh has called, "a highly variegated social and intellectual landscape" which requires that "simple models of conspiracy or opposition between well-defined and organized opponents have to be replaced with a more nuanced interpretation of the interchange between different cultures."[69] The Middle Ages is different from the contemporary, but its alterity is not that of a single world.

---

[67] *Medievalism and the Modernist Temper*, ed. R. Howard Bloch and Stephen G. Nichols (Baltimore: Johns Hopkins University Press, 1996), esp. Nichols' article "Modernism and the Politics of Medieval Studies," 24–56. "Modernism" here refers largely to the nineteenth and early twentieth centuries. An example of a work that moves in and out of the medieval and modern, the learned and the popular, showing their mutual conceptual reinforcement is Boureau, *Le droit de cuissage*.

[68] Carl Landauer, "Ernst Robert Curtius and the Topos of the Literary Critic," in *Medievalism and the Modern Temper*, 334–54. See also Alain Boureau, "Kantorowicz, or the Middle Ages as Refuge," in the same volume, 355–67.

[69] Waugh, introduction to *Christendom and its Discontents*, ed. Waugh and Diehl, 5.

Marvelous Peoples
or Marvelous Races?
Race and the Anglo-Saxon
Wonders of the East

Greta Austin

A SPIRITUAL WRITER IN YORKSHIRE at the end of the twelfth century rebuked a slow-witted disciple:

> If you were as English in the quickness of your mind as you are by nationality, and had truly considered what I said before, about there being only four things we ought to love, and how the world and the things that are in the world must not be loved, you would have avoided such a question. But since you are acting like a German without the intelligence to get off the ground, I will have to tackle the point again.[1]

---

[1] *The Bridlington Dialogue*, ed. and trans. by a "Religious of C. S. M. V." (London: A. R. Mowbray, 1960), 66: "si sic esses anglus vivacitate sensus quemadmodum es natione, et bene considerasses quod supra dictum est quatour tantum esse diligenda, et quomodo mundus vel que in mundo sunt diligenda non sunt, talem modo questionem non fecisses. Sed quia sensu theutonicus es et propterea etiam heres in plano . . . necesse est michi . . . epilogum facere." As quoted by Paul Meyvaert, "'Rainaldus est malus scriptor Francigenus'—Voicing National Antipathy in the Middle Ages," *Speculum* 66 (1991), 751.

In his 1991 presidential address to the Medieval Academy of America, Paul Meyvaert quoted this example of national pride and antagonism as an example of how medieval Europeans viewed each other across linguistic and national boundaries.[2]

I wish to ask a related question, but one that focuses on medieval European perceptions of peoples very distant from them—not just across the English Channel, but as far away as India. This paper looks at the *Mirabilia*, or the *Wonders of the East*, and concentrates on one *Wonders* manuscript to ask how it depicts and describes Eastern peoples. This question is posed by examining a specific problem of translation. The *Wonders* repeatedly uses the Latin word *genus* and the Old English word *cyn* to describe the Eastern peoples. *Genus* and *cyn* are often translated as 'race.'[3] This translation, however, may be misleading. *Race*—although a number of alternative definitions could be proposed— has come to refer very frequently to certain broad divisions among humans, divisions which are made on the basis of physical appearance and place of national origin.[4] But the word *race* seems to have been coined only in the seventeenth century,[5] when it was taken up as a way

---

[2] Meyvaert, "Rainaldus," 743–63.

[3] See, for example, *The Letters of Saint Boniface*, trans. and intro. by Ephraim Emerton (New York: Columbia University Press, 1940), or R. W. Southern, "England's First Entry into Europe," in *Medieval Humanism and Other Studies* (New York: Harper and Row, 1970), 142.

[4] The Oxford English Dictionary gives one definition of *race* as "one of the great divisions of mankind, having certain physical peculiarities in common." It notes, "The term is often used imprecisely; even among anthropologists there is no generally accepted classification or terminology."

[5] See François Bernier, "Nouvelle division de la terre, par les differentes espèces ou races d'hommes qui l'habitent . . . ," *Journal des sçavans* 12 (1684), 148–55. Bernier identified four distinct human races, saying that his system differed from previous ones because it did not take into account the different countries or regions of the world but, rather, judged according to "the exterior form of the body, and principally of the face" (148). Bernier devoted the latter half of his article to a comparison of the beauty of the world's women. For example, he spoke highly of the attractiveness of women in the Indies, Persia, and

of classifying the natural world.[6]

This paper will argue that the *Wonders* discusses and depicts Eastern peoples in a way fundamentally different from modern conceptions of race, and that *race* is not an accurate translation of *genus* and *cyn* in the *Wonders*. Word searches provide hints but not conclusive evidence about how to translate *genus* and *cyn*.[7] The most effective way to determine what the *Wonders* may have meant by *genus* and *cyn*

Egypt but had nothing good to say of the appearance of women in India (152–55). Yet Bernier classed certain kingdoms of North Africa and South Asia as "European" (149). He seems to have been working from an assumption that these peoples exhibited a level of political and social organization commensurate with Europe's.

[6] See Londa L. Schiebinger, *Nature's Body: Gender in the Making of Modern Science* (Boston: Beacon Press, 1993), and the bibliography cited, esp. n. 6, 243–44.

[7] Three relevant definitions of *genus* can be isolated in the Oxford Latin Dictionary, the *Thesaurus Linguae Latinae*, and Lewis & Short. Most generally, *genus* is defined as "stock, descent, birth, origin." It also could mean "all human people," or "nationality or nation." The *Thesaurus Linguae Latinae* enlarges upon this latter meaning of *genus*, describing it as "a wider notion concerning the entirety of those who, although unaware among themselves of shared blood, nonetheless speak of one lineage [*stirps*] and origin." The Anglo-Saxon translation seems to support the idea that *genus* describes a division of peoples into certain broad groups. The Old English translator used *cyn(n)* to translate *genus*. *Moncyn(n)* is used as a translation for *genus* in the *donestre* marvel (British Library MS Cotton Tiberius B.v, fol. 83r). *Genera bestiarum* is rendered as *wildeora cynn* (85r). Yet the translator also employed *cyn(n)* generally, in places where *genus* does not appear, such as in the translation for *arbores* as *treowcyn*, "kinds of trees." *Cyn(n)* seems here to mean simply "type, kind", and not "race." The Anglo-Saxon glossaries I have consulted give the following translations for *cyn(n)*: "race, kind, kindred, family," in *Word-Hoard*, ed. Stephen Barney, 2nd ed. (New Haven: Yale University Press, 1985); "every being of one kind, a kindred, kind, race, nation, people, tribe, family, lineage, generation, progeny, kin," in *An Anglo-Saxon Dictionary*, ed. Bosworth and Toller; and "race, family, kindred," in *Bright's Old English Grammar & Reader*, ed. F. G. Cassidy and Richard Ringler. Barney points out the etymological connections between *cyning* (king), *cyne-* (royal), and *cynn*, and notes their roots in *ge-cynde* (innate, natural), *cennan* (beget), and *-cund* (deriving from, kind). In translating *genus* in the *Wonders*, therefore, I have used "type" or "kind," or even "tribe" instead of "race," as an *ex tempore* measure.

is to look closely at the "wonders" themselves. This essay suggests that the *Wonders'* understanding of *genus* does not correspond to that of *race* in two important ways.

First, the illustrations and text suggest that the *Wonders* views Eastern peoples not with distaste but, rather, with curiosity and an interest in hierarchical order. The *Wonders* has an arrangement different from other related texts. The anonymous compiler re-arranged the order of the texts and images so that the marvels begin with animals, progress to humans with bestial characteristics, and end with humans who enjoy cooked food, clothing, and political organization.[8] This paper will argue that the structure of the *Wonders* is important and that it reveals something about why the work's compiler, copyists, and readers might be interested in the Eastern peoples.

Second, it might seem that the *Wonders* represents Eastern peoples in order to categorize them scientifically or, put another way, simply in order to understand their positions in the natural world. I will suggest, however, that the *Wonders'* interest in these peoples is soteriological: the individual marvels are arranged to show the hierarchical spectrum of those people to whom God offers grace. An interest in salvation can be deduced from internal evidence, such as a Christian, apocryphal fragment which is attached to the *Wonders*. Soteriological concerns also can be seen by considering how the *Wonders* fits into the volumes in which it appears and, at a second level, how it was copied and used in a particular historical context. I now turn to the *Wonders* to demonstrate that it understands other peoples in a way different from the modern meanings of race.

---

[8] See the comparisons with the old French translations, as collated by J. D. Pickles, *Studies in the Prose Texts of the Beowulf Manuscript* (Ph.D. diss., Cambridge, 1971), 61–82.

The *Wonders of the East*[9] describes animals and, particularly, the legendary peoples of the East,[10] such as headless men with faces in their chest.[11] These stories, which date back to the ancient Greeks, were transmitted to the medieval Latin West through a number of channels, primarily Pliny's *Natural History*.[12] Excerpts from Pliny formed the basis of a rich variety of medieval stories about the Eastern wonders, stories that generally concerned Alexander the Great's travels in India.[13] One of these stories was a letter that claimed to have been written by a Greek traveling with Alexander the Great. The *Wonders* appears to have been compiled from this letter, although the original epistolary framework is absent. Three copies of the *Wonders* exist today: (1) British Library MS Cotton Tiberius B.v, fols. 78v–87v [hereafter

---

[9] Montague Rhodes James, *Marvels of the East: A full reproduction of the three known copies, with introduction and notes*, Publications of the Roxburghe Club 191 (Oxford: Oxford University Press, 1929).

[10] Some of the peoples are described as living "in Gallia," but most live in what was considered "Asia" on medieval maps, such as the map in one of the *Wonders* copies. See p. 49 below .

[11] Elsewhere called *blemmyae*; see John Block Friedman, *The Monstrous Races in Medieval Art and Thought* (Cambridge, Mass.: Harvard University Press, 1981).

[12] See Friedman, *Monstrous Races*, 5–25, 34–35; and Rudolf Wittkower, "Marvels of the East: A Study in the History of Monsters," *Journal of the Warburg and Courtauld Institutes* 5 (1942), 159–68. On the translation of the Greek romance of Pseudo-Callisthenes by Julius Valerius in the fourth century and on the tenth-century translation by Archpriest Leo of Naples, see Walter Berschin, *Greek Letters and the Latin Middle Ages: From Jerome to Nicholas of Cusa*, trans. J. C. Frakes, rev. ed. (Washington, D.C.: Catholic University of America Press, 1988), 84, 171.

[13] On the medieval Alexander literature see George Cary and David J. A. Ross, *The Medieval Alexander* (Cambridge: Cambridge University Press, 1956); and Ross, *Alexander Historiatus*, Altertumswissenschaft Bd. 186 (London: Warburg Institute, 1963; repr. Frankfurt: Athenaeum, 1988), and *Studies in the Alexander Romance* (London: Pindar, 1985). See also Gerrit H. V. Bunt, *Alexander the Great in the literature of Medieval Britain*, Mediaevalia Groningen 14 (Groningen: Egbert Forsten, 1994); and Paul Meyer, *Alexandre le Grand dans la littérature français du moyen âge* (1886; Geneva: Slatkine Reprints, 1970).

"Tiberius"]; (2) British Library MS Cotton Vitellius A.xv, fols. 98v–106v, in the portion of the manuscript known as the "Nowell Codex," which existed independently until bound with other texts in the seventeenth century [hereafter "Vitellius"]; and (3) Oxford, Bodleian Library, Bodley 614, fols. 36–51 [hereafter "Bodley"].[14] All three date to the eleventh and early twelfth centuries and were copied in England.[15] All are illustrated. Tiberius contains Latin and Anglo-Saxon texts; Vitellius provides only Anglo-Saxon; and Oxford has only the Latin.[16]

---

[14] British Library MS Cotton Tiberius B.v is reproduced in facsimile in Patrick McGurk, Anne Knock, et al., *An Eleventh-Century Anglo-Saxon Illustrated Miscellany*, Early English Manuscripts in Facsimile 21 (Baltimore: Johns Hopkins University Press, 1985). British Library MS Cotton Vitellius A.xv is reproduced in *The Nowell Codex (British Museum Cotton Vitellius A.xv, Second ms.)*, ed. Kemp Malone, Early English Manuscripts in Fascimile 12 (Copenhagen: Rosenkilde & Bagger, 1983). For descriptions of Tiberius and Vitellius, respectively, see N. R. Ker, *Catalogue of Manuscripts containing Anglo-Saxon* (Oxford: Oxford University Press, 1957), no. 193, pp. 255–56, and no. 216, pp. 281–83. For Bodley see Falconer Madon and H. H. E. Craster, *A Summary Catalogue of Western Manuscripts in the Bodleian Library at Oxford*, vol. 2 (Oxford: Clarendon Press, 1922), no. 2144, part 2, pp. 229–30. See also Elzbieta Temple, *Anglo-Saxon Manuscripts, 900–1066*, A Survey of Manuscripts Illuminated in the British Isles 2 (London: Harvey Miller, 1976), 72 (no. 52) for Vitellius, and 104–05 (no. 87) for Tiberius. All three manuscripts are reproduced in James, *Marvels*.

[15] Bodley 614 is dated by James (*Marvels*, 6) to the early twelfth century. Temple (*Anglo-Saxon Manuscripts*, 72) places Vitellius in the late tenth century but Malone (*Nowell Codex*, 119) suggests the late tenth or early eleventh century and Kenneth Sisam (*Studies in the History of Old English Literature* [Oxford: Clarendon Press, 1953], 94) dates it to ca. 1000 C.E. Tiberius is dated to the second quarter of the eleventh century (Temple, 104; and Michelle Brown, *Anglo-Saxon Manuscripts* [Toronto: University of Toronto Press, 1991], 32). Tiberius may have been produced in Winchester or Canterbury. Winchester has been suggested because it is the only capitalized name in the list of bishops that appears on fols. 20v–22 (Ker, *Catalogue*, 255). The list of bishops, however, concludes with Sigeric, archbishop of Canterbury (989–95 C.E.), and fols. 23v–24 contain his itinerary in and from Rome in 990 C.E. (Ker, 255). According to McGurk and Knock (*Anglo-Saxon Illustrated Miscellany*, 34), it is impossible to suggest a home for Tiberius on paleographical grounds.

[16] The Latin cited here is from Tiberius. In general, I have translated from the Latin, with some consultation of the Old English. See Pickles, *Prose Texts of the Beowulf*

The complicated textual and pictorial relations of the three manuscripts lie outside the scope of this essay.

In order to understand how a particular text and its images function as a whole, this essay focuses on the Tiberius *Wonders*. All three copies differ from each other in significant ways, and for practical purposes it is important to look carefully at how one particular text works. Tiberius offers two advantages: it has both the Latin and the Anglo-Saxon; and it is the most richly illustrated.[17]

A brief overview of the structure of the Tiberius *Wonders* is necessary. Tiberius opens by describing and depicting animals, but it then introduces a number of groups who have both human and animal characteristics, although nearly all are called "human beings," *homines*. Among these are the following: the *cynocephali*, who breathe fire and have "horses' manes, boars' teeth, and dogs' heads";[18] the tri-colored men, *homines*, with lions's heads and mouths like fans;[19] the headless men who "have eyes and mouths in their breast";[20] and the *homodubii*, the "dubious men" (82v), half-man and half-ass. All these peoples are depicted naked. One can see a gradual movement up the scale of humans towards groups with increased social or linguistic organization, such as "barbarous men who have 110 kings under them,"[21] and a treacherous tribe of humans (*hominum genus*), who are called *donestre* and who use language to seduce, capture, and eat other men (fig. 1). Then the balance shifts towards peoples whom the text describes more

---

Manuscript, 61–81, for collations of the Latin and Anglo-Saxon *Wonders* texts and the related Old French texts. James, *Marvels*, collates only the Latin.

[17] See n. 14 above.

[18] ". . . ibi nascuntur cenocephali quos nos conopoenas appellamus habentes iubas equorum, aprorum dentes, canina capita, ignem et flammam flantes" (80r).

[19] "Item liconia in gallia nascuntur homines tripertito colore quorum capita capita leonum pedibus xx ore amplissimo sicut vannum . . ." (81r).

[20] ". . . nascuntur homines sine capitibus qui in pectore habent oculos et ores . . ." (82r).

[21] "Est et alius locus hominum barbarorum habens sub se reges numero cx" (82v).

Figure 1. *Donestre* [on left]. London: British Library MS Cotton Tiberius B.v, fol. 83r.
By permission of The British Library.

approvingly. There are priests in temples (84r); honest men who have a kingdom by a red sea (84v); and "kind," long-lived people who have many kings and give their guests women, apparently as tokens of hospitality (85v). In this way, the text and illustrations of the Tiberius *Wonders* move gradually along the scale from animals to humans who enjoy clothing, political organization, cities, and kings.[22]

The *Wonders* in Tiberius provides important visual and written clues about its creators' attitude to the distant peoples. The illustrations and the text, taken together, seem to encourage the reader to adopt certain viewpoints. I will look first at the illustrations and then at the language of the *Wonders*.

The Tiberius illustrations have two features that are important in determining the attitude towards the marvelous peoples: first, the frame; and second, a figure whom I call "the visitor." The frames around the Tiberius images are employed in at least two ways.[23] First, the

---

[22] It should be noted that the Tiberius *Wonders*' organization is not entirely consistent. At certain points, marvels focus on peoples who do not fit into the movement of the text. I would identify five such interruptions: (*a*) The gold-digging ants marvel (80v) and (*b*) an elephant marvel (80v–81r) occur between the first "homines" at 80r and the next humans of 81r. (*c*) A passage on women with tails, camel feet, boars' tusks and teeth, and hair to their feet occurs at 85r, just as the *Wonders* moves up the scale of increased humanity and describes honest men and kind, hospitable kings. The text comments that Alexander the Great killed these women "because of their obscenity" [*Quarum multe ex ipsis ceciderunt pro sua obscenitate a magno nostro Macedone Alexandro . . .*]. This marvel may have been placed here because the previous marvel (84v) also describes women. (*d*) At the end of the *Wonders*, there are brief descriptions and images of black men called *biopes* (86r) and (*e*) black men on a burning mountain (87r). These peoples are depicted as dressed only in tunics from the waist and then naked. As I discuss below, the gradual "undressing" of the peoples depicted may prefigure the naked bodies in hell shown in the Jamnes-Mambres marvel at 87r–v. It is also worth noting that flora and fauna occasionally are described and depicted between marvels concerning peoples: namely, at 83r, 84v, and twice at 86r and 86v with an additional third illustration on the former.

[23] Vitellius and Oxford also have frames and use them in similar ways. For example, the frame is violated in Vitellius by hands in speaking gestures (e.g., 102r, 102v).

frame creates a boundary or a distance between the reader and marvel, between West and East. Second, the frame is employed to play with and cross over that boundary. For example, the headless man, a *blemmya*, wraps his long fingers around the frame and grasps it with his prehensile feet (fig. 2). He seems to be "literally stepping out of it [the frame] into the real world of the spectator."[24] The foreground is foreshortened, pushing the figure up towards the reader, so that the sense of immediacy is even greater. The frame is a boundary that the Eastern man and the reader share: the *blemmya* steps on it and grasps it; the reader sees it as a decorative device, as part of the page's layout.[25]

The violation of the frame suggests that the man is too large, perhaps even too "real," to be contained by the frame. The *blemmya* exists in a space very close to the reader. The frame is used here as a common denominator between reader and marvel. It collapses much of the distance between reader and headless man and, perhaps, between East and West. The centaur of 82v, for instance, is humanized by breaking the frame (fig. 3).[26] Although the accompanying text does not say that the centaur speaks, the violation of the frame draws attention to his speaking gesture. The implication, as I will discuss below, seems to be that the centaur is human because he is capable of using language. The frame is used slightly differently here from the frame of the *blemmya*. The *blemmya* directly confronts the viewer, like a man in a zoo. Other marvels, such as the centaur, seem to brush away the frame, as if their world extended out into the three-dimensional space above the page.

What are we to make of these two uses of the frame? I would suggest that the answer is linked to the actions of reading and looking.

---

[24] Herbert Broderick, "Some Attitudes toward the Frame in Anglo-Saxon Manuscripts of the Tenth and Eleventh Centuries," *Artibus et Historiae* 5 (1982), 35.

[25] Feet crossing the frame occur frequently in Tiberius: the *homodubius* (80r); the two-faced man (81r); the lion-headed man (81v); the *donestre* (83v); the man feeding dogs (85r); and the man eating raw meat (85v).

[26] See also the *donestre* of 83v, the priest of 84r, and the black man of 86r.

Figure 2. *Blemmya* [on right]. London: British Library MS Cotton Tiberius B.v, fol. 82r. By permission of The British Library.

Figure 3. Centaur. London: British Library MS Cotton Tiberius B.v, fol. 82v. By permission of The British Library.

Yet a viewer's interaction with a text is too complicated to generalize further about how an Anglo-Saxon viewer might have looked at the *Wonders*. I would only suggest that a figure, whom I call the visitor, reveals certain implicit attitudes in the Tiberius *Wonders* towards the Eastern peoples. The visitor, who is dressed in a tunic and tights, appears in a number of illustrations. For example, the visitor is depicted being eaten by a tall cannibal (fig. 4). The accompanying text voices one of its rather rare opinions: ". . . we rightly call them enemies [*hostes*], for they eat whomever they capture."[27] The visitor, as a victim, stands for the viewpoint of the anonymous "we." Here, as elsewhere, clothing establishes a difference between eater and victim: the visitor's clothing contrasts with the cannibal's nakedness.

The visitor figure is revealing, I think, of subtle and usually implicit attitudes toward the various Eastern peoples, whether he is being eaten by a tall cannibal, deceived by a wily *donestre* cannibal, or given women as gifts by kind kings. A set of values emerges in these interactions. These criteria, such as the use of clothes, the choice of foods, and political organization, are used to organize the *Wonders*. The marvelous peoples appear in the order in which they share in these values. For example, the "most evil and barbarous people" who oppress 110 kings appear about two-thirds of the way through the *Wonders*. The bad people soon are followed by the good men, who have kings and oppress 110 tyrants. What seems implicit here is that the *Wonders* values "good" kingly authority, as opposed to tyranny. These kings, the accompanying text tells us, give their guests women. We see two scenes of the kings: first some of the kings speaking among themselves, and then the happy visitor being given a woman by three kings (figs. 5 and 6). The kings wear English three-pointed crowns and are engaged in

---

[27] "Trans Brixontem flumen ad orientem nascuntur homines longi et magni habentes foemora et surras xii pedum, latera cum pectore vii pedum colore nigro quos hostes rite appellamus. Nam quoscumque capiunt comedunt" (81v).

Figure 4. Cannibal [on right]. London: British Library MS Cotton Tiberius B.v, fol. 81v. By permission of The British Library.

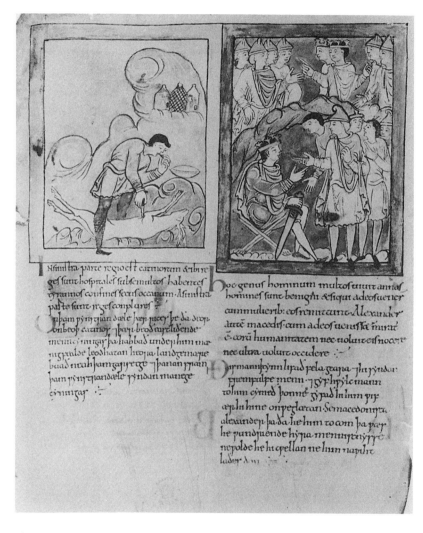

Figure 5. Kings. London: British Library, MS Cotton Tiberius B.v, fol. 85v. By permission of The British Library.

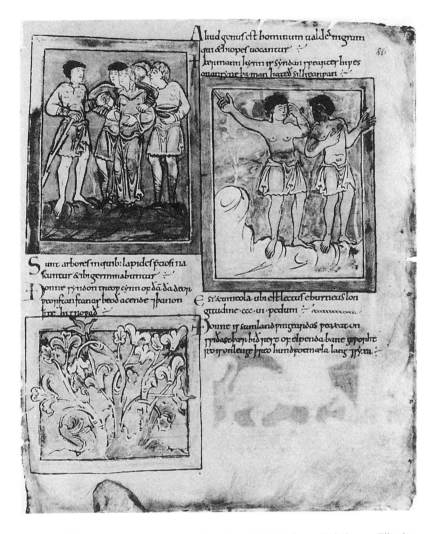

Figure 6. Kings being given a woman. London: British Library MS Cotton Tiberius B.v, fol. 86r. By permission of The British Library.

energetic dialogue.[28] Thus the *Wonders* privileges good, kingly authority over tyranny. The text notes, "Alexander of Macedonia . . . wondered at their *humanitas* and did not wish to harm them, nor, further, to kill them."[29] *Humanitas* can mean "humane conduct towards others," "good breeding," or simply "the qualities, feelings, and inclinations of mankind." To be commended for *humanitas* is, perhaps, the highest award the *Wonders* bestows. In this way, the *Wonders* organizes the different types of Eastern peoples into a hierarchical order. This scale begins with the "least human" of the peoples and moves toward the "most human."

It is worth pausing briefly to note that the *Wonders* conceives of the human body in a manner different from modern conceptions of it. I would suggest that we tend today to think of a clear division between human beings and animals. In the *Wonders*, however, the human body could be shaded by relative degrees of humanity and "bestiality." Certain peoples might have bodies which brought together combinations of human and animal: men with dog's heads; or "homodubii," men to the waist and asses below. The *Wonders* is not alone in seeing the human

---

[28] The kings of Tiberius (85v) have three-pointed crowns, with a three-petaled acanthus-shaped leaf for each point. This style of crown is found in another Anglo-Saxon manuscript of the first part of the eleventh century, British Library MS Cotton Claudius B.iv. See Ker, *Catalogue*, 178–79. See also the crowns in figs. 152–53 and 155–56 in Gale Owen-Crocker, *Dress in Anglo-Saxon England* (Manchester: Manchester University Press, 1986), 152–54. The kings of Tiberius 85v also wear cloaks fastened over one shoulder with a brooch, which Owen-Crocker sees as English, figs. 151 and 153, pp. 150, 152. This cloak style appears in Cambridge, Corpus Christi College 183, an early tenth-century Anglo-Saxon manuscript (Ker, 64–65). The Tiberius kings are wearing striped leg coverings on 86r similar to those depicted in another Anglo-Saxon manuscript of the eleventh century, British Library Cotton Julius A.vi. See Owen-Crocker, fig. 168, p. 165, and Ker, 202–05. Bodley has similar crowns and cloaks on 45v and 48r.

[29] "A sinistra parte sunt reges conplures. // Hoc genus hominum multos vivit annos. Homines sunt benigni et si qui ad eos venerint cum mulieribus eos remittunt. Alexander autem Maced[on]is, cum ad eos venisset miratus est eorum humanitatem nec voluit eis nocere nec ultra voluit occidere" (85v).

body as a flexible, fluid quantity. After describing numerous Eastern peoples in his *Etymologies*, Isidore of Seville points out how men could be transformed into beasts.[30] The line between human and animal in the early Middle Ages could be blurry: no category or taxonomy existed which might drive a firm, comforting wedge between human being and animal. Yet a human had a soul and was, as Augustine put it, "a mortal rational creature."[31]

The *Wonders* indicates the humanity of the Eastern peoples—as "mortal and rational"—both through the speaking gestures of the illustrations and the descriptions of the peoples as *homines* in the text. The *Wonders* does not question whether these Eastern peoples were human *per se*. One compelling piece of evidence for this position is the word choice of the *Wonders*: all but two of the Eastern tribes are called *homines*, "men."[32] Furthermore, nearly all the peoples are depicted

---

[30] *Isidori Hispalensis Episcopi Etymologiarum sive originum libri xx*, ed. W. M. Lindsay, vol. 2 (1911; New York: Oxford University Press, 1985), XI.iv.

[31] ". . . homo, id est animal rationale mortale . . ." (*De civitate Dei* 16.8).

[32] I argue that the *Wonders* considered all the Eastern tribes to be human peoples and, therefore, worthy of salvation. There are two groups whose humanity could be questioned, the *homodubii* and the *cynocephali*. The *homodubii* are described as having "the appearance of men to the bellybutton" but are asses below the bellybutton, with long bird-like feet ["Ubi nascuntur homodubii qui usque ad umbilicum hominis speciem habent reliquo corpore onagro similes longis pedibus ut aves, lena voce sed hominem cum viderint longe fugiunt . . ." (82v)]. Half-animal and half-human, they are, literally, "dubious men," floating on the boundary between human and animal. The drawing, however, suggests that the *homodubii* may be considered by the anonymous illustrator to be human. A *homodubius* points over the edge of the frame, with one finger and a thumb extended in a speaking gesture. The violation of the frame further calls attention to the significance of the gesture. Language is used in the *Wonders* as an index of humanity, as I argue (p. 42 above). The other group whose humanity may have been in question is the *cynocephali*, who breathe fire and have "horses's manes, boars' teeth, and dogs' heads." In the illustration of the Tiberius *Wonders*, however, the *cynocephalus* has everything but the head of a man, and his right hand is engaged in a speaking gesture. Furthermore, theological, literary, and, perhaps, pictorial contexts may have caused Anglo-Saxon readers to assume the *cynocephali* to be men. Isidore

with speaking gestures. Even the two groups not called *homines* are en-gaged in speaking, which seems to be the visual sign of the human. The *Wonders* assumes that these apparently semi-human peoples were, on the whole, human beings (*homines*), even if they happened to have bird's feet, two heads, a lion's head, or another quirky anatomical feature. The organization of the *Wonders* seems not to be designed to figure out which of the Eastern peoples are human and which not. Rather, it arranges these peoples into a scale of ascending humanity, from humans with bestial characteristics to humans who are fully "human."

This brings me to my second point about how the *Wonders* per-ceived these other peoples. Why would the *Wonders* be organized into a hierarchy? I believe that the *Wonders* was interested in other peoples in order to represent, in pictures as in words, the order and diversity of those to whom God offers his salvific grace.[33] The *Wonders* implicitly

---

of Seville clearly identifies the *cynocephali* as belonging to all "human kind." Although he comments later that their barking makes them seem "more beasts than men," he notes that language is not limited to speech but can take the form of signs or motions: "Sicut autem in singulis gentibus quaedam monstra sunt hominum, ita in universo genere humano quaedam monstra sunt gentium, ut gigantes, cynocephali, cyclopes . . . cynocephali appellantur eo quod canina capita habeant, quosque ipse latratus magis bestias quam homines confitetur. . . . Nonnulli sine linguis esse dicuntur, invicem sermonis utentes nutum sive motum" (*Etym.* XI.iii). As Friedman (*Monstrous Races*, 72–74) has pointed out, St. Christopher was dog-headed in some early versions of his legend, particularly Irish ones, which were influential in England. The only two images of Christopher as dog-headed in Western art come from the western part of the British Isles. It seems not coincidental that one of the three *Wonders* manuscripts includes a homily on St. Christopher (Vitellius, fols. 94–98, followed by the *Wonders* [fols. 98v–106v]) and that Christopher and *Wonders* are copied in the same hand (Ker, *Catalogue*, 281). The Christopher legend in Vitellius seems to refer only to the saint's enormous size and not to his dog head. See Vitellius 94r and the text printed in Stanley Rypins, *Three Old English Prose Texts in MS Cotton Vitellius A.xv*, Early English Text Society, O. S. 161 (1924; Millwood, N.Y.: Kraus, 1987), 68, lines 17–19.

[33] Consuelo Dutschke, Rare Books and Manuscripts, Columbia University, kindly pointed out the article on the history of alphabetization by M. A. and R. H. Rouse in the *Dictionary of the Middle Ages*. Rouse and Rouse suggest that the earlier Middle Ages

takes a theological position: that the various peoples of the East were descended from Adam and could be saved.[34] The *Wonders* considered different *genera* as examples of the diversity of the descendants of Adam and was interested in such wondrous humans, I believe, not only out of curiosity but also because of soteriological concerns. Four aspects of the *Wonders* point to soteriological interests in the text and illustrations in their organization.

The first and, perhaps, most compelling, evidence that soteriological concerns color the organization, language, and images of the *Wonders* is the Latin and Anglo-Saxon apocryphal fragment which appears in two copies of the *Wonders*.[35] The fragment appears to have been taken from the "Penitence of Jamnes and Mambres," an apocryphal Christian text from antiquity which concerned two Egyptian magicians.[36] The two *Wonders* exemplars describe and show how Mambres opened his brother Jamnes's magic books and how Jamnes's spirit, now in hell, cautioned him against magic.[37] The *Wonders* has a very fragmentary text but a full-page illustration—the only full-page image

---

reject artificial order, which weights each item equally, in favor of a "real" order, whereby, for example, *Deus* must precede *angelus*.

[34] For a related problem see Cindy L. Vitto, *The Virtuous Pagan in Middle English Literature*, Transactions of the American Philosophical Society 79.5 (Philadelphia: American Philosophical Society, 1989).

[35] Tiberius, 87r–v; Bodley, 51v. The absence of this fragment in the Beowulf manuscript may suggest that its text is less closely related than the other two. The drawings in Tiberius and Bodley also resemble each other more than those in Vitellius. See McGurk and Knock, *Anglo-Saxon Illustrated Miscellany*, 92–94.

[36] M. Förster, "Das lateinischaltenglische Fragment der Apokryphe von Jamnes und Mambres," *Archiv* 108 (1902), 15–28; and M. R. James, "A Fragment of the 'Penitence of Jannes and Jambres'," *Journal of Theological Studies* 2 (1900–01), 572–77.

[37] As James notes, the illustration on 87r (which depicts two naked men in conversation among rocks) may illustrate either the Jamnes-Mambres fragment or else the last section of the *Wonders*, which describes men who live on burning mountains ("Fragment," 573). Given, however, that the illustrations invariably follow the text, the illustration would be of the preceding text, namely, the men on burning mountains.

in these two *Wonders*—of the magician Jamnes, naked in the mouth of hell, and his brother, who stands, holding an open book, on the rim of the world (fig. 7). The text and images warn of the dangers of magic and of the fate of magicians, the great mouth of hell that swallows up the unbeliever.[38]

Such apocryphal fragments, which were appended to the older, pagan text of the *Wonders*, appear at the end of two copies. The Jamnes-Mambres images and text appear at the end of the Tiberius *Wonders* and about two-thirds of the way through Bodley. Bodley contains an additional twelve marvels. These extra marvels may be an accretion, or they are original to the Tiberius-Bodley exemplar and Tiberius has lost them.[39] Bodley ends with a different Christian fragment, the "Accursed Dancers."[40] The Accursed Dancers fragment depicts and describes three different versions of a story in which women, forbidden by their priest to dance on a feast day, are cursed by him to dance until Doomsday.[41]

Why were these apocryphal Christian fragments added, at some unknown point, to the *Wonders*? I suggest that they provide a Christianizing gloss to a text that was originally pagan. The Jamnes-Mambres and Accursed Dancers fragments remind the reader that the threat of hell and the glories of heaven were ultimately at stake in the wonders and in the order of the natural world.

---

[38] The presence of the Jamnes-Mambres fragment suggests an intriguing relationship between magic and marvel; unfortunately, the question lies beyond the scope of this essay.

[39] James, *Marvels*, speculates that these marvels were lost in Tiberius. Sisam, however, (*Studies*, 71) calls the Vitellius marvels an "accretion." The comments made below are not irrelevant to Vitellius's structure. The general movement from animal-human to human, with corresponding changes in the representation of clothing, language, and so on, can be seen in the additional Vitellius marvels, and the story of the "Accursed Dancers" of 50v adds a further Christianizing gloss. See p. 45 above.

[40] Bodley, 51v.

[41] James, *Marvels*, 31–32, n. 50.

Figure 7. The magician Jamnes and his brother Mambres. London: British Library MS Cotton Tiberius B.v, fol. 87v. By permission of The British Library.

Soteriological concerns also can be seen by locating the *Wonders* in a context of theological thought about the marvelous peoples. The Eastern peoples were discussed by Augustine and other theologians because they posed two problems pertaining to salvation: Could the Eastern marvelous peoples be saved? That is, they could be saved if they were human, so were these peoples human?[42] In *The City of God*, Augustine asked whether the legendary "monstrous tribes of men"[43] could claim descent from Adam and could, therefore, be saved. Augustine argued that, yes, they are Adam's offspring, and they can be saved, because everyone who possesses reason, regardless of how peculiar that person might appear to us, is human.[44] Augustine compared the monstrous peoples to the individual monstrous births, such as babies with two heads, which occur among us, here in the known world. We should not question, Augustine emphasized, God's plan as creator, because we are unable, with our earth-bound and limited viewpoint, to see the whole plan of creation and see how each part fits into it. God as creator selects the various elements "from whose likeness and diversity he weaves the beauty of the universe."[45] So, just as we should not question the humanity of individual aberrant births, based on their appearance, neither should we rule out the possibility that the Eastern peoples are rational and, therefore, human. In this way, Augustine left the humanity of the marvelous peoples an open question.

---

[42] On Augustine's influence on Anglo-Saxon verse see Bernard Huppé, *Doctrine and Poetry: Augustine's Influence on Old English Poetry* (Albany: State University of New York Press, 1959).

[43] ". . . quaedam monstrosa hominum genera . . ." (*De civitate Dei* 16.8).

[44] "Verum quisquis uspiam nascitur homo, id est animal rationale mortale, quamlibet nostris inusitatam sensibus gerat corporis formam seu colorem sive motum sive sonum sive qualibet vi, qualibet parte, qualibet qualitate naturam, ex illo uno protoplasto originem ducere nullus fidelium dubitaverit" (*De civitate Dei* 16.8).

[45] "Deus enim creator est omnium . . . sciens universitatis pulchritudinem quarum partium vel similitudine vel diversitate contexat" (*De civitate Dei* 16.8).

The *Wonders* stakes out a theological position more definitive than Augustine's. Tiberius seems to suggest that all the Eastern peoples were indeed human and that they therefore were capable of being saved. The organization of the *Wonders* reflects a grand scheme of salvation. A helpful way to think about the soteriological organization of the *Wonders* is to compare it to Isidore of Seville's hierarchical structure of the *Etymologies*. Isidore organized his work according to a grand hierarchical scheme, which began with God, the angels and the saints, moved on to human peoples, turned next to marvelous peoples, then to the animal world, the earth's geography, and so on. The *Wonders* presents a similar hierarchy of salvation, but in reverse order.[46] As such, the *Wonders* witnesses not only to the variety of God's creation but also to the order of creation.

In understanding the *Wonders'* approach to other human beings, one also must consider how and where the *Wonders* was copied and in what context—that is, along with what other texts—it appears. These considerations raise problems. The *Wonders* cannot be dated precisely, nor has its manuscript *stemma* been precisely determined.[47] It is unclear whether the compiler of the *Wonders* was Anglo-Saxon or whether the *Wonders* was copied from earlier exemplars, perhaps Carolingian or Ottonian ones.[48] It would be far more convenient to be able to say that the *Wonders* reflected Anglo-Saxon concerns at a particular time. Yet at least two factors—the presence of what seem to be Anglo-Saxon cloaks and crowns in the illustrations and the translations into Old

---

[46] On the chain of being see Arthur Lovejoy, *The Great Chain of Being: A study of the history of an idea* (1936; Cambridge, Mass.: Harvard University Press, 1964).

[47] The exact relationships among the three manuscripts are still debated. For example, Tiberius's drawings are closely related to those in Bodley, and the illustrations in Vitellius appear to be copied from a different exemplar. See McGurk and Knock, *Anglo-Saxon Illustrated Miscellany*, 89–94.

[48] Sisam (*Studies*, 75–76) argues that the *Wonders* was compiled and illustrated in England, but McGurk and Knock (*Anglo-Saxon Illustrated Miscellany*, 91) question his conclusions.

English—suggest that an English hand was active in copying and translating an exemplar and in adding distinctive touches to the illustrations. The manuscripts containing the *Wonders* probably were copied in English monasteries during the century before, or perhaps soon after, the Norman Conquest. Perhaps the dual legacy of conquests and of missionary work sharpened the Anglo-Saxon eye to the varieties of peoples in the world.[49]

Finally, it should be noted that curiosity and a sense of wonder seem to flavor the *Wonders'* soteriological concerns. The Tiberius and Bodley *Wonders* were bound with texts such as calendars, treatises on the heavenly bodies, and maps.[50] One of these maps is the map famous for first depicting the British Isles in a realistic way.[51] One could say

---

[49] In an article on theological resistance to the Antipodes, Valerie I. J. Flint suggests that the possible existence of the Antipodes—on the other side of the globe, and unreached by any known humans—threatened the idea of one single descent from Adam ("Monsters and the Antipodes in the Early Middle Ages and Enlightenment," *Viator* 15 [1984], 63–86; repr. in *Ideas in the Medieval West: Texts and their Contexts*, ed. Flint [London: Variorium Reprints, 1988], 65–80). "To accept such habitation would be to sever the human race into non-communicating parts and to bring Augustine's construction, with all its inner ingenuity and moral urgency, tumbling about his ears" (74). Flint places such resistance in its context of missionary efforts in Germany and points out that the idea of one common origin was important in incorporating new, and perhaps "very strange," converts into the existing German church (75).

[50] The "scientific" texts in Tiberius include a zone map, a now-lost map of the heavens, a calendar, charts of the lunar cycles, Priscian's *Periegesis*, Cicero's translation of *Aratea*, and a world map famous for showing the first realistic image of the British Isles. Bodley contains, in the same hand as the *Wonders*, a calendar with some illustrations of the occupations of the months and an illustrated tract on the heavenly bodies, based on the *Aratea*.

[51] The *mappa mundi* in Tiberius at fol. 56v well may have been used as a guide to reading the *Wonders* as natural history. Inversely, perhaps the *Wonders* was a picturebook to accompany the map. Six of the sixteen cities or regions mentioned in the *Wonders* appear also on the map, as do the "Cinocephales," the Nile, and the "Griphorum gens" (*Wonders*, 80r, 80v, 86v). The map's mention of a region full of beasts and serpents might refer to the two-headed serpents of the *Wonders* (79r–v). There is also a parallel between the map's "Hic dicitur esse mons ardens" and the "mons ardet" of the *Wonders* (86v).

that the overall theme of these two volumes is "natural history." One must note, however, that in the case of Tiberius this interest is the result of compilation: the *Wonders* appears in the same hand as Ælfric's selections and translations from Bede's *De temporibus anni* [fols. 24–28v] and lists of popes, emperors, bishops, and English kings [fols.19v–23v], while the treatises and illustrations that concern the natural world were added when the present-day Tiberius codex was created. Similarly, J. R. R. Tolkien suggested that the theme of the Nowell Codex, which includes *Beowulf*, is "monsters," although it also includes the story of the giant St. Christopher and *The Wonders*, both of which concern peoples who can be or are saved.[52] Thus it appears that the common thread linking the three *Wonders* codices is an interest in natural curiosities and in the variety of God's creation. As in a bestiary, one can observe in the *Wonders* a process of sorting out natural phenomena, namely, the different peoples of the earth.[53] Unlike a bestiary, however, the *Wonders* orders that diversity into a hierarchical scheme of the universality of salvation for all the descendants of Adam.

The *Wonders* can be seen to take the theological position that the marvelous peoples were human and could, therefore, be saved. The *Wonders* represents the Eastern peoples as existing in a hierarchy of increasing humanity, a hierarchy inspired by soteriological concerns. I find it revealing that the *Wonders* was copied in England at this

---

[52] J. R. R. Tolkien, "Beowulf: The Monsters and the Critics," *The Monsters and the Critics and other Essays*, ed. Christopher Tolkien (1983; Boston: Houghton Mifflin, 1984), 5–48.

[53] By considering the Anglo-Saxon *Wonders'* similarity to bestiaries, one can better understand how a medieval reader or compiler might have looked at the *Wonders*. Like a bestiary, the *Wonders*, particularly the Tiberius copy, gives pride of place to the illustrations. Bestiaries and the *Wonders* have similar purposes: to identify natural phenomena, to illustrate the impressive variety of animals or peoples, and, probably, to inspire wonder in the viewer. One can assemble pictures of different types of peoples, just as one collects those of animals.

important, transitional point in English history. Its existence suggests a curiosity about the types of humans on earth and in the order of the natural world.

The *Wonders* does not depict or describe these marvelous peoples in terms that parallel the modern conceptions of race. Modern ideas of race divide human peoples into a few broad groups, originally on the basis of physical appearance. The *Wonders* does not categorize the Eastern peoples in the same way. *Genus* and *cyn* are used of particular groups who share certain characteristics or live in a particular place, as in "There is an island in the red sea in which a human kind. . . ."[54] Soteriological concerns of the *Wonders* suggest an additional definition of *genus* and *cyn*. Because all *genera* and *cyn* traced their ultimate origin to Adam, *genus* and *cyn* as a whole might refer to "omne hominum genus," "all human kind."[55] *Genus* and *cyn* may have two meanings in the *Wonders*: (1) a specific group of humans who share physical characteristics and place of origin; and (2) "all human people," the entirety of humans who are descended from Adam, who can be saved. The question of translation thus opens up larger problems that are significant both to the origins of the idea of race and to the history of particular understandings in Christendom of distant neighbors.

---

[54] Tiberius, 83r: "Itaque insula est in rubro mari in qua hominum genus est. . . ."

[55] Acts 17:26.

WONDERS OF THE BEAST: INDIA IN CLASSICAL AND MEDIEVAL LITERATURE

ANDREA ROSSI-REDER

CLASSICAL ACCOUNTS OF INDIA, and the medieval European "Wonders" accounts that they influenced, depict India as a land of marvels and monstrosities. In works such as Ktesias's *Indika* and the Anglo-Saxon *Wonders of the East,* India's inhabitants are portrayed as bizarre and often frightening creatures, half-beast, half-human, who behave strangely and sometimes even aggressively toward Westerners. These works show clearly that European prejudice toward non-Westerners was documented as early as the classical and medieval periods and that an early relative of what now is termed colonial discourse was already the literary method used to create difference between West and East. Until now, scholars generally have examined the roots of colonial discourse only as far back as the Renaissance, but, in fact, classical and medieval literature, long before colonial expansion, contained the seeds of colonial thinking about natives of non-European countries such as India.[1]

In her essay "Race Thinking Before Racism," Hannah Arendt contends that "race-thinking, with its roots deep in the eighteenth century,

---

[1] For the sake of brevity I concentrate this study on India, but almost identical portrayals of Africa appear in classical and medieval texts as well.

emerged simultaneously in all Western countries during the nineteenth century."[2] Although she is correct about nineteenth-century racism growing out of the eighteenth century, she fails to acknowledge that racist beliefs already were deeply ingrained in Western thinking. Early Western accounts of India portray non-European peoples as misfits and monsters. In these works, foreign characteristics and customs perceived as different, and therefore unusual or bizarre, indicate to European observers presumed levels of barbarity and bestiality among non-Western peoples. These early accounts of India presuppose the superiority of Western peoples over non-Western peoples. Classical and medieval accounts often portray non-Europeans as monstrous, half-human and half-animal hybrid beings, less developed than "civilized," fully human Europeans. Such hybridity—a recognition of familiar (human) characteristics combined with unfamiliar (animal) traits—is, as we shall see, related to the hybridity spoken of by post-colonial critics such as Homi K. Bhabha. Furthermore, early accounts of the East portray Indians and other Eastern races as abject, base, and made to feel or appear ashamed of themselves in the face of "superior" European observers. Such projections of baseness, oddity, and "ex-centricity" upon others betray a European sense of its own centrism. A culture that perceives itself as the norm often will believe in its right to hold up or even bring standards of normalcy to other cultures. This study examines the literary roots of the perceptions of difference between East and West and, in so doing, looks at the roots of racism and imperialism in Western literature and society.

Much ancient Greek literature betrays a Graecocentrist attitude related to an imperialist impulse. James S. Romm notes that "in the Greek experience of India, nearly all major accounts of that distant land came from agents of the imperial rulers who invaded it."[3] Those who

---

[2] Hannah Arendt, *Origins of Totalitarianism* (New York: Harper & Row, 1978), 518.

[3] James S. Romm, *The Edges of the World in Ancient Thought* (Princeton: Princeton University Press, 1992), 83–84.

had occasion to travel would have been connected with diplomatic or imperialistic missions. Scylax, supposedly the first Greek to visit India, was a sea captain under Darius of Persia in the fifth century B.C. On a voyage that took him westward down the Indus and into the Indian Ocean, Scylax recorded accounts, now lost, of a host of bizarre peoples, including *Skiapodes* (one-legged, one-footed creatures who use their foot as a parasol), *Otoliknoi* (creatures with huge, fan-like ears), and *Monopthalmoi* (one-eyed beings).[4] Romm states that Scylax's work was:

> addressed not to the Persians . . . but to a Greek audience who delighted in marvelous tales. Archaic myth and legend had long fostered the notion that peoples of the distant world could be monstrous or deformed by comparison with those of the *oikoumene* [humans of the known world]. . . . Scylax seems to have been consciously working within this tradition, gratifying his culture's expectations of the distant world as a gallery of bizarrely formed monsters and marvels.[5]

It seems entirely possible that Scylax recorded not what he actually saw but, instead, what his own cultural prejudice and expectations led him to see or believe—not unlike the observations of many eighteenth- and nineteenth-century British in India, who, influenced by the vestiges of the *Wonders* tradition, fully expected to see strange inhabitants there—and so did.[6] Indeed, Scylax's portrayals influenced a long line of paradoxographers, natural historians, philosophers, and scientists, even into the early Renaissance, and set up a precedent for early modern and modern accounts of India as a land of marvels.

Scylax's account of India seems to have been the basis for that of Ktesias, a Persian court physician under Artaxerxes in the late fifth and

---

[4] Ibid., 84–85.

[5] Ibid., 85.

[6] See Katherine George, "The Civilized West Looks at Primitive Africa, 1400–1800," *Isis* 49 (Mar. 1958), 62–72.

early fourth century B.C.[7] Although Ktesias may have never ventured
into India at all, his position at Sousa, the gateway to the East, would
have put him in touch with travelers coming in and out of India,[8] and
indeed, Ktesias claims to have gathered information from "firsthand
. . . inquiry" and "reliable informants."[9] Ktesias's account, *Indika,*
preserved in Photius's *Bibliotheka* (ninth century A.D.), is fascinating
because it presents India as a land of absolute marvel.[10] In keeping with
his fellow paradoxographers, Ktesias describes a land filled with wonders at every turn—strange animals, plants, and bizarre races and their
odd customs. Ktesias's India contains rivers flowing with honey and
lakes covered with rich oils. According to Ktesias, in India dwells the
martichora, or man-eating beast with a human head, leonine body, and
a tail that ejects poison darts.[11] Ktesias also writes of seven different
races of people, including the one-eyed *Monopthalmoi,* the long-eared
Panotii or *Pandae,* and pygmies.[12] Of the dog-headed *Kunokephaloi,*
Ktesias says:

> In the mountains dwell men who have the head of a dog; they wear skins of
> wild beasts as clothing, and they speak no language, but bark like dogs and
> in this way understand one another's speech. They have teeth bigger than a
> dog's, and nails like those of a dog, but larger and more rounded. . . . They
> understand the speech of the Indians, but cannot respond to them; instead
> they bark and signal with their hands and fingers, as do mutes.[13]

---

[7] Romm, *Edges of the World,* 78.

[8] Ibid. See also John Block Friedman, *The Monstrous Races in Medieval Art and Thought*
(Cambridge, Mass.: Harvard University Press, 1981), 5.

[9] Romm, *Edges of the World,* 86.

[10] J. W. McCrindle, *Ancient India as Described by Ktesias the Knidian* (London:
Trubner, 1882).

[11] Romm, *Edges of the World,* 87.

[12] Ibid., 88.

[13] Ibid., 79

Two aspects of this passage stand out: the creatures' hybridized, half-beast, half-human, appearance; and their inability to communicate with outsiders, a form of what I shall call discursive abjection. *Kunokephalos* hybridization shares differences and similarities with postcolonial notions of hybridity. As we shall see, for critics such as Homi K. Bhabha, hybridity is the result of two cultures coming together to produce another hybridized culture. The colonial power looks upon the members of this hybridized culture as only partly human, somewhat similar to the way in which Ktesias sees the *Kunokephaloi* as only half human. The postcolonial view on hybridization suggests that the hybridized beings lack not only full humanity but also fully human capabilities, such as language acquisition and use. The *Kunokephaloi* cannot communicate "properly," and this lack of articulateness that Ktesias and other early writers attribute to a number of Eastern creatures constitutes a form of discursive abjection. In discursive abjection the subject attributes to the object inhumanity and lack of suitable speech. As a result, the Other often is made to feel shame about its inability to communicate in a civilized manner.

In *The Location of Culture*, Homi Bhabha discusses hybridity as a necessary component of colonial discourse.[14] For Bhabha, the coming together of two cultures as a result of colonialism creates cultural and racial hybridity, and the power of postcolonial writing basically stems from this exchange. Bhabha states:

> The discriminatory effects of the discourse of cultural colonialism, for instance, do not simply or singly refer to a "person," or a dialectical power struggle between self and other, or to a discrimination between mother culture and alien cultures. Produced through the strategy of disavowal, the *reference* of discrimination is always to a process of splitting as the condition of subjection: a discrimination between the mother culture and its bastards, the self and its doubles, where the trace

---

[14] Homi K. Bhabha, *The Location of Culture* (London and New York: Routledge, 1994), 112.

of what is disavowed is not repressed but repeated as something
different—a mutation, a hybrid.[15]

Although Bhabha speaks of hybridity as the product of colonialism,
Ktesias and *Wonders of the East* present a discriminatory Western view
of creatures who cannot be fully human and so must take on non-human
features as well. The result is that India's inhabitants are human
enough to warrant the reader's attention but mutated enough to create
a sense of wonder, even horror and disgust. The observer's description
of the objectified calls the latter's humanity into question. The *Indika*'s
Kunokephalos has a dog-head, and, although he appears human below
the neck, his wearing animal skins further reduces his status to that of
a non-civilized wildman (if indeed a man). He is neither human nor
bestial but somewhere in between, and anyone familiar with European
colonial writing about other races recognizes the attempt to subhu-
manize or even dehumanize the observed race. Take, for instance, a
passage from Meredith Townsend's early twentieth-century observations regarding his first-hand "experience" with Indians and other races
incapable of Europeanization "despite" colonialism:

> . . . the Indian civilization of itself by the law of its being *cannot* suppress
> suttee, female infanticide, Thuggeeism—though self-defence may order the
> killing of the individual Thug—phallic worship, or the unrestricted wander-
> ing of naked devotees of both sexes in front of palaces. . . . The chain of
> civilization breaks before the claim of religious freedom, and admits a rush
> of barbarism which affects all external as well as all internal life in India.[16]

Townsend believes that Indians possess an uncontrollable nature,
partially related to their paganism, that results in "savage" practices
such as these. No matter how much English civilization Indians are
exposed to, they nevertheless revert to their old habits. For Townsend,

---

[15] Ibid., 111.

[16] Meredith Townsend, *Asia and Europe* (New York: Putnam's, 1905), 350–51.

Indians possess a hybrid nature, consisting of a "true" savage nature, which at times can be covered up, but not eradicated, by imitating European behavior. Despite their dark skin, Indians may look human and may even occasionally act it, but eventually they will betray their true selves, just as Ktesias's *Kunokephalos*, despite his half-human features, cannot hide his half-dog appearance and behavior.

Ktesias's *Indika* recounts a bizarre world of aberrant peoples who not only look different but also live in a manner decidedly un-Greek and, therefore, uncivilized. The ancient Greeks—with their system of laws, government, education, theater, literature, and philosophy— perceived themselves as superior to other races.[17] The words *xenophobia* and *barbarian* were Greek coinages to describe their feelings toward those living outside the city-state; *xenophobia* meaning 'fear of strangers' and *barbarian* from the Greek imitation of the sounds others seemed to make in their own languages.[18] The etymology of the latter word relates directly to Ktesias's comment regarding the dog-headed *Kunokephaloi*'s barking instead of uttering human speech. Their language is somewhere between human and animal speech.[19] *Kunokephaloi* can understand human speech but are not sophisticated enough to replicate the sounds. Instead, they produce non-sense, or what Roland Barthes might call non-sentence.[20] In this regard Bhabha comments: "[t]he non-sentence is not before (either as the past or *a priori*), or inside (either as depth or presence), but outside (both spatially and temporally ex-centric, interruptive, in-between, on the borderlines, turning inside out)."[21]

---

[17] Friedman, *Monstrous Races*, 26; and David Spurr, *The Rhetoric of Empire* (Durham and London: Duke University Press, 1993), 102–03.

[18] Friedman, *Monstrous Races*, 26.

[19] Romm, *Edges of the World*, 79.

[20] Roland Barthes, *The Pleasure of the Text*, trans. Richard Miller (New York: Hill and Wang, 1975), 49.

[21] Bhabha, *Location of Culture*, 182.

This turning inside-out is one of the steps toward abjection, which involves the divulging of the inner core of one's being either by the self or by another. Medieval mystics often employ abjection to attain unity with the Divine. The mystic is able to turn herself or himself inside out, exposing the raw vulnerability of the soul to the Divine, thus becoming abject in the presence of the Godhead.[22] The turning inside-out can occur at the hands of another; a literal example would be Apollo's flaying alive the satyr Marsyas, thus exposing his inner nature.[23] A similar, but not identical, type of abjection occurs in colonialist texts. In the mind of the colonizer, the true inferior state of the colonized must be exposed, and the colonized must be left to feel humbled and abject. In the classical and medieval precursors of colonial literature, inhabitants of the East are portrayed as only partly human. The bestiality of the beings' inner natures appears outwardly, so that it manifests itself in their appearance and behavior. The hybridized creatures become abject because their true natures have been exposed, causing them shame and humility in the presence of the "superior" European.

Kunokephalos language, like the hybridized creature himself, is marginalized also because it cannot be comprehended by Western ears. The language of the Other remains outside the sphere of "normal" human language. The Other's language is ex-centric—away from the *civitas* and as strange, incomprehensible, and perhaps useless—at least to Westerners—as dog-barking.

In *The Rhetoric of Empire,* David Spurr identifies a rhetorical tradition in Western colonial writing in which:

> non-Western peoples are essentially denied the power of language and are
> represented as mute or incoherent. They are denied a voice in the ordinary

---

[22] Mystical abjection involves denial and debasement, often through the use of negation or by means of the *via negativa*. This negative approach to abjection ties in with Spurr's view of negative discourse (discussed in this essay), an idea very close to my idea of discursive abjection.

[23] See Dante, *Paradiso* I.

idiomatic sense—not permitted to speak—and in a more radical sense—not recognized as capable of speech.[24]

Such a denial of speech necessarily involves abjection. By denying speech to non-Westerners, the Western observer forces the notion of abjection upon the observed; the observed cannot survive or even communicate without the presence of the European and is meant to feel inferior for this "lack" of Western intelligibility. As an example of the projection of unintelligibility upon the Other, Spurr cites a particularly revealing passage from Kipling. In it, Kipling describes an Indian:

> He was absolutely unintelligible, and stammered almost to dumbness. . . . the man clicked and choked and gasped in his desperate desire to make the Sahib understand. But it was no use; and in the end he departed as he had come— bowed, abject, and unintelligible.[25]

Kipling's Indian leaves "abject" because he cannot communicate— or, rather, because he does not have the means to communicate with Kipling. Julia Kristeva explains that abjection involves the subject's debasement of and pushing away of the object: "It [abjection] becomes what culture, the *sacred*, must purge, separate and banish, so that it may establish itself as such in the universal logic of catharsis."[26] Abjection occurs when the empowered subject, convinced of the object's vileness, marginalizes or even discards the Other. The subject regards that vileness as existing in the Other's inner nature but manifested in the outer nature as well. In both aforementioned passages from Ktesias and Townsend, bestial appearance and behavior betray a

---

[24] Spurr, *Rhetoric of Empire*, 104.

[25] Rudyard Kipling, "From Sea to Sea" (1900), in *Collected Works of Rudyard Kipling*, vol. 17 (New York: AMS Press, 1970), 154–55, cited in Spurr, *Rhetoric of Empire*, 104.

[26] Julia Kristeva, "The Politics of Interpretation," in *The Kristeva Reader,* ed. Toril Moi (New York: Columbia University Press, 1986), 317. See also Kristeva, *Powers of Horror: An Essay on Abjection*, trans. Leon S. Roudiez (New York: Columbia University Press, 1982), 16–18.

savage core. Likewise, Ktesias's denying the *Kunokephaloi* human
language reduces that race to an unintelligible, uncultured group who
must resort to the frustration of barking and using hand signals "as do
mutes" in order to communicate at all with civilized people. The *Kunokephaloi* are reduced to looking and behaving in a manner which
Westerners would deem ridiculous or abject. David Spurr acknowl-
edges the ties between incoherence and abjection in colonialist writing.[27]
The "negation of linguistic capability in non-Western peoples" has
been used systematically to deny cultural value to other races.[28] Spurr
labels this practice whereby a race or culture is reduced to "a cultural
zero degree" as rhetorical negation.[29] The disempowered, marginalized
one cannot communicate effectively with the colonial power because
the latter projects unintelligibility upon the former. This projection of
unintelligibility demands abjectification, a turning inside-out of the
represented Other to show the inner, inhuman, unintelligible core. The
process by which the Western observer denies the Other's coherence—thereby denying the Other's intelligence, humanity, and civilization and also causing the Other to feel inadequate and ashamed—is
discursive abjection.

Whereas hybridization in Ktesias and in *Wonders of the East* is
obvious and literal, the use of abjection, discursive and otherwise, especially in *Wonders*, is not quite so explicit. Yet, a close examination of
the language of *Wonders of the East* shows a detachment that subtly
debases the inhabitants of Eastern countries described in the work.

Wonders of the East is an early medieval compendium that describes
the bizarre animals and human-like creatures which inhabit the far,

---

[27] Spurr, *Rhetoric of Empire*, 104.

[28] Ibid., 105–06. Spurr speaks of this occurring today, as in the case of a *Manchester Guardian* reporter who evaluates an entire country (Saudi Arabia) based on the brief contacts he makes with "airline attendants, taxi drivers, minor functionaries of the Information Ministry, and other foreign journalists."

[29] Ibid., 104–06.

eastern reaches of the world. *Wonders* describes fire-breathing chickens, snakes with lantern-like eyes, and camel-abducting ants, along with (now using the medieval Latin spellings) Sciapods, *Cynocephali*, *Panotii*, and the like. Although three versions of *Wonders of the East* remain extant, I will discuss just one of these.[30] Bound with its related text *The Letter of Alexander to Aristotle* in Cotton Vitellius A. xv, the *Beowulf* manuscript, this version of *Wonders*, written in Old English, is probably a tenth- or eleventh-century work.[31] Along with *Alexander's Letter*, *Wonders* is related to earlier works of Greek paradoxography, as the descriptions of the East and of its inhabitants indicate. *Wonders*'s geography is vague, but it is safe to assume that the *Cynocephalus* (*Kunokephalos*)—and other creatures mentioned by Ktesias and other paradoxographers as inhabitants of India—are supposed to dwell there or thereabouts. In *Wonders*, the *Cynocephali*, also called *Conopenae*, complete with "horses' manes and boars' tusks and dogs' heads and their breath like a fiery flame,"[32] live in or near Egypt, but since the classical and medieval worlds believed India and Africa to be attached, this would not have been perceived as far from India. However, for the sake of variety, let us look at other hybridized creatures from *Wonders*. The description of one race includes a reference to Alexander:

> Then there are other women who have boar's tusks and hair down to their heels and ox-tails on their loins. These women are thirteen feet tall and their bodies are of the whiteness of marble. And they have camel's feet and boar's teeth. Because of their uncleanness they were killed by Alexander the Great

---

[30] The other two extant versions not mentioned here are those in British Museum Cotton Tiberius B.v. (Latin and Old English) and Oxford Bodleian Library Bodley 614 (Latin). For more on this see Paul Allen Gibb, *"Wonders of the East": A Critical Edition and Commentary* (Ph.D. diss., Duke University, 1977); and Andy Orchard, *Pride and Prodigies: Studies in the Monsters of the Beowulf Manuscript* (Cambridge: D. S. Brewer, 1994).

[31] Orchard, *Pride and Prodigies*, 1–2.

[32] Ibid., 189.

of Macedon. He killed them because he could not capture them alive, because they have offensive and disgusting bodies.[33]

These immense, half-human, half-animal women repulse Alexander, who must kill them because of their vileness. In a weird twist of logic, Alexander kills the women because they are too offensive to capture alive. Furthermore, their uncleanness seems to indicate more than unsatisfactory hygiene: Alexander appears to judge the purity of the boar-tusked women as well. For Kristeva, Alexander's action would betray a conflict with his own sense of impropriety:

> This other, before being another subject, is an object of discourse, a non-object, an abject. This abject awakens in the one who speaks archaic conflicts with his own improper objects, his ab-jects, at the edge of meaning, at the limits of the interpretable. And it arouses the paranoid rage to dominate those objects, to transform them, to exterminate them.[34]

According to Kristeva, the abject is loathed for the filthiness projected upon it and must undergo a purification ritual at the hands of the subject.[35] Although it is impossible to determine Alexander's projected issues in this instance, the matter-of-fact attitude employed by the *Wonders* narrator reveals little or no embarrassment or remorse concerning Alexander's behavior, nor any justification for his action. The women's vileness seems to be reason enough for Alexander to kill them.

All of *Wonders of the East* is characterized by this detached voice reporting the situation with hardly a suggestion of meaning attached, aside from an occasional comment regarding ugliness, ferocity, barbarity, and even a few infrequent compliments. Take, for instance, the report concerning the elephant-eared *Panotii*, who, according to tradition and in the strange geography of *Wonders,* inhabit India:

---

[33] Ibid., 201.

[34] Kristeva, "Politics of Interpretation," 318.

[35] Kristeva, *Powers of Horror*, 72–73.

> Going from there is a place where people are born who are in size fifteen feet tall and ten broad. They have large heads and ears like fans. They spread one ear beneath them at night, and they wrap themselves with the other. Their ears are very light and their bodies are as white as milk. And if they see or perceive anyone in those lands, they take their ears in their hands and go far and flee, so swiftly that one might think that they flew.[36]

Despite the inherent wonder of such creatures, the narrator does not betray an overt sense of wonder about the creatures described. This lack of interpretation in *Wonders*'s language has parallels with a modern colonialist text. In E. M. Forster's description of the Marabar Caves in *A Passage to India*, Aziz takes on a tour to the caves a group that includes Adela Quested and Mrs. Moore, but a loud, incomprehensible boom causes them, and in particular Adela, great alarm. The echo is "entirely devoid of distinction: If one had spoken vileness in that place, or quoted lofty poetry, the comment would have been the same—'ou-boum'."[37] As David Spurr demonstrates, these caves represent the essence of India, "which can be described but not interpreted, so that if they [the caves] have any meaning at all, they stand for the utter absence of meaning."[38]

In the same way, *Wonders* can describe the *Panotii* and their sleeping-bag ears but cannot comment on this trait or explain why they run when they see others. The *Panotii* simply disappear into the Indian landscape. Similarly, in *A Passage to India,* when Ronny and Adela attempt to identify a bird, Forster remarks that they cannot identify it because "nothing in India is identifiable, the mere asking of a question causes it to disappear or to merge into something else."[39] Likewise, the observer in *Wonders* cannot seem to grasp the *Panotii*, either physically or conceptually.

---

[36] Orchard, *Pride and Prodigies*, 197.

[37] E. M. Forster, *A Passage to India* (New York: Harcourt Brace, 1924), 149.

[38] Spurr, *Rhetoric of Empire*, 102.

[39] Ibid., 86, cited in Edward Said, *Culture and Imperialism* (New York: Vintage, 1993), 201.

In *Wonders of the East,* India is identical to the India depicted by Forster, a place of mystery and imagination that does not make any sense. India is a land of intuition rather than reason, and *Wonders's* creatures seem to act intuitively rather than rationally. The *Blemmya,* a creature who would look human except that his head is embedded in his chest, is a literal example of this lack of rationality in monstrous creatures. The *Blemmya's* heart, seemingly lodged in the creature's forehead, appears to substitute for his brain.[40] The Other represents a being, even a culture, without Western laws, morals, or organization— something to be feared. The Western viewer attempts not to understand or to communicate but, merely, to project his own fear of non-European-ness onto the object. By attributing to the Other abject signs— such as outward bestiality, irrationality, and even unintelligibility— works such as Ktesias's *Indika* and the Anglo-Saxon *Wonders of the East* employ what might be termed an incipient colonial or even a proto-colonial discourse to assert Western superiority and justification for dominance over the strange creatures encountered, either face to face or through the tradition of armchair paradoxography. Such prejudices about India's inhabitants as monsters affected Renaissance explorers' expectations about the peoples they would encounter. After all, Cortes expected to encounter *Panotii* and *Cynocephali* in his travels, and Ralegh believed in the existence of *Blemmyae*, even after his voyages.[41] Nineteenth- and early twentieth-century xenophobia was influenced by a long tradition of thinking of other races as monsters. Colonial discourse rationalizes conquering and subordinating indigenous peoples by projecting subalternness upon them, by portraying the colonized as abject and less than human. The Eastern creatures in works such as Ktesias's *Indika* and *Wonders of the East* are clearly the precursors of colonialist images of Indians and demonstrate that colonial discourse has its roots in classical and medieval literature.

---

[40] For more on the *Blemmya's* irrationality see Friedman, *Monstrous Races*, 158.

[41] Friedman, *Monstrous Races*, 198.

THE BOOK OF JOHN MANDEVILLE AND THE GEOGRAPHY OF IDENTITY

MARTIN CAMARGO

SOONER OR LATER, every commentary on *The Book of John Mandeville* attempts to account for the work's immense and enduring popularity, a popularity that "has been greater than that of any other prose work of the Middle Ages," according to Mary B. Campbell.[1] It has been a long-standing topos to wonder at the credulity of so many generations of readers who found its amalgam of facts, half-truths, and outright fabrications more interesting, if not truer, than authentic eyewitness accounts of journeys to the East, including those out of which the unknown author of *The Book of John Mandeville* fashioned his fiction. Measured as a practical guidebook, the book clearly is deficient: even if the fabulous lands are omitted, Mandeville's route is physically impossible to follow. Geographical accuracy in the modern sense was not the reason for the book's popularity.

Since the publication of Josephine Waters Bennett's pioneering reappraisal, scholars increasingly have been willing to accept the fictional nature of *The Book of John Mandeville* and try to appreciate it for what it is rather than criticize it for what it is not. Unburdened by

---

[1] Mary B. Campbell, *The Witness and the Other World: Exotic European Travel Writing, 400–1600* (Ithaca: Cornell University Press, 1988), 122.

a Marco Polo's or an Odoric of Pordenone's responsibility to describe what he actually had seen or to retrace an actual itinerary, the unknown author was free to construct an ideal journey for his ideal traveler, the fictional Englishman Sir John Mandeville. In the studies by Josephine Waters Bennett, Donald R. Howard, Christian K. Zacher, and, more recently, Stephen Greenblatt, the fictional persona of the objective, curious, and tolerant Mandeville is given most of the credit for engaging the imaginations of medieval and early modern readers, not to mention a growing number of contemporary readers.[2] The same freedom that allowed the author to construct a convincing narrative voice also allowed him to shape his eclectic and derivative materials so that, despite the clutter and occasional diffuseness at the surface level, the resulting narrative as a whole exhibits a thematic and structural clarity and coherence that I would argue are among the most important reasons for its enduring authority. As Donald R. Howard puts it, "The book, for all its digressiveness, is remarkably structured; its two parts are set against each other so as to reveal a common truth from different perspectives."[3]

---

[2] Josephine Waters Bennett, *The Rediscovery of Sir John Mandeville*, MLA Monographs Series 19 (New York: MLA, 1954); Donald R. Howard, "The World of *Mandeville's Travels*," *Yearbook of English Studies* 1 (1971), 1–17, and *Writers and Pilgrims: Medieval Pilgrimage Narratives and Their Posterity* (Berkeley and Los Angeles: University of California Press, 1980), 53–76; Christian K. Zacher, *Curiosity and Pilgrimage: The Literature of Discovery in Fourteenth-Century England* (Baltimore: Johns Hopkins University Press, 1976), 130–57, 183–89; and Stephen Greenblatt, *Marvelous Possessions: The Wonder of the New World* (Chicago: University of Chicago Press, 1991), 26–51. "The most consistent appeal of the work," says Ralph Hanna III, "an appeal responsible for its ceaseless republication, translation, and use well into the eighteenth century, is that of a definable personality. Over and above the obvious marvels that the text relates, *Travels* attracts by the creation of a narrative personality— 'Mandeville'—a personality constantly vivifying and informing the marvelous Asian world described" ("Mandeville," in *Middle English Prose: A Critical Guide to Major Authors and Genres*, ed. A. S. G. Edwards [New Brunswick: Rutgers University Press, 1984], 121).

[3] Howard, *Writers and Pilgrims*, 67. Campbell also emphasizes the importance of the book's "form and purpose": constructed out of "building blocks" selected from a wide

Geography in *The Book of John Mandeville* has what I would call a rhetorical function: the shape of the world and the customs of those who inhabit it teach a moral lesson. That lesson is spelled out at the beginning, the middle, and the end of the book—in Mandeville's Prologue; at the end of his account of the Holy Land, when he reports his conversation with the sultan who rules there (chap. 15); and again near the end of the book, as he reflects on his travels to the most remote regions of the earth (chap. 34). Each of these sections—and the explicit statement of the book's theme that it contains—also is associated with one of the three places that delimit Mandeville's image of the world: the Prologue with his point of origin, England; the sultan's remarks in chapter 15 with the center of the world, Jerusalem; and the reflections in chapter 34 with England's antipodes, the realm of Prester John. Finally, those symmetrically situated thematic statements are supported and developed by the travelogue they frame to make of the whole an extended, rhetorically effective exhortation to recover the lost integrity of Christian identity.[4]

The symmetry is especially significant because the account of Mandeville's travels takes the form of an increasingly detailed image rather than a chronologically structured narrative: the journey unfolds

---

array of written sources, *The Book of John Mandeville* "was true because coherent; like any good building, it was used and it lasted" (*Witness*, 141). Douglas R. Butturff explicitly links the coherence of the work's "overall structure" to the author's skillful use of the narrator as "traditional satiric persona: the visionary who returns from a journey through strange places to report the unadorned truth about European Christianity, society, and the times" ("Satire in *Mandeville's Travels*," *Annuale Mediaevale* 13 [1972], 155–56).

[4] Modern critics who read *The Book of John Mandeville* as a call to reform Western Christianity include Howard, "World," esp. 12–17, and *Writers and Pilgrims*, esp. 67–75; Butturff, "Satire"; Iain M. Higgins, "Imagining Christendom from Jerusalem to Paradise: Asia in *Mandeville's Travels*," in *Discovering New Worlds: Essays on Medieval Exploration and Imagination*, ed. Scott D. Westrem (New York: Garland, 1991), 91–114, esp. 100–04; and Higgins, *Writing East: The "Travels" of Sir John Mandeville* (Philadelphia: University of Pennsylvania Press, 1997).

in space rather than in time.[5] Time, in fact, serves chiefly as a measure of distance—how many days or months it takes to get from one point to another. Structurally speaking, the account of Mandeville's travels resembles a map more than it does an itinerary. And the rhetorical function performed by that structure is exactly analogous to the function of a medieval *mappamundi*. According to David Woodward, there is "overwhelming evidence that the function of the *mappaemundi* was primarily didactic and moralizing and lay not in the communication of geographical facts."[6] Likewise, *The Book of John Mandeville* constructs a meaningful image of the world even as it provides a key for reading that meaning. That medieval readers did in fact approach this book as a verbal map is evident from the famous interpolation near the end of chapter 34, in which Mandeville claims to have presented his book to the pope at Rome for verification and correction:

> And oure holy fader of his special grace remytted my boke to ben examyned and preued be the avys of his seyd conseille, be the whiche my boke was preeued for trewe; in so moche that thei schewed me a boke that my boke was examynde by that comprehended fulle moche more be an hundred part, be the whiche the *Mappa Mundi* was made after.[7]

---

[5] Campbell makes a similar point about the way the smaller units of the book are organized: "The bonds between the pieces of data conveyed in any one chapter are usually eidetic, contributing enormously to our overall sense of being presented with an 'image of truth'—an image that, qua image, is more amenable to interpretation than simple belief" (*Witness*, 151).

[6] David Woodward, "Medieval *Mappaemundi*," in *The History of Cartography*, vol. 1: *Cartography in Prehistoric, Ancient, and Medieval Europe and the Mediterranean*, ed. J. B. Harley and David Woodward (Chicago: University of Chicago Press, 1987), 342.

[7] *Mandeville's Travels*, ed. M. C. Seymour (Oxford: Clarendon Press, 1967), 229. All quotations from the English version of *The Book of John Mandeville* in British Library, MS Cotton, Titus C.xvi are taken from this edition (hereafter cited parenthetically in the text as *Mandeville's Travels*). Aside from interpolations, the Cotton Version is generally a faithful translation of the Insular Version (England; before 1390), which I quote from the edition by George F. Warner, in *The Buke of John Maundeuill being the Travels of Sir John Mandeville, Knight 1322–56. A Hitherto Unpublished English*

The standard of truth against which Mandeville's account is measured is ultimately the symbolically significant image conveyed by a world map.[8]

Like the typical fourteenth-century OT map, Mandeville's world is circumscribed by a circle of which the midpoint is Jerusalem.[9] The very fact that so much emphasis is placed on Jerusalem's centrality is evidence of the importance of symbolism over geography and of cartography over narrative. In chapter 20 it is argued at some length that the world is a globe and that it is possible to travel completely around it, eventually arriving at the point from which one departed (*Buke of Maundeuill*, 90–93; *Mandeville's Travels*, 132–37). But a globe's midpoint obviously is not to be found on its surface, unless that globe is viewed at a distance—that is, from a cartographer's perspective. Mandeville seems to recognize the inconsistency, as evidenced by his various attempts to resolve it. To prove that despite the earth's sphericity Jerusalem is its center, he first invokes some spurious empirical evidence and then the authority of the Psalter:

> Ore auez oy dire auant qe Ierusalem est en mylieu de monde; et ceo poet homme moustrer par de la par vne lance fichee en terre sur la houre de mydy al equinocte, qi ne fait point de vmbre a nulle coustee. Et ceo qe ceo soit en mylieu de monde, Dauid le tesmoigne en le psalter, la ou il dit, *Deus operatus est salutem in medio terre.* (*Buke of Maundeuill*, 91)

> Also yee haue herd me seye that Ierusalem is in the myddes of the world. And that may men preuen and schewen there be a spere that is pight into the erthe vpon the hour of mydday whan it is equenoxium that scheweth no schadwe on no syde. And that it scholde ben in the myddes of the world

---

Version from the Unique Copy (Egerton MS. 1982) in the British Museum edited together with the French Text, Notes, and an Introduction (Westminster: Roxburghe Club, 1889) (hereafter cited parenthetically in the text as *Buke of Maundeuill*).

[8] Malcolm Letts believes that the interpolator may have had in mind the great *Mappa Mundi* at Hereford Cathedral (*Sir John Mandeville: The Man and his Book* [London: Batchworth Press, 1949], 101–06).

[9] Woodward, "Medieval *Mappaemundi*," 341–42.

Dauid wytnesseth it in the Psauter where he seyth, *Deus operatus est salutem in medio terre.* (*Mandeville's Travels*, 134)

Most significantly, he observes that the extremes of the known world are equidistant from Jerusalem:

> Dunqes cils qi se partent de celles parties doccident pur aler vers Ierusalem, atant des iournees come ils mettent a monter pur aler iusqes la, en atant de iourneies poient aler de Ierusalem iusqes as autres confins de la superficie de la terre par de la. Et, quant homme vait outre celles iourneies vers Ynde et vers les isles foraches, tot est enuironant la reondesse de la terre et de la mer par dessouz noz pais de cea. (*Buke of Maundeuill*, 91)

> Thanne thei that parten fro tho parties of the west for to go toward Ierusalem, als many iorneyes as thei gon vpward for to go thider, in als many iourneyes may thei gon from Ierusalem vnto other confynyes of the superficialtee of the erthe beyonde. And whan men gon beyonde tho iourneys toward Ynde and to the foreyn yles, alle is envyronynge the roundnesse of the erthe and of the see vnder oure contrees on this half. (*Mandeville's Travels*, 134–35)

Symbolically, Jerusalem's position exactly halfway between England and the realm of Prester John, at opposite ends of the globe, is as important as its position at the center of the *mappamundi*. Hence, Mandeville makes a point of having his geography both ways: the world is a globe that also can (and must) "be read" as if it were a disk.[10] Jerusalem is the center of Christian identity because Christ chose it as the site for his Passion. It is the focal point of the Holy Land, which:

---

[10] Zacher notes the incompatibility of viewing the world as the three joined continents of the OT map, centered around Jerusalem, with viewing it as a completely inhabited sphere. While the former perspective, that of the Christian pilgrim, informs the first part of *The Book of John Mandeville* and the latter perspective, that of the *curiosus*, informs the second part (*Curiosity and Pilgrimage*, 149–50), in the end, he maintains, the two parts are complementary, as "pilgrimage converts to exploration" (154). Campbell also draws attention to the presence of competing views, relating the fact that the "center of a spherical world cannot be found on its surface, and the edge cannot be found at all" to Mandeville's innovative "avoidance of the absolute and its closure" (*Witness*, 161). See also Greenblatt, *Marvelous Possessions*, 41–43.

soit benoite et seintefie et consacree dul precious corps et du sang nostre
seignur Ihesu Crist; en la quelle terre il ly plesoit soy enombrer en la virgine
Marie et char humaigne prendre et noricion, et la dite terre marcher et
enuironer de ses benureez piez. (*Buke of Maundeuill*, 1)

is blessed and halewed of the precyous body and blood of oure lord Ihesu
Crist; in the whiche lond it lykede Him to take flesch and blood of the vir-
gyne Marie to envyrone that holy lond with His blessede feet. (*Mandeville's
Travels*, 1)[11]

But according to Mandeville, Christ chose this land in the first place
because it is the center of the physical world and, hence, in spatial
terms the ideal point from which to proclaim his new law:

Auxi le Creour de tot le monde veolt mort soffrir pur nous a Ierusalem, qest
en my lieu de monde, a la fyn qe la chose fuit pupplie et sceue de touz les
cousteez de monde. (*Buke of Maundeuill*, 2)

Right so He that was formyour of alle the world wolde suffre for vs at
Ierusalem, that is the myddes of the world, to that ende and entent that His
passioun and His deth that was pupplischt there myghte ben knowen euenly
to alle the parties of the world. (*Mandeville's Travels*, 2)

Thus, the circle marking the spot where Christ's body lay, at the center
of the circular church of the Dome of the Rock, at the center of
Jerusalem, marks not only the physical but also the spiritual center of
the world; and the fact that Christians have no dominion over this circumscribed spot and the Promised Land that encircles it signifies the
off-centeredness of contemporary Christians, their alienation from their
true identity.[12]

---

[11] On the physical presence of sacred history in the Holy Land, of which the very
"rocks function . . . as tangible materializations of the sacred stories," exhibiting
imprints of sacred events that become ever more densely clustered as the "religious
core" at Jerusalem is approached, see esp. Greenblatt, *Marvelous Possessions*, 38–42.

[12] Zacher, *Curiosity and Pilgrimage*, 134–35, 138–39, also has noticed Mandeville's
persistent interest in "roundness" and its symbolism.

What keeps Christians off center and at a distance from their true home is their perverseness: they know the true law but choose not to obey it. They are unable to reclaim "la terre qe nostre Seignur nous promist en heritage" ["the same lond that oure lord behighte vs in heritage"] because their hearts are so enflamed with "orgoil couetise et enuye" [pryde, couetyse, and envye] that they strive to dispossess one another instead (*Buke of Maundeuill*, 2; *Mandeville's Travels*, 2–3). This is obvious even to the Saracens, who say that "ly Cristiens sont malueis . . . qar ils ne gardent mie les preceptz des Euuangelies qe Ihesu Crist lour deuisa" (*Buke of Maundeuill*, 69) ["the Cristene ben cursed . . . for thei kepen not the commandementes and the preceptes of the gospelle that Ihesu Crist taughte hem" (*Mandeville's Travels*, 100)]. Part of that curse is the loss of the Holy Land, which the sultan admits his people will keep only so long as Christians persist in sin:

> Et sy sauons bien par noz prophecies qe Cristiens regaigneront ceste terre, quant ils seruiront lour Dieu pluis deuoutement. Mes tant qils serront de si orde vie come sont ore endroit, nous nauons point de paour de eaux; qar lour Dieu ne les eidera mie. (*Buke of Maundeuill*, 69)

> And that knowe we wel be oure prophecyes that Cristene men schulle wynnen ayen this lond out of oure hondes whan thei seruen God more deuoutly. But als longe as thei ben of foul and of vnclene lyvynge as thei ben now, wee haue no drede of hem in non kynde, for here God wil not helpen hem in no wise. (*Mandeville's Travels*, 101)

More than simply a call to a physical pilgrimage or crusade, then, the appeal with which Mandeville ends the initial statement of his theme exhorts his fellow Christians to resume their true identity:

> Mes sil plesoit a nostre seint piere lapostoille, qar a Dieu plerroit il bien, qe les princes terrienz fuissent a bon acorde et ouesque ascuns de lour comune voisissent emprendre la seint viage doutre meer, ieo quide estre bien certein qen brief terme serroit la terre de promission reconcilie et mise en mayns des droitz heirs filz Ihesu Crist. (*Buke of Maundeuill*, 2)

But wolde God that the temperel lordes and alle worldly lordes were at gode acord, and with the comoun peple wolden taken this holy viage ouer the see, thanne I trowe wel that within a lityl tyme oure right heritage beforeseyd scholde be reconsyled and put in the hondes of the right heires of Ihesu Crist. (*Mandeville's Travels*, 3)

That the journey Mandeville has in mind is both spiritual and physical is emphasized when he turns to the task of showing how one approaches the Holy Land from Europe, for the means by which he brings his reader to Jerusalem are anything but efficient. The multiple, uncompleted journeys toward Jerusalem and the studied circumscribing of the Holy Land mimic the spiritual distance separating sinful Christians from their true home at the world's center. And because this first part of Mandeville's travels traverses *terra perdita* rather than *terra incognita*, lands that were more familiar to a fourteenth-century Christian European than the more distant lands of the Far East, it is likely that at least some readers would have been aware of the deliberate avoidance of the most direct route to that center. Mandeville himself draws attention to contemporary knowledge of the various routes to the Holy Land, observing of the shortest route to Egypt that "Il ne couient mie a nomer les cites ne les villes de ceo chemin, qar ly chemin est comun et si est scieuz et conuz de mointez nacions" (*Buke of Maundeuill*, 28) ["It nedeth not to telle you the names of the cytees ne of the townes that ben in that weye, for the weye is comoun and it is knowen of many nacyouns" (*Mandeville's Travels*, 39)].[13]

---

[13] Scott D. Westrem emphasizes the accuracy and the detail of the opening sections of *The Book of John Mandeville*: "In the first third of his book, Mandeville offers an almost obsessively accurate description of pilgrimage routes from Europe to places of Christian significance in Palestine, noting the reason for their importance, their contemporary appearance, and their spatial relationships to one another. Had he ended his account at Jerusalem, Mandeville would have created an accomplished and rhetorically sophisticated *peregrinatio*" ("Two Routes to Pleasant Instruction in Late-Fourteenth-Century Literature," in *The Work of Dissimilitude: Essays from the Sixth Citadel Conference on Medieval and Renaissance Literature*, ed. David G. Allen and Robert A. White [Newark: University of Delaware Press, 1992], 70). Bennett makes a case for the

The main route that Mandeville traces is much longer: it leads overland through central and southeastern Europe to Constantinople and thence by sea to Palestine, with stops at several islands along the way. From Cyprus, the main stop on the way from Constantinople, "vait homme par meer vers Ierusalem" (*Buke of Maundeuill*, 15) ["men gon to the lond of Ierusalem be the see" (*Mandeville's Travels*, 20)]; but even after we have reached the coast of Palestine, and despite repeated references to the ultimate destination of the trip, Mandeville refuses to proceed immediately along the direct route to Jerusalem. Instead, he takes us first in the opposite direction, from Tyre north to Sarepta, to Sidon, and to Beirut, then east to Sardenar and Damascus. Next he marks out a longer sea voyage from Cyprus, to the port of Jaffa, which "est la pluis pres part de la cite de Ierusalem, qar de ce port iusqes a Ierusalem ny ad qe vne iournee et demie" (*Buke of Maundeuill*, 16) ["is the nexte hauene to Ierusalem, for fro that hauene is not but o day iourneye and an half to Ierusalem" (*Mandeville's Travels*, 21)]. Then he returns to Tyre, this time proceeding south along the coast to "Tholomaida" or Acre (which, he points out, also may be reached directly from Venice, Calabria, or Sicily). Here again he seems deliberately to avoid a direct route to Jerusalem, providing instead a back-and-forth approach to Jaffa by leaping first over Jaffa to Gaza, four days' journey south of Acre, then back over Jaffa to the "chaustel des Pelerins" ["castelle of Pylgrymes"], north of Caesarea, then southward over Jaffa once again to Ashkelon, between Gaza and Jaffa, and finally northward to Jaffa itself (*Buke of Maundeuill*, 17; *Mandeville's Travels*, 22–23).

For a Jerusalem-bound pilgrim, this constitutes an exceptional amount of dallying on the coast, an impression confirmed by the fact

---

Mandeville author's actually having traveled to the Holy Land (*Rediscovery*, 54–68) but admits that the evidence is "tenuous" (67). Less skeptical is Dorothee Metlitzki, *The Matter of Araby in Medieval England* (New Haven: Yale University Press, 1977), 220–39, 296–99.

that even after he has brought us back to Jaffa, Mandeville proceeds to describe yet another detour, this time through the Sinai to Egypt. By this point it appears that Mandeville is doing more than just showing us how to reach Jerusalem. I would suggest that his impossible itinerary is designed to circumscribe the Holy Land, to mark clearly and explicitly its boundaries. This is confirmed by the fact that he interrupts his description of Egypt, at the end of chapter 6, to draw the rest of the circle formed by the lands contiguous to the Holy Land. First he indicates the distance between Cairo (Babylon the Lesser) and Babylon (the Great) in Persia (forty days' journey); then he describes Arabia and briefly mentions Chaldea and Mesopotamia, before concluding the chapter by explaining how the Nile originates in the Terrestrial Paradise and flows underground until it surfaces under Mt. Aloth, whence it flows through Ethiopia and Egypt (*Buke of Maundeuill*, 21–23; *Mandeville's Travels*, 29–31).

If the movement in chapters 1–15 is centripetal, and the center being sought is always Jerusalem, the rhetorical figure that best describes that movement is *praeteritio*. The ultimate destination of every Christian pilgrim is evoked constantly only to be deferred, and this dialectic of approach and deferral serves to represent the alienation of actual Christians from their true home. All roads may lead to Jerusalem, but to show in greater or lesser detail each of those roads only postpones our arrival and emphasizes the distance to be traversed. And when a particular route finally is chosen, it turns out to be the least direct of all, taking us first to Egypt and then by a roughly spiral path through the Promised Land before finally bringing us to Jerusalem.

The rhetorical purpose of this indirection is confirmed by the frequent association between loss of land and fragmentation of identity in the regions that delineate the boundaries of the Holy Land. A case in point is the first of many marvels catalogued by Mandeville. Before the church of Santa Sophia in Constantinople, the city that marks the boundary between the Christian West and the Moslem East, stands:

lymage Justinien lemperour, coeuere dor; et est a chiual coronez. Et soleit
tenir vn pomme rounde dooree en sa mayn; mes elle piecea est cheue fors. Et
ceo dit homme qe signefie ceo qe lemperour ad perdu grant partie de sa terre
et de sa seignurie. . . . Et ascuns ount quidez plusours foythz a remettre le
pomme en le mayn, mes elle ne veolt tenir. Celle pome signifieoit la seignurie qil auoit sur le monde qest roundez. Et lautre mayn il tient leuee contre
lorient, en signe de manacer les malfaitours. (*Buke of Maundeuill*, 4–5)

the ymage of Iustynyan the emperour couered with gold, and he sytt vpon an
hors ycrowned. And he was wont to holden a round appelle of gold in his
hond, but it is fallen out thereof. And men seyn there that it is a tokene that
the emperour hath ylost a gret partie of his londes and of his lordschipes. . . .
And men wolden many tymes put the appulle into the ymages hond ayen, but
it wil not holde it. This appulle betokeneth the lordschipe that he hadde ouer
alle the world that is round. And the tother hond he lifteth vp ayenst the est
in tokene to manace the mysdoeres. (*Mandeville's Travels*, 6)[14]

This explicitly interpreted image of loss and ineffectual threats of repos-
session is extended as we are told how Tyre (*Buke of Maundeuill*, 15;
Mandeville's Travels, 20), Acre (*Buke of Maundeuill*, 16; *Mandeville's
Travels*, 21), Tripoli (*Buke of Maundeuill*, 19; *Mandeville's Travels*, 26),
Damietta (*Buke of Maundeuill*, 24; *Mandeville's Travels*, 33), and other
cities along the edges of the Holy Land once had been possessed by
Christians but have long since fallen into the hands of Saracens.

Balancing such reminders of loss are the many "fragments" of the
Holy Land (and hence of Christian identity) that are particularly abun-
dant in the border regions of Constantinople and Egypt. Constantinople
holds such important relics of the Passion as the True Cross, Christ's
seamless tunic, the sponge and reed used to offer Christ vinegar and

---

[14] Campbell maintains that the story of the missing apple is a "lie" and would have
been recognized as such by anyone who had traveled to Constantinople, but that it is
"aesthetically justified" by its important structural function within the book as a whole
(*Witness*, 144–45). Higgins, *Writing East*, 72–77, is more willing to grant the exemplum some grounding in actual events and locates its significance in the way it has
been "moralized."

gall, one of the nails that held Christ to the cross, and half of the crown of thorns that Christ wore on the cross (*Buke of Maundeuill*, 5–7; *Mandeville's Travels*, 7–10), along with many other relics. Egypt contains the temple at Heliopolis, whose round shape is modeled on the temple at Jerusalem (*Buke of Maundeuill*, 41–44; *Mandeville's Travels*, 60–64), just as the Phoenix to whom it is dedicated figures forth the resurrected Christ (*Buke of Maundeuill*, 25; *Mandeville's Travels*, 34); and the apples of paradise (i.e., bananas), which reveal the shape of the cross when cut open (*Buke of Maundeuill*, 25; *Mandeville's Travels*, 35). Both regions thus are doubly marked with signifiers of Christian identity and loss of Christian ownership.

The symbolic significance of this doubleness once again is made explicit in the account of Constantinople, which is "la primere pais variant et descordant en foy et en lettres de nostre pais de cea" (*Buke of Maundeuill*, 11) ["the firste contree that is discordant in feyth and in beleeue and varieth from oure feyth on this half the see" (*Mandeville's Travels*, 15)]. Just as Constantinople is not yet the Holy Land but is filled with pieces of the Holy Land and reminders of its loss, so too it is part of Christendom without sharing "our"—that is, Western—Christianity: "Et, combien qe les Gregeois soient Cristiens, totefoithz ils varient mult de nostre droite creance" (*Buke of Maundeuill*, 9) ["And yif alle it so be that men of Grece ben Cristene, yit thei varien from oure feith" (*Mandeville's Travels*, 13)]. The last half of the third and final chapter describing Constantinople enumerates the ways in which Greek Christianity deviates from Roman Catholicism, as if to underscore the city's meaning as a locus of fragmented Christian identity (*Buke of Maundeuill*, 9–10; *Mandeville's Travels*, 13–14). The same strategy is used to make the same point at the end of chapter 13 (*Buke of Maundeuill*, 58–60; *Mandeville's Travels*, 85–88). As Mandeville approaches the boundary of the Promised Land from within, he pauses first to sketch its boundaries one last time and then to describe the practices of the "Iacobites," the "Suriens," the "Georgiens," and seven other Christian sects that "totdyz faillent . . . en ascun article de nostre foy" (*Buke of Maundeuill*, 58) ["alleweyes fayle . . . in somme articles of oure feyth" (*Mandeville's Travels*, 86)], despite sharing the same basic beliefs.

The general outlines and many details of Mandeville's journey toward Jerusalem are already present in the chief source for this part of the book, William of Boldensele's *Liber de quibusdam ultramarinis partibus* (1336).[15] The *Mandeville*-author has highlighted the symbolic potential of this structure by expanding William's text from other sources, not only providing additional examples of fragmentation but also, in the process, prolonging the time spent on the margins of the Holy Land and thus postponing still further the much-anticipated arrival at the center. Among his additions is what is perhaps the most interesting image of fragmented Christian identity associated with the boundaries of the Promised Land, the "monstre" who sought the prayers of "vn seint prodhomme heremite" in the "desertz de Egipte":

> As desertz de Egipte encontra vn seint prodhomme heremite vn monstre, auxi come vn homme as ii. grant cornz trenchantz en front, et auoit cors de homme iusqes al vmbrilioun et dessouz auoit le corps come chieure. Et ly prod-homme luy demandoit, qil estoit; et ly monstre respondy, qil estoit creature mortelle tiele qe Dieu lauoit crie et demorroit en ces desertz en purchaciant sa sustinance. Pria al heremite qil vousist celluy Dieu prier pur luy, qi pur sauuer le humaigne lignage descendy de ciels et nasqui de la pucelle et passion et mort soeffrist, si qe nous le sauons et par qi nous viuons et sumes. Et vncore est la teste ouesqes les cornz de ceo monstre a Alexandre pur le meruaille. (*Buke of Maundeuill*, 24)

> And this monstre that mette with this holy heremyte was as it hadde ben a man that hadde ii. hornes trenchant on his forhede, and he hadde a body lyk a man vnto the navele, and benethe he hadde the body lych a goot. And the heremyte asked him what he was, and the monstre answerde him and seyde he was a dedly creature such as God hadde formed and duelled in tho desertes

---

[15] On the relationship between William of Boldensele's *Liber* and the first fifteen chapters of *The Book of John Mandeville*, see Higgins, *Writing East*, 64–66, 69–77, 83–85, 92–99, 103–07, and 122–23.

> in purchacynge his sustynance; and besoughte the heremyte that he wolde
> preye God for him, the whiche that cam from Heuene for to sauen alle man-
> kynde, and was born of a mayden, and suffred passioun and deth, as wee wel
> knowen, be whom wee lyuen and ben. And yit is the hede with the ii. hornes
> of that monstre at Alisandre for a merueyle. (*Mandeville's Travels*, 33–34)

Both man and goat, both monster and Christian, this creature embodies the very borders he inhabits. He can be read both as a sign of the fragmentation of Christianity that permits the Saracens to control the center of Christian identity and as a reminder that no corner of the round earth is isolated from the power of the message that emanates from that center.

If the centripetal movement in the first fifteen chapters of *The Book of John Mandeville* emphasizes the fragmentation of Christian identity, the centrifugal movement of the last nineteen chapters emphasizes its pervasiveness. Paradoxically, as we move toward the geographical focus of Christian identity, we become aware of Christianity's current fragmentation;[16] while as we move away from that focus toward the geographical periphery, we become aware of Christianity's ubiquity. The "journey in" reminds us of the Christians' willful withdrawal from the center; the "journey out" reminds us of man's unavoidable proximity to the center.

As Mandeville moves away from Jerusalem (chaps. 16–34), he encounters increasingly outlandish creatures as well as societies that seem to exist for the sole purpose of flouting such Christian taboos as those against cannibalism, incest, polygamy, public nudity, and human sacrifice. Yet no matter how far removed in space from the center of Christian identity, every culture that Mandeville encounters betrays some trace of Christian truth. As he observes very near the end of his book:

> de toutz ces pais don't iay parle, et de toutes cellis isles et de toutz ces diuerses
> gentz qe ieo vous ay deuises et des diuers loys et des diuersez creaunces qils

---

[16] Howard extends this fragmentation to the Holy Land itself, which is presented as a kind of "relic" that acquires meaning and coherence through Christian faith and the stories in the Bible (*Writers and Pilgrims*, 70–72).

ount, il ny ad nulle gent, pur quoy ils ayent en eux resoun et entendement, qi
nayent ascuns articles de nostre foy et ascuns bons pointz de nostre creaunce
et qils ne croient en Dieu qy fist le mounde, qils appellent Dieu de nature. . . .
Mes ils ne scieuent mie parfitement, qar ils nount qi lour deuise, forsqe ensi
qils entendent de lour sen naturel. (*Buke of Maundeuill*, 154)

of alle theise contrees and of alle theise yles and of alle the dyuerse folk that
I haue spoken of before and of dyuerse lawes and of dyuerse beleeves that
thei han, yit is there non of hem alle but that thei han sum resoun within hem
and vnderstondynge—but yif it be the fewere—and that han certeyn articles
of oure feith and summe gode poyntes of oure beleeve; and that thei beleeven
in God that formede alle thing and made the world and clepen Him God of
Nature. . . . But yit thei cone not speken perfytly, for there is no man to techen
hem, but only that thei cone deuyse be hire naturelle wytt. (*Mandeville's
Travels*, 227)

The marvelous East is thus analogous rather than antithetical to the
Christian West, and the traces of Christianity in creatures ignorant of
the Gospels (and often scarcely recognizable as images of God) underscore by contrast the willful fragmentation of Christian identity among
those to whom the truth has been revealed and who define themselves
as followers of Christ.

Geography serves to make this point rhetorically above all through
the representation of India—in particular the island realms of the
Christian king Prester John—as the antipodes of Western Europe, in
particular England. The spatial relationship between Mandeville's home-
land and Prester John's domain first is noted in chapter 18 (*Buke of
Maundeuill*, 81; *Mandeville's Travels*, 119–20),[17] elaborated in chapter

---

[17] In chap. 18, Mandeville confines himself to the astrological opposition between the
men of India, who are dominated by Saturn and therefore "ont . . . nature et voluntee
qils ne querent point a mouoir" ["han of kynde no wille for to meve ne stere to seche
strange places"], and the men of England, who are dominated by the moon and therefore have "nature et voluntee de mouoir legierement et de chemyner par diuerses voies
et de sercher choses estranges et diuersitees du monde" ["wille of kynde for to meve
lyghtly and for to go dyuerse weyes and to sechen strange thinges and other dyuersitees
of the world"] (*Buke of Maundeuill*, 81; *Mandeville's Travels*, 119–20). This seemingly

20 (*Buke of Maundeuill*, 91–92, 93; *Mandeville's Travels*, 134–35, 137), and reasserted one last time at the beginning of chapter 34 (*Buke of Maundeuill*, 152; *Mandeville's Travels*, 223). From a cartographer's perspective, both lands are on the world's periphery, equidistant from its center, Jerusalem. But the global perspective is equally emphasized: they are the obverse rather than the opposites of one another; each is the midpoint of a continuous circular journey that begins and ends at the other. From this perspective, when Mandeville reaches the lands of Prester John he is halfway home.

The paradox of traveling toward home by traveling away from it is the physical counterpart of the still greater paradox of Christian identity disclosed by Mandeville's journey. At England's antipodes belief is imperfect rather than fragmented. At this pole of Christian identity, those who lack perfect knowledge of God's laws serve God naturally; at the opposite pole, those who have perfect knowledge of God's laws unnaturally refuse to serve God.[18] East of Jerusalem Mandeville encounters men whose ignorance and, in some cases, physiognomy position them at the periphery but who seek the center—literally,

---

innocent contrast acquires thematic significance as the primitive Christianity of Prester John and the natural religion of such Eastern peoples as the inhabitants of the islands of "Bragmey" and "Gysonophe" (*Buke of Maundeuill*, 144–46; *Mandeville's Travels*, 211–15) are set against the fickle newfangledness of the Western Christians epitomized in the Englishman Mandeville. According to Zacher the association between Englishmen and wanderlust was well established by the beginning of the fourteenth century (*Curiosity and Pilgrimage*, 141–42) .

[18] Morton W. Bloomfield relates Mandeville's affirmation of man's natural inclination to believe in God to the "scholastic concept of natural reason" ("Chaucer's Sense of History," *Journal of English and Germanic Philology* 51 [1952], 310–11). See also Butturff: "the emphasis on the natural religions found in the lands described in the second half of the book suggests the unnatural practices of the Europeans" ("Satire," 164). On medieval views of Eastern peoples, in particular the Indians, as virtuous non-Christians or "noble savages," see Thomas Hahn, "The Indian Tradition in Western Medieval Intellectual History," *Viator* 9 (1978), 213–34, esp. 223–34], and John Block Friedman, *The Monstrous Races in Medieval Art and Thought* (Cambridge, Mass.: Harvard University Press, 1981), 163–77.

in the case of Prester John himself (*Buke of Maundeuill*, 147–48; *Mandeville's Travels*, 216), while west of Jerusalem he encounters men whose knowledge of the true law should place them at the center but who perversely seek the periphery. Which islands, we are left to ask, are inhabited by monsters?[19]

[19] This essay is expanded from a paper read at the Thirty-First International Congress on Medieval Studies, The Medieval Institute, Kalamazoo, May, 1996. The original paper grew in part out of conversations with Richard Glejzer. For valuable suggestions on an earlier draft of the essay, I wish to thank Alan T. Gaylord.

Froissart's "Debate of the Horse and the Greyhound": Companion Animals and Signs of Social Status in the Fourteenth Century

Kristen M. Figg

In his fifteenth-century treatise *Master of Game*, Edward Duke of York extols the virtues of hunting dogs:

> A hound is true to his lord and master . . . a hound is of great understanding and of great knowledge, a hound hath great strength and great goodness, a hound is a wise beast and a kind [one]. A hound has a great memory and great smelling, a hound has great diligence and great might, a hound is of great worthiness and of great subtlety. . . .[1]

Such statements expressing the affection of nobles for their hunting dogs are well known from medieval treatises. Less familiar are the role of dogs as travel companions and the way that the daily maintenance

---

[1] Edward of Norwich, 2nd Duke of York, *The Master of Game: The Oldest English Book on Hunting*, ed. William A. and F. Baillie-Grohman (New York: Duffield, 1909), 79–80. This fifteenth-century English treatise is an adaptation of *Le livre de la chasse* by Gaston II Phoebus, Count of Foix, cited in n. 14 below.

of both dogs and horses helped define upper-class behavior and ethno-centrism in the Middle Ages. These cultural assumptions about the sig-nificance of human-animal relations are particularly well illustrated in a short poem by Jean Froissart called *Le Debat dou Cheval et dou Levrier*, "The Debate of the Horse and the Greyhound."[2] In a *dittié* of about ninety-five lines that combines the marvel of talking beasts with the details of a real-life trip to Scotland, the fourteenth-century poet and chronicler not only offers a humorous view of animal personalities but also suggests indirectly some of the distinguishing marks of civi-lized English society in contrast to the strange and savage behavior of the tribal Scots.

When Froissart wrote a prose account of his trip to Scotland in 1365, contained within Book I of the *Chroniques*, he was not working within the traditional genre of the medieval travel narrative, which so often was filled with reports of monstrous races and marvelous crea-tures. While other writers, like John Mandeville, claim to have ven-tured into exotic lands and to have seen cannibals and giants, Froissart traveled only throughout the known world of Western Europe, which did not provide the kind of sensational material expected in travel literature. Instead, Froissart limited his accounts mainly to reporting on the well-known people and politics of the day; his attempts to depict the "marvelous" occur in his re-creation of the spirit of honor and chivalry that he recognized in noble behavior. Froissart did, however, express a sense of wonder at the surprising variations in human habits and attitudes, in particular those that reflected differences in class and culture. And so, while he maintained an undeviating focus on the world of battles and politics and negotiations in the *Chroniques*, he also chose to treat his experiences in Scotland poetically, in a whimsical debate between two marvelous animals—a talking horse and a talking

---

[2] For the complete text and an English translation see *Jean Froissart: An Anthology of Narrative and Lyric Poetry*, ed. Kristen M. Figg and R. Barton Palmer (New York: Routledge, 2001), 488–91.

greyhound—who reveal not a fanciful society beyond the limits of the known world but a keen non-human observational perspective on the very culture that Froissart himself represents.

In the literature of the Middle Ages, the talking animal, of course, makes its appearances in a number of contexts, some more "marvelous" than others. As Jan Ziolkowski has demonstrated amply in his study of medieval Latin beast poetry, there is a long tradition of using the persona of an animal to typify a set of moral characteristics for the purpose of teaching a lesson, or to represent a real-life human whose appearance in his own guise in a satirical text might prove dangerous to the author.[3] Likewise, animals might be made to take part in verbal debates, ranging from the well-known theoretical discussions of body and soul to arguments that Ziolkowski sees as more closely related to the tradition of "flyting," the exchange of insults for sport.[4] In all of these cases, however, the animals in question are to be seen anthropomorphically, representing in some way a human position to which they are suited

---

[3] Jan Ziolkowski, *Talking Animals: Medieval Latin Beast Poetry, 750–1150* (Philadelphia: University of Pennsylvania Press, 1993). Ziolkowski cites, for example, the instance of Eugenius Vulgarius, a tenth-century priest from Naples who lost his office when Pope Sergius II invalidated all the appointments made by his predecessor; his "Comic Visions" presents an assembly of birds who gather for a concert and are interrupted first by noisy beasts and then by characters with historical and mythical names probably pointing to "actual friends and acquaintances in Eugenius's circle" (115). For discussions of "human animals" and parodic animal depictions in the later medieval tradition see essays by Joyce E. Salisbury and David A. Sprunger in *Animals in the Middle Ages: A Book of Essays*, ed. Nona C. Flores (New York: Garland, 1996).

[4] No doubt the best known of the moral debate poems to readers of Middle English is the "Debate of the Owl and the Nightingale," but the tradition includes at least one greyhound—and a rather narrow moral disagreement focused on hunting—in the Latin *Concertacio leporarii et falconis*, translated in the fifteenth century by Robert du Herlin as *Le Debat du Faucon et du Lévrier*, ed. Gustaf Holmér (Stockholm: Almqvist & Wiksell, 1978). For a general discussion of debate poems see Hans Walther, "Das Streitgedicht in der lateinischen Literatur des Mittelalters," *Quellen und Untersuchungen zur lateinischen philologie des Mittelalters*, 15 (Munich: Beck, 1920). For a discussion of "flyting" see Ziolkowski, *Talking Animals*, 131–52.

symbolically, even when their behavior, aside from their surprising verbal ability, is more or less in keeping with their animal natures. They are "marvelous" in the sense of being interesting literary creations, but they do not invite the audience to think of them as real talking animals or to engage in any critical reappraisal of their place in the real world, since it is always so apparent that their behavior and discussions must be translated into an allegorical or satirical human context.

In contrast to talking animals such as these, the main characters in *Le Debat dou Cheval et dou Levrier* are at once more ordinary and more remarkable. For while they do not outwit anyone or teach any lessons in human morality—and they certainly bring no messages from the spiritual world as do the talking animals in medieval saints' lives[5] —their very fidelity to the actual conditions of life as the companion animals of aristocratic travelers makes them, for the present-day reader, the most dependable of witnesses to what Froissart must have seen as a distinguishing pattern of elevated human behavior. Taking a narrative stance not unlike that in his realistically detailed *pastourelles*,[6] Froissart fashions himself as a mere observer of a conversation that creates a convincing picture of a day in a particular time and place. By supplying his animals with distinctive personalities in keeping with their real-life traits and roles, he is able to provide two points of view on that day and to suggest through the animals' complementary perspectives a good deal

---

[5] See, for example, the story of "St. Brendan and the White Birds," translated from Plummer's *Vitae Sanctorum Hiberniae* (Oxford, 1910) by Helen Waddell in *Beasts and Saints* (1934; repr. Grand Rapids, Mich.: W. B. Eerdmans, 1996), 115–19. Here one of the "multitude of birds" in a single tree identifies the flock as the "great ruin of the ancient foe, who did not consent . . . wholly" to the will of God. Rather than being real animals endowed with the gift of speech, these birds are embodiments of human spirits who must sing the praises of God while remaining in estrangement from his presence.

[6] Though other works of medieval literature, such as Machaut's *Jugement du Roy de Behaigne* and Chaucer's *Book of the Duchess*, make use of the convention of a narrator happening onto a dialectical situation, Froissart is distinctive in his focus on class relations in the *pastourelles* and in his inclusion of the realistic details of daily life.

of what was valued, feared, and enjoyed by a group of weary travelers on the rugged road home from Scotland in 1365.

That Froissart intended the poem to be realistic in substance, though whimsical in tone, is suggested by the specificity of his opening line, which starts with his own name:

> Froissart was coming back from Scotland
> On a horse that was grey. . . . (1–2)

> Froissars d'Escoce revenoit
> sus un cheval qui gris estoit. . . .

Froissart refers elsewhere to his horse, Grisel, the name by which this one is soon to be addressed, and the trip to Scotland is clearly the tour described in his *Chroniques* as having taken place by commission of Queen Philippa in the mid-1360s. That the greyhound—again very specific in being described as white—is not an incidental companion is clear from the fact that he is "en lasse," that is, on a leash, and indeed it is recorded that Froissart brought back from Scotland, a country renowned for its greyhounds, a fine white specimen of the breed.[7] One thus can imagine the real Froissart traveling along at the end of a difficult journey and letting his mind wander to the issue of whether the travels had been any more or less taxing on the beasts who were his companions. The greyhound, who speaks first, sets the scene, and the horse follows immediately with visual details and the introduction of dramatic conflict:

> "Alas," says the greyhound, "I am tired,
> Grisel, when are we going to rest?
> It's time to eat."
> —"You're tired?" says the horse,

---

[7] John M. Gilbert, *Hunting and Hunting Reserves in Medieval Scotland* (Edinburgh: John Donald, 1979), 64–65. Gilbert provides here a history of the greyhound and other breeds as used in Scottish hunting.

"If you had carried a man and a trunk
Up hills and down dales
Then you could curse the day
When your mother gave birth to you. . . ." (4–11)

"Las!," dist li levriers, "je me lasse!
Grisel, quant nous reposerons?
Il est heure que nous mengons."
—"Tu te lasses?," dis li chevaus:
"Se tu avoies mons et vauls
Porté un homme et une male,
Bien diroies: lit heure est male,
Que je nasqui ongues de mere!"

The greyhound's question perhaps reflects the very fact that he is newly acquired and has no idea of how long such a journey might continue, but his response shows no lack of spirit or sense of his own importance. Indeed, he seems keenly aware of differences in treatment as he proceeds with his arguments. First he minimizes the horse's difficulties by pointing out that the horse is designed for such work, being "grans et fors" and supplied with four iron shoes while he, through all this, has a "bien petit corps" and has to go barefooted. He is, he says, designed for sport—"pour les gens esbanoyer"—not for work like a horse who is "ordonnés et fès" for carrying men and their belongings. Furthermore, the greyhound argues, the horse will get more attention at the end of the day, when the master will automatically bring him oats and look for signs of discomfort, even throwing his own cloak over him if he seems to be limping, while the dog is going to be left crouching off to the side somewhere.

The greyhound's description of how the horse is cared for—supplemented later by references to rubbing, scratching, currying, and cleaning of hooves—perhaps is not surprising by twentieth-century standards, and yet this careful consideration of the horse's needs is a recognition of his status as a valued commodity in the society, and it is characteristic of a particular, and relatively recent, cultural attitude. For Froissart, who considered himself to be in the service of one of the most advanced courts in Europe, this well-maintained and self-satisfied horse marked the boundary between a civilized society and one that was, by contemporary standards, markedly more primitive. We are, of course, familiar with the way that the quality of a horse could help distinguish between high and low status within English society, as demonstrated, for example, by the contrast in depictions in the Ellesmere manuscript of *The Canterbury Tales* between the Miller on his small, plain horse and the Prioress on her larger and fancier mount.[8] But the value of the particular kind of horse that Froissart presents to us is not merely visual and superficial, as can be better understood from Froissart's description of the differences between the movements of the English and Scottish armies in the wars of 1327, recorded in Book I of the *Chroniques*,[9] which Froissart apparently was composing at the very time of this trip.

As Froissart depicts it, the English military's very existence was dependent on just the kind of sturdy burden-bearing horse that the greyhound refers to, and the nobles' treatment of horses reflects the debt they owe them. In a passage remarkable for its specific detail, Froissart tells of 40,000 men of war waiting six weeks near York, supplied with good wine from Gascony, Alsace, and Rhine, plenty of food—and he adds in nearly the same breath that "there was dayly brought before their lodgyngis hey, ootes, and litter, wherof they were well served for their horses, and at a metly price" (47). His picture of

---

[8] For a color reproduction showing all the pilgrims and their mounts see Herbert C. Schulz, *The Ellesmere Manuscript of Chaucer's Canterbury Tales* (San Marino: The Huntington Library, 1966). For a full discussion of the various horses mentioned in *The Canterbury Tales* see Teresa McLean, *The English at Play in the Middle Ages* (Windsor Forest, Berkshire: Kensal Press, 1983), 30–32. McLean classifies the pilgrims' mounts from the poorest to the best, with the nun's priest on a jade, the canon on a hackney, the cook and ploughman on undistinguished mares, and the reeve on a "stot"; the more genteel riders include the shipman on his rouncy, the wife of Bath on her ambler, and the monk on his palfrey.

[9] All passages from the *Chroniques* are quoted from the Lord Berners translation, *The Chronicle of Froissart*, 5 vols. (London: David Nutt, 1901–03), 1:42–64.

the Scots, who lived in a "savage and wylde countrey" and a "ryght pore countrey of every thyng, saving of beastis" (48), is remarkably different, a point that he illustrates mainly by discussing distinctions in their mode of travel. While the English, with their massive supplies and wagons, could manage to move only six miles a day, the Scots, he says, in a day and a night "wyll dryve theyr hole host xxiii myle, for they are all a horsebacke" (49) except for those who follow behind on foot. The knights and squires are "well horsed" and "the comon people and other, on litell hakeneys and geldyngis" (49), and they pull no carts or wagons because of the ruggedness of the mountains. An important detail that Froissart adds is that these little horses are never tied at night nor "kept at hard meate" but, rather, are "lette go to pasture in the feldis and busshes" (49).

While such a distinction in the mode of travel might seem to the modern reader to work to the advantage of the less heavily encumbered Scots, the social implications lean strongly in the other direction. As Joyce Salisbury points out in her study of animals in the Middle Ages, the transition from small to large horses was an important development in northern Europe between the eighth century, when horses were pony-sized and selective breeding was still unknown, and the fourteenth century, when the noble war horse had reached a height of eighteen or nineteen hands.[10] This change in stature was important not only in battle but in transportation as well, since good pack horses carrying heavy loads could travel at a much greater speed than the oxen they had replaced. Members of the upper class, who could afford a luxury animal that required a diet of grain and had no residual value as food, could now carry with them the goods and belongings that displayed their status and maintained their high standard of living.

Thus it is significant when Froissart reports that the quick-moving Scots carry with them "noo purveyaunce of brede nor wyne" because

---

[10] Joyce Salisbury, *The Beast Within: Animals in the Middle Ages* (New York: Routledge, 1994), 29–30.

their habit is to get by with "flesshe halfe soden" and only river water to drink. They carry no pots and pans because they cook wild animals in their skins. Everything a rider has is carried with him on his horse:

> bitwene the saddyll and the pannell, they trusse a brode plate of metall, and behynde the saddyl, they wyll have a lytle sacke full of ootemele, to the entent that whan they have eaten of the sodden flesshe, than they ley this plate on the fyre, and tempre a lytle of the ootemele: and whan the plate is hote, they cast of the thyn paste theron, and so make a lytle cake in maner of a crakenell, or bysket, and that they eate to comfort with all theyr stomakis. (49)

Given his fascination with these homely details, it is clear that Froissart is conscious of an important trade-off in the level of the Scots' quality of life when he remarks, "Wherfore it is no great merveile, though they make greater journeys than other pepple do" (49). As penitential authors point out, eating raw meat, in particular, was considered a sign of bestiality;[11] what is gained by the Scots in mobility is offset by their lack of basic human dignity.

The potential results of such differences of habit become clear when, in the course of the campaign, the English decide to pursue the Scots through "marisshes and savage desertis, mountaignes and dales," braving conditions that cause them to become exhausted, "mervailously fortravailed" (51). In order to cut the Scots off at the river, the English settle on a plan in the Scottish style, each man on horseback taking with him only one loaf of bread, which he is to "trusse . . . behynde hym on his horse." They leave behind all the carriages and wagons, not just for speed but also to protect them from capture. Far from finding such a mode of travel efficient, however, the English experience a kind of cultural crisis. After riding a torturous twenty-four miles, they discover when they want to rest that there is nothing to tie

---

[11] Salisbury, *Beast Within*, 64. For a theoretical discussion of the role of cooking in defining boundaries between humans and animals see Claude Lévi-Strauss, *The Raw and the Cooked: Introduction to a Science of Mythology*, trans. John and Doreen Weightman (New York : Harper & Row, 1969).

horses to in the marshes, so they must hold onto the reins all night. The bread they have brought is inedible because it is permeated with the horses' sweat, and everyone is reduced to drinking river water except for a few lords who had brought along bottles of wine. Likewise, no one has any light to see by, except for those nobles who had thought to bring torches. Froissart says, "In this great trouble and daunger they passed all that nyght: their armour still on their backis, their horses redy sadled" (53). Having necessarily denied themselves access to their highly developed animal support system, the English are unable to function in the civilized manner to which they are accustomed.

The degree to which their dependence on large burden-bearing horses figures into their difficulties continues to be emphasized as Froissart describes the next day of the campaign. Though they were eager to fight just to escape the inconvenience of their position, they were delayed by rain; all they could do to feed the horses was cut down branches of trees and offer them leaves. Finally they sent to Newcastle for provisions, which were delivered, significantly, on "lytle nagges, charged with brede evyll bakyn, in panyers, and smalle pere wyne in barels" (54). Without their own supplies, the English were at the mercy of the local economy, and after a few days the price being charged went up considerably. As it continued to rain, the horses' saddles and reins were rotting, and "most part of their horses hurt on their backs: nor they had nat wherwith to shoo them, that were unshodde, nor they had nothyng to cover them selfe withall, fro the rayne and colde, but grene busshes, and their armour. . ." (55). The image of unshod, partially harnessed horses and men hovering under bushes or their own armor for shelter suggests nearly complete exposure to the elements, a condition associated with only the most primitive human societies.

Although one may assume that Froissart the traveler-narrator on his route home from Scotland among upper-class companions did not have to face the bitter hardships experienced by the English army, the fact that his *Debat* is set in Scotland at all certainly would have suggested to an aristocratic English or French audience the possibility of inclement weather, rough roads, and poor supplies, so that the importance of a sturdy and dependable horse would receive special emphasis. While the role of the traveling mount was not as showy or glorious as that of the heroic steed extolled in other kinds of poetry, such a horse was certainly a more basic element of everyday life among people who moved whole households from one location to another as a matter of course. Given this context, then, it is no wonder that Froissart's greyhound predicts at the end of the day that the master will tell his proper and dependable traveling mount, "Rest well, Grisel, for you have deserved the oats you are eating now" [Or pren ton repos, / Grisel, car bien l'as desservi / L'avainne que tu menges ci] (58–60).

If the dog's picture of the horse's status thus can be said to provide an accurate reflection of the attitudes of an audience with a firm general sense of the superiority of English or Anglo-French culture, the horse's picture of the dog's life is no less revealing, adding to the depiction of social norms an image of the more particular, and highly elevated, tastes of the nobility. Although the two animals are quarreling over whose life is harder—or, conversely, more pampered—the real difference between them is not the degree to which they are appreciated but the kind of role they play in the typical owner's life. This becomes immediately apparent in the horse's complaint about what the dog eats, for while the horse, in his functional, utilitarian role, is sure to get his oats, it is the dog who will be treated as if he were a companion, almost a member of the household. As Grisel puts it:

> I wish to God that I were a dog
> . . . .
> For then I would have bread and butter
> For breakfast, and rich soup.
>
> Pleuïst Dieu que je fuisse uns chiens,
> . . . .
> S'avroie dou pain et dou bure
> Au matin, et la gresse soupe. (34–37)

This menu is apparently no exaggeration, since Cotgrave's Dictionary of 1611 defines the French term "souppes de levrier"—literally greyhound soup—as being a concoction made of coarse brown bread soaked in the "last and worst fat of the beefpot."[12] Accounts from royal kennels document under the category of "dog food" large bills for bread,[13] and some medical treatises even describe a diet of butter for an ailing hound. While the famous Gaston de Foix recommends in his *Le livre de la chasse* only bread when hounds are not hunting, so that they associate meat with the hunt and "hunt more keenly," royal hounds sometimes were fed blood pudding, and sick ones got tripe, blood potage, or broth, not to mention the possibility of table scraps.[14] Thus the horse is not far from the mark when he says, "I know very well what he feeds you—if there is only one good morsel around, you'll have it in your muzzle" [Je sçai bien de quoi il te soupe: / S'il n'avoit q'un seul bon morsel, / Tu part en as te en ton musel] (38–40). To make things worse, the horse points out that the dog can go wherever he pleases and that no one dares strike or beat him. He, on the other hand, will feel the rider's heels in his side immediately if he does not keep up a good trot. While the horse is without doubt a carefully maintained cog in the machine of civilized living, it is the dog who represents the luxury of sport and leisure in aristocratic life.

---

[12] Randle Cotgrave, *A Dictionarie of the French and English Tongues, 1611* (Menston: Scolar Press, 1968).

[13] John Cummins, *The Hound and the Hawk: The Art of Medieval Hunting* (New York: St. Martin's, 1988), 26.

[14] Gaston Phoebus recommends a number of specific remedies in Section X of his treatise. For a cold he suggests that the owner hold the nostrils of the dog over a steaming pot of water that contains camomile, mint, sage, rue, and other herbs; for a sore throat, he suggests meat cut into tiny pieces and cooked in broth or the milk of a goat or cow. He comments that "le beurre aussi, et les oeufs font grand bien. . . ." For a translation of this treatise into modern French see Gaston Phoebus, *Le livre de la chasse/Gaston Phébus; texte intégral traduit en français moderne par Robert et André Bassuat* (Paris: P. Lebaud, 1986). For a convenient facsimile see *The Hunting Book of Gaston Phébus: Manuscrit français 616, Paris, Bibliothèque nationale*, introd. Marcel Thomas and François Avril (London: Harvey Miller, 1998).

The recreational element of dog ownership among nobles is particularly well illustrated in the way that dogs were bred and acquired for highly specialized purposes, in much the same way that modern sports enthusiasts pride themselves on owning exactly the right piece of equipment for every game. The idea of the functions of different breeds was highly developed, as can be seen in an illustration showing eight distinct types of dogs, from an elegantly illuminated copy of the medieval hunting treatise by Gaston de Foix, who was, some years later, in the 1380s, the recipient of an extended visit from Froissart himself (fig. 1).[15] As the fourteenth century's most eminent authority on hunting, Gaston, who called himself Febus (Phoebus, Phébus) to draw attention to his Apollonian good looks, details the functions of each kind of dog, including the highly prized scent hounds, which most often gained the rare distinction of being officially designated *beau chien*. The greyhound, classified as a sight hound, is especially valued for its "speed and willingness to seize and pull down running quarry," but it is noted that when it is not on the field it should "follow its master and do all his commands, being sweet, clean, joyous, willing and gracious in all its doings except towards the wild beasts, to whom it should be terrible, spiteful and hostile."[16]

The breeding of both dogs and horses, of course, was significant not only for the development of desirable skills and capabilities related to aristocratic activities but also for establishing and displaying the status of the owner. Froissart's horse's name—Grisel—indicates a grey or dappled color that puts him in the category of the prized, decorative mount, reminiscent of Charlemagne's "Ash-Grey"; the selective development of distinctive colors and markings separated such an animal

---

[15] In his study of hunting in medieval Scotland, Gilbert lists the following sporting breeds: Alaunt, Bloodhound, Brachet, Deerhound, Great Dane, Greyhound, German boarhound, Kennet, Limer, Mastiff, Rauch, Scenting hound, Sleuthhound, and Terrier (*Hunting and Hunting Reserves*, 64–66). The Scottish greyhound is most likely the ancestor of what is today known as a deerhound.

[16] *Le livre de la chasse*, Book II, chap. 18.

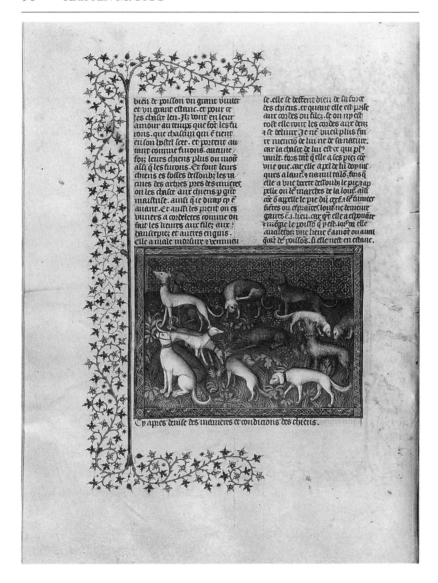

Figure 1. Medieval hunting dogs. Top, left to right: greyhound, running hound, lymer, bird dogs (spaniels). Middle: two small smooth-coated greyhounds, two mastiffs. Front: two alaunts, a greyhound-mastiff cross (known as "bastard"), and another lymer or running hound. From *Le livre de la chasse* by Gaston Phoebus, The Pierpont Morgan Library, New York: M.1044, fol. 28v.

from the ordinary dun-colored horse that was most common as a farm animal.[17] Likewise, Froissart's mention of the fact that his greyhound is white is consistent with a comment by John I of Portugal, who lists hounds of pure white and pure yellow as most desirable, followed by dogs of mixed color; it is his opinion that all black dogs are bad.[18] In a culture where such distinctions were common knowledge, the audience would have had no trouble discerning that both of these animals belonged to a man of some quality.

But although the status of the two animals may seem similar with regard to color, the horse's jealousy of the greyhound is not entirely misplaced, for the dog's purpose as a marker of his owner's rank is so predominant that it often relieves him of any practical duties whatso- ever, especially in the context of travel. Illustrations from the time show the greyhound being acquired as much for a "graceful presence" as for a hunting dog,[19] a function suggested clearly in the Ellesmere de- piction of the Monk, where the dogs seem to be running along merrily and their depiction is used to suggest the pilgrim's self-indulgent char- acter. Indeed, in her book on medieval travel, Margaret Wade Labarge includes in her description of Thomas à Becket's elegant embassy procession an image of two hundred members of a household on horse- back, large iron-bound chariots, each pulled by five horses, grooms walking alongside strong and shapely horses, and food servants in

---

[17] For a discussion of the development of purely decorative characteristics in the breeding of horses see Salisbury, *Beast Within*, 30–32. McLean identifies the grey horse as the most desirable, with the pale "grissel" as best, followed by "liards" (horses spotted with grey), the more common dappled greys, and the iron-grey "ferrant." References to chestnuts and black horses are, she points out, rare in horse's names, pictures, or stories (*English at Play*, 34).

[18] John I of Portugal, *Livro da montaria*, ed. Francisco M. Esteves Pereira (Coimbra: Imprensa da Universidade, 1918), 56. McLean points out in her discussion of colors of dogs that the name "greyhound" refers not to the dog's color but to its "grae" or "high grade" (*English at Play*, 41).

[19] Cummins, *The Hound and the Hawk*, 14.

small groups, singing as they went, followed by greyhounds and other hunting dogs with their runners and attendants.[20] To enhance the elegance of such a tableau, greyhound owners often provided their animals with splendid collars, examples of which appear not only in travel and hunting scenes but also in illuminations depicting the luxurious pleasure gardens of courting couples such as Maugis and la Belle Oriande (fig. 2). Such collars are described in one queen's wardrobe account as being constructed from "le tissue white and green with letters and silver turrets"; in another they are made from "soy chekerey vert et noir avec le tret, letters and bells of silver gilt."[21] Fine specimens of the greyhound breed were frequently offered as gifts, as Froissart himself documents in one of his *pastourelles* (VIII), where a shepherd has been given the job of delivering four fine dogs—heroically named Tristram, Hector, Brun, and Rollant—to the eminent Gaston himself.[22]

The association in this *pastourelle* between high praise of Gaston and the gift of four greyhounds is no coincidence, for Gaston, who was known for being "sage, large, noble et vaillant" and who was given credit for remarkable management of his territories, credited his virtues directly to his dogs. Gaston Phoebus "loved hounds of all beasts" and perceived hunting as a way of avoiding mortal sin and saving his soul.[23] He speaks of the pleasures of "uncoupling hounds, running with them, cheering them on" as activities that left no room for evil thoughts. He even associates nobility and gentility of heart with "the love of working

---

[20] Margaret Wade Labarge, *Medieval Travellers: The Rich and the Restless* (New York: Norton, 1982), xi.

[21] Cummins, *The Hound and the Hawk*, 24. These elegant collars seem to be peculiar to greyhounds, probably because they show up well on the long, thin neck typical of the breed. Running hounds are depicted with plainer collars, and mastiffs usually wear spiked collars, as if to indicate that they are aggressive and difficult to control.

[22] For a modern edition of Froissart's *pastourelles* see Rob Roy McGregor, *The Lyric Poems of Jehan Froissart* (Chapel Hill: University of North Carolina Press, 1975).

[23] D. H. Madden, *A Chapter of Mediaeval History: The Fathers of the Literature of Field Sport and Horses* (London: John Murray, 1924), 156.

Figure 2. A greyhound with an ornate collar, ca. 1475. From the *Roman de Renaud de Montauban*, Bibliothèque de l'Arsenal, Paris: MS fr. 5072, fol. 31v.

dogs," a stipulation no doubt intended to contrast with the fashion for lap dogs of the type to which Chaucer's Prioress fed choice morsels while people were going hungry. The only fault that Gaston finds in ten chapters on dogs is that they die too soon.[24]

Gaston was not alone in his affection for dogs, nor in his association of certain breeds with a noble style of life. Some greyhounds were for hunting and others were "kept in the palace as decorative display"[25]—distinguishing those given the name "greyhounds of the chamber" from those which lived a more active life. But even among hunting dogs, sometimes the finest specimens received as gifts became part of a household. A famous *beau chien* named Souillart, owned by Jacques de Brézé, was said in his old age to have slept in his master's

[24] Ibid., 196–98.

[25] Cummins, *The Hound and the Hawk*, 25.

chamber, near the fire. Likewise, John of Portugal reportedly had two alaunts "which he loved so much that he took them into his bed at night, and slept between them. . . ."[26] Dogs also were given careful medical attention (fig. 3), a fact documented already in the thirteenth century by Albertus Magnus, who describes detailed cures for the nine ailments of mange, maggots, tumors, thorn wounds, rabies, emaciation, indolence, fleas, and constipation.[27] The emotional scene of the death of a favorite dog is depicted in Alfonso of Castille's fourteenth-century treatise *Libro de la montería* (fig. 4).

Still, with a surprisingly realistic balancing note, Froissart's poem suggests that the attachment an aristocratic hunter felt for his favorite hunting dog might not save the animal from every discomfort, for while the treatises present a purist's point of view of breeds and training, in the everyday world of travelers a dog might still have been expected to fulfill certain functions of a more generic nature. In spite of his protestations that his body is built for sport, the greyhound in the poem claims that while the horse is allowed to sleep in a nice bed of clean soft straw, he, as the only available canine, will be put out back and told to guard the door. This duty, according to treatises, ordinarily belonged to the mastiff, who was "visually unsuitable, clearly, to act as a royal or aristocratic accouterment or gift as the greyhound or alaunt often did,"[28] or perhaps of the Talbot, the manor dog referred to in The Nun's Priest's Tale and described in the girdlebook owned by a certain Harry the Haywarde as "a large white or light-colored animal with long hanging ears, heavy jaws, and a large wide nose for good scenting ability."[29] Its fierceness, as it appears in a Tudor armorial roof painting

---

[26] Ibid.

[27] Albertus Magnus, *Man and the Beasts (De Animalibus, Books 22–26)*, trans. James J. Scanlan, Medieval and Renaissance Texts and Studies 47 (Binghamton: Center for Medieval and Early Renaissance Studies, 1987), 83.

[28] Cummins, *The Hound and the Hawk*, 15.

[29] John B. Friedman, "Harry the Haywarde and Talbat his Dog: An Illustrated Girdlebook from Worcestershire," in *Art Into Life: Collected Papers from the Kresge*

Figure 3. Maladies and remedies of dogs. From *Le livre de la chasse* by Gaston Phoebus, The Pierpont Morgan Library, New York: M.1044, fol. 31v.

Art Museum Medieval Symposia, ed. Carol Garrett Fisher and Kathleen L. Scott (East Lansing: Michigan State University Press, 1995), 139–40.

Figure 4. Alfonso XI of Castile lamenting the death of a hound after a boar hunt. From the *Libro de lat Montería del Rey de Castilla Alfonso XI*. Patrimonio Nacional, Madrid: M.II/2105, fol. 34v.

Figure 5. A Talbot dog. Tudor armorial roof painting, Haddon Hall, Derbyshire. Photo by John B. Friedman.

(fig. 5), suggests its importance in "apprehending evil-doers" more than in fulfilling one of the specified roles in the formal chase. Furthermore, Albertus Magnus states that "not every dog is suitable for detecting thieves," recommending mongrels over greyhounds and explaining a thorough method of training watch dogs that involves a victim clad in leather body armor who allows the dog to practice biting, in a manner not unlike that used in modern attack dog training.[30] But though these specialized animals might have been preferred, Froissart's greyhound reminds us that even in an age when the hunting dog was considered a noble animal, the fears of travelers on a dangerous route at night might outweigh the accepted function of a particular dog.

---

[30] Albertus Magnus, *Man and the Beasts*, trans. Scanlan, 82.

Indeed, the cultural attitude towards Froissart's greyhound is given further nuance when the dog points out that if anything is stolen out of the kitchen, he is the one who will end up getting beaten: "If anyone covers with a cloth any bread, meat, butter, cheese or milk," he says, "and the serving wench or the valet eats it" [. . . j'en ai toutes les tapes, / Car s'on envolepe ens es nappes / Pain, char, bure, frommage ou let / Et la meschine ou li vallet / En menguent par aucun cas . . .] (69–73) all the blame will fall on him, and he will not even have had a taste of the delicacies. He will, he claims, get beaten just on suspicion, a reflection perhaps of an older and broader underlying cultural perception of the dog as a lowly, untrustworthy creature whose very name is used as an insult to human beings.[31] Horses, the greyhound points out, never get blamed for such things, and nothing is required of the horse once he has put in his good day's work. If the horse suffers more by day, then the dog, with his closer physical and emotional proximity to humans, bears his share of the burden by night.

The apparent balance between the two positions at this point in the poem turns out to be the signal for resolution, for at this moment the dog sees a town up ahead and tells the horse to go at a gallop, to which the horse agrees, since he, too, is hungry. While the stolid working horse has made his case in a mere twenty-seven lines to the sporting greyhound's more recreational and showy sixty, neither has really won out in the argument. The final line says simply that Froissart manages to "reconcile" them, saving both the author and the audience from any obligation to choose a winner. Froissart thus throws the focus of the poem backwards onto the detailed descriptions presented by the animal

---

[31] For a discussion of the dog as a moral outcast see Salisbury, *Beast Within*, 132–33. The degree to which dogs could be used as a symbol of low morality and inhumanity perhaps nowhere is better illustrated than in Dante's *Inferno*, where references to "canni" and barking and howling occur throughout the lower regions. As Salisbury points out, it is probably the very fact that dogs lived in such close and privileged proximity with people that made them seem morally threatening in a culture that was struggling to maintain a distinction between humans and animals.

characters themselves, avoiding any possible debate or any tendency on the part of the reader to associate the horse or the dog with a human moral position. Much as the observer-narrator of Froissart's *pastourelles* provided a glimpse into the "exotic" lives of the shepherds and shepherdesses who depended on the nobility for their living, the narrator of this debate offers Froissart's patrons a surprisingly accurate and complete report on an aspect of their own courtly world which would ordinarily have remained unexamined and unarticulated.

Like much of the travel literature of the day, of course, Froissart's poem was intended mainly to entertain. Though the debate might raise some interesting questions about the differences in treatment between horses and dogs, and even suggest some inconsistency in the prevailing attitudes towards canine character, its tone is lighthearted and certainly not intended to confront the audience with awareness of their sense of cultural superiority (which they no doubt felt was well-founded) or aristocratic excess (which, in the guise of refinement, was considered both their privilege and their right). It does, however, present the kinds of specific and visual details of daily life that are so rare in medieval literature, creating a new perspective that invites the audience to take a fresh look at the known world. Like travelers in a foreign land, Grisel and the greyhound provide the outlines of "indigenous" behavior, raising their relations with humans to a new level of consciousness which in its own time must have elicited many a smile of recognition and which today provides rare insight into the interlinkings of animals, nationality, and social class.

THE MIRACLE
OF THE LENGTHENED BEAM
IN APOCRYPHAL AND
HAGIOGRAPHIC TRADITION

THOMAS N. HALL

IN A 1982 ESSAY on the hagiographic motif of the lengthened beam, Baudouin de Gaiffier drew attention to some twenty examples of a miracle story in Latin saints' lives and miracle collections from the sixth to the sixteenth century in which a wooden board intended for use in a construction project is at first found to be of inadequate size but is then miraculously stretched to its requisite length.[1] The story in its typical form involves a scene in which a group of workers is charged with building a tower or bridge or some other kind of edifice but find their work interrupted when they realize that a single beam has been cut too short. The problem is remedied when, in one common scenario, the saint whom the life commemorates observes the workers' plight and offers a prayer or word of instruction to his audience, or in an alternative scenario, in which a secondary figure such as a bishop or priest prays to the departed saint for help. In both cases, the result is that through the saint's intercession the beam is miraculously lengthened,

---

[1] Baudouin de Gaiffier, "Le thème hagiographique de la poutre allongée," *Mittellateinisches Jahrbuch* 17 (1982), 18–25.

sometimes growing even longer than the workers require. More often than not, the beam is then deemed a relic, and fragments taken from the elongated portion are said to work miracles for many years afterward.

An early and well-known example of this miracle is reported by Gregory of Tours in his *On the Glory of the Martyrs* in a chapter on the reconstruction of a shrine in honor of Saint Lawrence. The story Gregory tells is that a church in Italy dedicated to Saint Lawrence had become so decayed after years of neglect that its roof completely collapsed. The local residents made preparations for its repair by traveling to a nearby forest, where they cut down oak trees, planed new beams, carted them back to the church, and laid them side by side on the ground for alignment, only to discover that one of the beams had inadvertently been cut too short. The bishop in charge of the project then raised a prayer to Saint Lawrence, lamenting the fact that his meager resources would not permit him to have another beam cut and brought from the forest. As Gregory explains:

> Suddenly, to the surprise of all, the beam grew to such a length that it was necessary for a long piece to be cut off. After this task the people thought it improper to lose this blessing; so, in the belief that this beam had been touched and lengthened by the hand of the martyr, they cut the leftover piece into little splinters and often drove off various illnesses [with these splinters].[2]

---

[2] English trans. by Raymond Van Dam, *Gregory of Tours: Glory of the Martyrs*, Translated Texts for Historians, Latin Series 3 (Liverpool: Liverpool University Press, 1988), 64. Gregory, *In gloria martyrum* § 41, "De basilicae sancti Laurentii trabe" (*BHL*, no. 4776), ed. Br. Krusch, *Gregorii Turonensis Opera*, MGH, Scriptores rerum Merovingicarum 1 (Hanover: Hahn, 1885), 516, lines 4–7: "Ilico cunctis attonitis, trabes crevit in tanto spatio longitudinis, ut necesse esset, partem magnam incidi. De qua industria plebis, beneficia perdere nefas putans, credens eam manu martyris tactam ac prolongatam, partem quae superfuerat frustratim decerpens, diversas infirmitates saepe submovit." Gregory's story is repeated by Vincent of Beauvais, *Speculum historiale* XII.94, parte priore (Nuremburg: Anton Koberger, 1483). It also is mentioned briefly in the thirteenth-century *Speculum laicorum* sometimes attributed to John of Hovedon: *Le Speculum Laicorum. Edition d'une collection d'exempla, composée en Angleterre à la fin du XIIIe siècle*, ed. J. Th. Welter, Thesaurus exemplorum 5 (Paris:

The tale of the beam miraculously lengthened by Saint Lawrence, Gregory goes on to say, was found so worthy of commemoration that it even had been set to verse by Venantius Fortunatus, and in continuing his own account Gregory quotes the opening lines of Fortunatus's poem:

> Lawrence, you who were burned in the life-giving flames because of your merit and who returns with burning faith as a victor over the fire, when the people restored the church with a beam that was too short, the beams grew, and their precious faith grew too. Although the log had been cut too short, it stretched itself because of your excellence. To the extent that it had previously been too short, it was cut afterwards. The tree that was cut by axes was worthy to grow longer, and the dry foliage learned to become longer.[3]

But the effects of the miracle did not stop here, Gregory says. He himself once knew a man whose toothache had been cured when he touched a splinter of the beam to his tooth, while other fragments more recently had been transported to Limoges, where they were entrusted to Abbot Aredius and are known to have brought about additional cures far from the site of the original miracle.

Auguste Picard, 1914), 47 (cap. XXX, no. 213); and it is summarized in the chapter on Saint Lawrence (cap. CXVII) in the *Legenda aurea: Jacobi a Voragine Legenda Aurea Vulgo Historia Lombardica Dicta*, ed. Th. Graesse, 3rd ed. (1890; Osnabrück: Zeller, 1969), 494.

[3] *Gregory of Tours: Glory of the Martyrs*, trans. Van Dam, 64. Gregory, *In gloria martyrum*, 516, lines 9–16:

> Laurenti, merito flammis vitalibus uste,
>   Qui fervente fide victor ab igne redis,
> Dum templa novant breviore robore plebes,
>   Creveruntque trabes, crevit et alma fides;
> Stipite contracto tua se mercede tetendit,
>   Quantum parva prius, postea caesa fuit.
> Crescere plus meruit succisa securibus arbor,
>   Et didicit sicca longior esse coma.

See also Venantius Fortunatus, *Carmen* IX.14, "De basilicae sancti Laurenti trabe" (*BHL*, no. 4775), lines 1–16, ed. F. Leo, *Fortunati Opera*, MGH, Auctores antiquissimi 4.1 (1881; Munich: MGH, 1981), 218.

For Gregory and Fortunatus, this story is worth repeating because it witnesses to the superabundance of productive, generative, and curative powers that result from a prayer to a saint. In both tellings of the story, Saint Lawrence's response to the bishop is not so much to fulfill his request as to exceed it, and a defining feature of the miracle is the extravagant growth of the beam beyond its ideal length. If Lawrence had simply accomplished what the bishop had asked of him and had made the beam grow only to the point that it was of equal length with the others, then the effect would have been simply to annul the beam-cutter's mistake, complete and perfect the beam, and render it suitable for use in the construction project, all to the glory of Saint Lawrence. But something quite different seems to be intended here. The beam's inordinate growth brings glory to Lawrence, but the miracle ironically fails to answer the bishop's prayer and makes the beam unfit for use. As miracles go, this one seems rather impractical, but it has the important consequence of demonstrating by means of a concrete and vivid example a saint's capacity to outperform human need or expectation. In this respect, the story's emphasis on the beam's excessive growth helps classify the miracle as an act of supererogation, a display of miraculous power that is greater than required.[4] Among New Testament miracles, its closest analogue is the miracle of the loaves and fishes, which likewise results in a bountiful surfeit. In medieval saints' lives and miracle collections, the events that most closely recall this pattern are miracles in which a lamp or well or fountain bubbles over with a

---

[4] On supererogatory acts see J. Hennessey, "Supererogation, Works of," in *New Catholic Encyclopedia*, 15 vols. (New York, etc.: McGraw-Hill, 1967), 13:810–11. The significance of supererogation as an ethical concept is discussed most fully by David Heyd, *Supererogation: Its Status in Ethical Theory* (Cambridge: Cambridge University Press, 1982); and Gregory Mellema, *Beyond the Call of Duty: Supererogation, Obligation, and Offence* (Albany: SUNY Press, 1991). In contemporary ethical theory a supererogatory act is understood to be a morally praiseworthy act (such as an act of charity) performed voluntarily and in an altruistic spirit by someone who has no obligation to do so and who expects no reward for it. The idea that saints are able to perform meritorious works over and above any requirements God places on them is the foundation upon which the late medieval practice of selling indulgences rests.

profusion of oil, or in which a river overflows its bounds, in each case a sign of overabundance.[5] However, in the story of Saint Lawrence and the lengthened beam, the excessive growth is actually governed by strict measures of balance and proportion. The miracle compensates for the error of the improperly cut beam on a scale of measured equivalences: just as the intensity of Lawrence's martyrdom by burning is equivalent to the intensity of his burning faith, so the growth of the beam is matched by the growth of the people's faith, and the quantity of the excess growth is in direct proportion to the gap that first rendered the beam useless. Thus even though the miracle is supererogatory, it is hardly without control or limitation, and the lengthening of the beam in fact adheres to a calculated plan of mathematical precision.

What most interested de Gaiffier in this story is the frequency with which it is repatterned in other saints' lives, from Gregory's day through the early Renaissance, a valuable testimony, he suggested, to the manner in which certain miracles are retold and reformulated in hagiographic literature over the course of several centuries. A variation of the same story emerges, for instance, in the eleventh-century account of the miracles of Saint Augustine of Canterbury by Goscelin, who reports that just such an incident took place during the construction of a tower adjacent to the monastery of Ethelingey. When one of the beams for the tower was found to be a foot and a half short, the worried abbot appealed to Saint Augustine, and the beam at once expanded by three feet—twice the length of the original deficiency.[6] In Braulio of

---

[5] Gerd Theissen, *The Miracle Stories of the Early Christian Tradition*, trans. Francis McDonagh, ed. John Riches (Philadelphia: Fortress Press, 1983), 103, defines miracles of this sort as "gift miracles," ones that "make material goods available in surprising ways; they provide larger-than-life and extraordinary gifts, food transformed, increased, richly available." In Theissen's thinking, however, gift miracles such as the miracle of the loaves and fishes "are never initiated by requests, but always by an act of the miracle-worker" (103), a qualification which clearly does not apply to the miracle of the lengthened beam.

[6] Goscelin, *Miracula s. Augustini ep. Cantuariensis, Historia maior* (*BHL*, no. 779), ptd. *Acta Sanctorum*, ed. Socii Bollandiani, 1st ed., 68 vols. (Antwerp, etc.: Meursium,

Saragossa's seventh-century *Life of St. Aemilianus Cucullatus*, a similar miracle is said to take place in the building of a barn. When the workers find one beam short, Saint Aemilianus turns to God with imploring eyes and asks that the work not be left unfinished. The workers return to their project and find that the beam has become longer than all the rest.[7] Virtually the same miracle is told of the fifteenth-century Minorite Saint Matthaeus Agrigentinus (Saint Matthew of Sicily) in the collection of miracles assembled by Luke Wadding in the *Annales Minorum*, only in this case the lengthened beam permits a group of carpenters to complete their construction of a bridge.[8] These and other versions of the miracle from a variety of times and places confirm de Gaiffier's impression that the story had a remarkable longevity as a literary phenomenon, and show how saints' lives typically feed off one another for narrative material. But much of the story's prolific career remains undocumented, and in what follows I would like to build upon de Gaiffier's observations about the evolution of this miracle story by reconstructing a formative stage in its early history—in its history before Gregory of Tours, that is—and by suggesting a connection between this story and two other groups of medieval narratives that reflect a common structure and that offer some evidence for the oral transmission of medieval miracle tales.

---

etc., 1643–), Mai VI, 397–411, this miracle at 400–01: "Apparuit trabi trium pedum spatium excrevisse, hoc est tantum iam illi superesse, quantum ante claruerat defuisse"; see also de Gaiffier, "Le thème hagiographique," 19–20.

[7] Braulio, *Vita s. Aemiliani Cucullati conf. Tarracone* (*BHL*, no. 100), ed. Ignazio Cazzaniga, "La Vita di S. Emiliano, Scritta da Braulione Vescovo di Saragozza: Edizione Critica," *Accademia Nazionale dei Lincei, Bollettino del Comitato per la preparazione della edizione nazionale dei Classici Greci e Latini*, nuova serie, fascicolo 3 (1954), 7–44, at 34; English trans. by A. T. Fear, *Lives of the Visigothic Fathers*, Translated Texts for Historians 26 (Liverpool: Liverpool University Press, 1997), 33–34; see also de Gaiffier, "Le thème hagiographique," 18.

[8] *Annales Minorum seu Trium Ordinum a S. Francisco Institutorum*, ed. A. R. P. Luke Wadding, 3rd ed., 25 vols. (Florence: Quaracchi, 1932), 10:139; see also de Gaiffier, "Le thème hagiographique," 22.

Although unremarked by de Gaiffier, the basic form of the miracle of the lengthened beam can be traced back to an episode in the *Infancy Gospel of Thomas*, an originally Greek or Syriac apocryphon of the second or third century that consists of a series of anecdotes about the young boy Jesus, who manifests his divine powers at an early age by performing a number of miracles.[9] These discrete vignettes, drawn probably from an ancient cycle of religious folklore with analogues in Indian, Egyptian, and Greco-Roman myth, feature an alternately playful and mischievous Jesus who acts out his divine gifts by riding a sunbeam, bringing to life twelve sparrows fashioned from clay, striking a boy dead who happened to bump him on the shoulder by mistake, and confounding his teacher at school by reciting a mystical allegory of the alphabet extracted from Pythagorean models. From a literary-historical perspective, this cycle of stories is remarkable for its early manipulation of the *puer senex* topos and for its development of a class of amusing miracles which have an important later reflex in the pranks played by medieval saints known as the *joca sanctorum*.[10] One of the

---

[9] On the *Infancy Gospel of Thomas* see *BHG*, nos. 779p–779pb; Mauritius Geerard, *Clavis Apocryphorum Novi Testamenti*, Corpus Christianorum Series Apocryphorum (Turnhout: Brepols, 1992), 34–39 (no. 57); Friedrich Stegmüller, *Repertorium Biblicum Medii Aevi*, 11 vols. (Madrid: Consejo superior de investigaciones cientificas, 1950–80) [hereafter *RBMA*], nos. 175, 2–23; the discussion by Oscar Cullmann in Edgar Hennecke, *New Testament Apocrypha*, ed. Wilhelm Schneemelcher, English trans. ed. Robert McL. Wilson, 2 vols. (Philadelphia: Westminster, 1963–65) [hereafter *NTA*], 1:388–401; and J. K. Elliott, *The Apocryphal New Testament: A Collection of Apocryphal Christian Literature in an English Translation* (Oxford: Clarendon Press, 1993), 68–83.

[10] On the *puer senex* topos see Adolf Hofmeister, "Puer, iuvenis, senex. Zum Verständnis der mittelalterlichen Altersbezeichnungen," in *Papsttum und Kaisertum. Forschungen zur politischen Geschichte und Geisteskultur des Mittelalters Paul Kehr zum 65. Geburtstag dargebracht*, ed. Albert Brackmann (Munich: Verlag der Münchner Drucke, 1926), 287–316; J. de Ghellinck, "Iuventus, gravitas, senectus," in *Studia mediaevalia in honorem admodum Reverendi Patris Raymundi Josephi Martin, Ordinis Praedicatorum s. theologiae magistri LXXum natalem diem agentis* (Bruges: De Tempel, 1948), 38–59; Ernst Robert Curtius, *European Literature and the Latin Middle Ages*, trans.

more benign episodes of the Infancy Gospel tells how Jesus helped his elderly father Joseph by lengthening a board Joseph needed in order to build a piece of furniture.[11] In the version of the apocryphon that preserves the fullest form of this anecdote, the Greek B text, the story unfolds as follows:

> And when Jesus had reached his eighth year, Joseph was ordered by a certain rich man to construct a bed for him, for he was a carpenter. And he went out in the field to collect wood, and Jesus also went with him. And having cut two pieces of wood, he fashioned one and he laid it beside the other; and when he had measured it he found it too short. And when he saw it, he was grieved and sought to find another. And when Jesus saw it he said to him, "Lay these two together so as to make both ends equal." And Joseph, being in doubt what the child meant by this, did what was ordered. And he said to him again, "Take hold firmly of the short piece of wood." And Jesus made that piece of wood equal to the other. And he said to Joseph, "Grieve no more but do your work without impediment." And he, when he saw, was exceedingly amazed and said within himself, "Blessed am I that God gave me such a child."[12]

Willard R. Trask (1952; Princeton: Princeton University Press, 1973), 98–101; and J. A. Burrow, *The Ages of Man: A Study in Medieval Writing and Thought* (Oxford: Clarendon Press, 1988), 95–102, 105–06, 111–16, 120–23, 137–41. On the *joca sanctorum* see Benedicta Ward, *Miracles and the Medieval Mind: Theory, Record and Event 1000–1215*, rev. ed. (Philadelphia: University of Pennsylvania Press, 1987), 211–13; and Kathleen Ashley and Pamela Sheingorn, *Writing Faith: Text, Sign, & History in the Miracles of Sainte Foy* (Chicago and London: University of Chicago Press, 1999), 91–94.

[11] The earliest known Greek version of this story appears in the *Evangelium Thomae Graece A* cap. XIII, ed. Constantinus de Tischendorf, *Evangelia apocrypha*, editio altera (Leipzig: Mendelssohn, 1876), 152; reproduced with a Spanish trans. by Aurelio de Santos Otero, ed. and trans., *Los evangelios apócrifos*, 3rd ed. (Madrid: Biblioteca de autores cristianos, 1979), 296–97. An English trans. of the Greek text by A. J. B. Higgins appears in *NTA* 1:396–97. On the apocryphon's textual history see Stephen Gero, "The Infancy Gospel of Thomas. A Study of the Textual and Literary Problems," *Novum Testamentum* 13 (1971), 46–80, who identifies literary and folkloric analogues for many of the miracles, though not for the one discussed in this essay.

[12] Elliott, *The Apocryphal New Testament*, 82. Compare the analogous episode in the Greek A text, trans. Elliott, 78–79.

This form of the story (from the Greek B text) is attested only in manuscripts of the fourteenth century and later but is believed to descend from a lost parent text in Greek or Syriac from the second or third century, which would thus predate de Gaiffier's earliest example of the lengthened beam miracle by a comfortable margin.[13] However, the same anecdote about Jesus lengthening Joseph's beam would have been known to an even wider medieval audience through the extracts of the *Infancy Gospel of Thomas* incorporated into a second and better-known apocryphon, the Latin *Gospel of Pseudo-Matthew*.[14] This later work, essentially a compilation of Nativity and Infancy narratives from the *Protevangelium of James* and the *Infancy Gospel of Thomas*, survives in manuscripts from as early as the eighth century, though the recension that includes the beam-stretching miracle is known only from the eleventh century and later. Its version of the anecdote about the lengthened beam is modified and elaborated, in part, it seems, to absolve Joseph of any responsibility for the improperly cut beam:

> Now Joseph was a carpenter, and used to make nothing else of wood but ox-yokes, and ploughs, and implements of husbandry, and wooden beds. And it came to pass that a certain young man ordered him to make for him a

---

[13] The earliest known Latin manuscript is described and edited by Guy Phillipart, "Fragments palimpsestes latins du Vindobonensis 563 (Ve siècle?). Évangile selon s. Matthieu, Évangile de l'Enfance selon Thomas, Évangile de Nicodème," *Analecta Bollandiana* 90 (1972), 391–411, at 406–08. On the Latin versions of the apocryphon see Gero, "The Infancy Gospel of Thomas," 50–51.

[14] *BHL*, nos. 5334–42c; *RBMA*, no. 168; *NTA* 1:406; and Geerard, *Clavis Apocryphorum*, 29–30 (no. 51). Until recently, the *Gospel of Pseudo-Matthew* was thought to have been composed by Paschasius Radbertus, but it is now dated ca. 550–700 and is regarded as anonymous; see Jan Gijsel, *Die unmittelbare Textüberlieferung des sog. Pseudo-Matthäus*, Verhandelingen van de Koninklijke Academie voor Wetenschappen, Letteren en Schone Kunsten van België, Klasse der Letteren, jaargang 43, Nr. 96 (Brussels: Paleis der Academiën, 1981), who catalogues 130 manuscripts. José M. Canal-Sánchez independently catalogued 108 manuscripts in his "Antiguas Versiones Latinas del Protevangelio de Santiago," *Ephemerides Mariologicae* 18 (1968), 431–73, at 453–56.

couch six cubits long. And Joseph commanded his servant to cut the wood
with an iron saw, according to the measure which he had sent. But he did not
keep to the prescribed measure, but made one piece of wood shorter than the
other. And Joseph was in perplexity, and began to consider what he was to
do about this. And when Jesus saw him in this state of cogitation, seeing that
it was a matter of impossibility to him, He addressed him with words of com-
fort, saying: Come, let us take hold of the ends of the pieces of wood, and let
us put them together, end to end, and let us fit them exactly to each other,
and draw them to us, for we shall be able to make them equal. Then Joseph
did what he was asked, for he knew that He could do whatever He wished.
And Joseph took hold of the ends of the pieces of wood, and brought them
together against the wall next to himself, and Jesus took hold of the other ends
of the pieces of wood, and drew the shorter piece to Him, and made it of the
same length as the longer one. And He said to Joseph: Go and work, and do
what thou hast promised to do. And Joseph did what he had promised.[15]

In this second version of the story, from the *Gospel of Pseudo-Matthew*,
the wood for the couch is prepared not by Joseph himself but by an

---

[15] *Apocryphal Gospels, Acts, and Revelations*, trans. Alexander Walker, Ante-Nicene
Christian Library 16 (Edinburgh: T. & T. Clark, 1870), 48. *Pseudo-Matthaei Evangelium* cap. XXXVII, ed. Tischendorf, *Evangelia apocrypha*, 105–06: "Et cum esset
Ioseph faber lignarius et nihil aliud ex ligno operaretur nisi iuga bobum et aratra et
terrae versoria et culturae apta, ligneosque faceret lectos, contigit ut quidam iuvenis illi
faciendum grabatum cubitorum sex demandaret. Et iussit Ioseph puero suo incindere
lignum seca ferrea secundum mensuram quam miserat. Qui non servavit definitum sibi
modum; sed fecit unum lignum brevius altero. Et coepit Ioseph aestuando cogitare quid
faciendum ei esset super hoc. Et ut vidit Iesus eum sic aestuantem cogitatione, cui res
gesta impossibilis erat, consolatoria voce alloquitur eum dicens: Veni teneamus capita
singulorum lignorum, et coniungamus ea caput ad caput, et coaequemus ea ad se et
trahamus ad nos: poterimus enim ea facere aequalia. Tunc Ioseph obtemperavit iubenti;
sciebat enim quod posset facere quicquid vellet. Et apprehendit Ioseph capita lignorum
et iunxit ad parietem et iuxta se, et tenuit Iesus altera capita lignorum et traxit ad se
brevius lignum et coaequavit ligno longiori. Et dixit ad Ioseph: Vade operari, et fac
quod facturum te promiseras. Et fecit Ioseph quod promiserat." This passage, from the
Pars altera of the apocryphon (caps. XXV–XLII), is evidently a late addition to the
text that first shows up in manuscripts of the eleventh century and is not included in the
recent edition by Jan Gijsel, *Libri de natiuitate Mariae: Pseudo-Matthaei Euangelium*,
Corpus Christianorum Series Apocryphorum 9 (Turnholt: Brepols, 1997), whose edition ends with cap. XXIV.

anonymous apprentice, so that the beam's inadequacy is no fault of Joseph's, who comes across as a more competent craftsman than he does in the *Infancy Gospel of Thomas*. The young Jesus, too, assumes a more authoritative bearing in *Pseudo-Matthew*, which concludes this episode not with an exclamation of Joseph's pride in his son but with Jesus's admonition that his father quit gaping in amazement at the elongated beam and get back to work.

That the story of the beam miraculously lengthened by Christ for Joseph would have been familiar to a large medieval audience goes without saying, since these two apocrypha served as the foundational texts for a vast assortment of medieval legends about the infancy and childhood of both the Virgin Mary and Christ. It was principally through the *Gospel of Pseudo-Matthew*, for instance, that medieval audiences encountered stories of Christ's mischievous antics as a child. It was largely on the authority of the *Protevangelium* and *Pseudo-Matthew* collectively that the liturgies for the feasts of the Nativity of the Virgin, her Presentation at the Temple, her Conception, and her Assumption were introduced into the Western Church during the seventh and eighth centuries,[16] and it was *Pseudo-Matthew* as well that inspired the traditional iconography of the Flight into Egypt.[17] Several medieval works

---

[16] Simeon Vailhé, "La fête de la Présentation de Marie au Temple," *Echos d'Orient* 5 (1901–02), 221–24; Sister Mary Jerome Kishpaugh, *The Feast of the Presentation of the Virgin Mary in the Temple: An Historical and Literary Study* (Washington, D.C.: Catholic University of America Press, 1941), 36; and Mary Clayton, *The Cult of the Virgin Mary in Anglo-Saxon England*, Cambridge Studies in Anglo-Saxon England 2 (Cambridge: Cambridge University Press, 1990), 27–28. On the influence of the apocryphal Infancy Gospels collectively on medieval liturgy see Achim Masser, *Bibel, Apokryphen, und Legenden: Geburt und Kindheit Jesu in der religiösen Epik des deutschen Mittelalters* (Berlin: E. Schmidt, 1969), 98–105.

[17] Karl Vogler, "Die Ikonographie der 'Flucht nach Aegypten'" (Diss. Heidelberg 1930; Arnstadt, 1930); and Sheila Schwartz, "The Iconography of the Rest on the Flight into Egypt" (Diss. New York University, 1975). Fritz Saxl proposes *Pseudo-Matthew* as the inspiration for the depiction of the Flight into Egypt on the Ruthwell Cross: "The Ruthwell Cross," *Journal of the Warburg and Courtauld Institutes* 6 (1943),

on the lives of the Virgin and Christ, including the celebrated poems by Hrotsvita of Gandersheim and Konrad von Fußesbrunnen, are indebted directly to *Pseudo-Matthew*,[18] and a large number of readers would have been introduced to the apocryphal anecdote about Jesus and the lengthened beam through translations of these Infancy Gospels into one or more medieval vernaculars: the *Infancy Gospel of Thomas* was rendered into Irish verse before the close of the seventh century,[19]

1–19, repr. in *England and the Mediterranean Tradition: Studies in Art, History, and Literature* (New York and London: Oxford University Press, 1945), 1–19, at 4–5. For a partial list of patristic and medieval authors who allude to the miracle of the falling idols from the Flight into Egypt story see James DeQuincey Donehoo, *The Apocryphal and Legendary Life of Christ* (New York: Hodder & Stoughton, 1903), 89, n. 2. On the influence of the *Gospel of Pseudo-Matthew* on medieval iconography of the Nativity and Infancy of Christ and Mary see F. Witte, "Apokryphe, legendarische und volkstümliche Elemente in den Weihnachtsbildern des ausgehenden Mittelalters," *Zeitschrift für Christliche Kunst* 32 (1919), 119–26; and Gertrud Schiller, *Ikonographie der christlichen Kunst*, 4 vols. in 6 (Gütersloh: Mohn, 1966–80), 1:36–135 (on Christ), 4:2, 31–82 (on Mary). As Elliott, *The Apocryphal New Testament*, 84, remarks, "Much medieval art is indecipherable without reference to books such as Pseudo-Matthew."

[18] The source of Hrotsvita's *Historia nativitatis laudabilisque conversationis intactae Dei genitricis* (*BHL*, no. 5346), composed ca. 975, is discussed by R. ten Kate, "Hrotsvits Maria und das Evangelium des Pseudo-Matthäus," *Classica et Mediaevalia* 22 (1961), 195–204; and by Jan Gijsel, "Zu welcher Textfamilie des Pseudo-Matthäus gehört die Quelle von Hrotsvits Maria?" *Classica et Mediaevalia* 32 (1971–80), 279–88. On the debt of Konrad von Fußesbrunnen's early thirteenth-century poem *Die Kindheit Jesu* to *Pseudo-Matthew* see Masser, *Bibel, Apokryphen und Legenden*, 70–87. On the use of *Pseudo-Matthew* in the Middle High German *Passional* see Karl Bartsch, "Die Kindheit Jesu und das Passional," *Germania: Vierteljahrsschrift für deutsche Alterthumskunde* 5 (1860), 432–44.

[19] *The Poems of Blathmac Son of Cú Brettan together with the Irish Gospel of Thomas and a Poem on the Virgin Mary*, ed. James Carney, Irish Texts Society 47 (Dublin: Irish Texts Society, 1964), 89–105; English trans. in *Irish Biblical Apocrypha. Selected Texts in Translation*, ed. Máire Herbert and Martin McNamara (Edinburgh: T. & T. Clark, 1989), 44–47. In translation, the relevant verses read: "(47) A piece of craftwork was brought to the house to Joseph to be adjusted, for it projected too far on one side, with one side exceeding the other. (48) Jesus said: 'You take hold of your end, and I will take mine.' He stretched the shorter side until it was equivalent to the other" (47).

and translations of the *Gospel of Pseudo-Matthew* survive in Old and Middle English,[20] Anglo-Norman,[21] Old French,[22] medieval Italian,[23]

For discussion see Martin McNamara, "Notes on the Irish Gospel of Thomas," *Irish Theological Quarterly* 38 (1971), 42–66, and *The Apocrypha in the Irish Church* (1975; Dublin: Dublin Institute for Advanced Studies, 1984), 52–53.

[20] An anonymous Old English sermon on the Nativity of Mary surviving in three manuscripts translates chaps. 1–12 of the *Gospel of Pseudo-Matthew*, beginning with the infertile marriage of Anna and Joachim and continuing through the doubting of Mary. A second partial Old English translation appears in Vercelli Homily VI, which incorporates material from chaps. 13, 17–18, and 22–25. For discussion and other evidence of the knowledge of this apocryphon in Anglo-Saxon England see Mary Clayton, *The Apocryphal Gospels of Mary in Anglo-Saxon England*, Cambridge Studies in Anglo-Saxon England 26 (Cambridge: Cambridge University Press, 1998). The Middle English verse *Pseudo-Matthew*, a poem in octosyllabic couplets composed ca. 1280–90, is edited by Carl Horstmann under the title "Die Kindheit Jesu" in *Altenglische Legenden: Kindheit Jesu, Geburt Jesu, Barlaam und Josaphat, St. Patriks Fegfeuer* (Paderborn: Schöningh, 1875), 3–61. (The "Geburt Jesu" in Horstmann's title is an unrelated Middle English translation of the *Protevangelium of James*, one of the sources of the *Gospel of Pseudo-Matthew*). For discussion see Reinhold Köhler, "Zu einer Stelle der altenglischen Gedichts von der Kindheit Jesu," *Englische Studien* 2 (1878–79), 115–16 (with a *Nachtrag* by E. Kölbing); and Ferdinand Holthausen, "Zum mittelenglischen Gedicht 'Kindheit Jesu' (Ms. Laud 108)," *Archiv für das Studium der neueren Sprachen und Literaturen* 127 (1911), 318–22.

[21] The Anglo-Norman version, in octosyllabic quatrains from the end of the thirteenth century, is edited by Maureen Boulton, *Les Enfaunces de Jesu Crist*, Anglo-Norman Texts 43 (London: Anglo-Norman Text Society, 1986). In her introduction, Boulton observes that "neither the French nor the Anglo-Norman Évangile depends directly on any known version of the *Pseudo-Matthew*, as both contain episodes which have analogues only in Syriac, Arabic, or Armenian, and others which are unattested elsewhere" (9).

[22] The Continental French version, also in octosyllabic couplets and from the early fourteenth century, is edited by Maureen Boulton, *The Old French Évangile de l'Enfance: An Edition with Introduction and Notes*, Studies and Texts 70 (Toronto: Pontifical Institute of Mediaeval Studies, 1984).

[23] To clarify a passage in Tischendorf's edition of the Latin *Pseudo-Matthew*, Silvio Ferri prints excerpts from a fourteenth-century Italian translation of *Pseudo-Matthew* which, to my knowledge, is nowhere fully edited: Ferri, "Nota al testo latino dell' 'Evangelium Infantiae'," *Studi Mediolatini e Volgari* 1 (1953), 119–25.

Provençal,[24] Welsh,[25] and Czech.[26] So widely disseminated were these two works (and in particular *Pseudo-Matthew*) that it is difficult to avoid the conclusion that the anecdote they contain about Christ and Joseph must have provided the central model for later formulations of the miracle of the lengthened beam in the writings of medieval hagiographers. And this, of course, makes perfect sense when one considers the hagiographic context of those later formulations: any medieval audience familiar with the anecdotes in the Infancy Gospels would have immediately understood a miracle story in which a saint lengthens a wooden beam as a classic illustration of the principle of *imitatio Christi*, a recollection and recapitulation of a miracle once performed by Christ, even as a child.[27]

---

[24] At least three rhymed versions of *Pseudo-Matthew* also exist in Provençal (see *RBMA*, no. 168,9), surviving in at least nine manuscripts which, to my knowledge, have not been systematically classified and edited. The most recent edition is by Giovanni Caravaggi, *Vangeli provenzali dell'infanzia*, Istituto di filologia romanza dell'Università di Roma, collezione di testi e manuali 47 (Modena: Società Tipografica Editrice Modenese, 1963), who prints the text of only one manuscript. Others are described and/or printed in *Denkmäler der provenzalischen Litteratur*, ed. Karl Bartsch, Litterarischer Verein in Stuttgart, Bibliothek 39 (1856; Amsterdam: Editions Rodopi, 1966), 270–305; Paul Meyer, "L'Évangile de l'Enfance," *Bulletin de la Société des anciens textes français* 1 (1875), 76–82; Adolf Kressner, "Die provenzalische Bearbeitung der Kindheit Jesu," *Archiv für das Studium der neueren Sprachen und Literaturen* 58 (1877), 291–310; Edmund Suchier, "Über provenzalische Bearbeitungen der Kindheit Jesu," *Zeitschrift für romanische Philologie* 8 (1884), 522–69; V. Crescini and A. Rios, "Un frammento provenzale a Conegliano," *Zeitschrift für romanische Philologie* 19 (1895), 41–50; Paul Meyer, "L'Évangile de l'Enfance en Provençal (Manuscrit du Marquis de Cambis-Velleron et de Raynouard)," *Romania* 35 (1906), 337–64; and Joseph Huber, "L'Évangile de l'Enfance en Provençal (Ms. Bibl. nat. nouv. acqu. fr. 10453)," *Romanische Forschungen* 22 (1907), 883–989.

[25] The Welsh prose translations, surviving in three manuscripts from the late thirteenth and early fourteenth centuries, are printed with a partial translation by Mary Williams, "Llyma Vabinogi Iessu Grist," *Revue celtique* 33 (1912), 184–248.

[26] Francis J. Thomson, "Apocrypha Slavica: II," *The Slavonic and East European Review* 63 (1985), 73–98, at 78.

[27] On the theme of *imitatio Christi* in medieval saints' lives see Francis Wormald, "Some Illustrated Manuscripts of the Lives of Saints," *Bulletin of the John Rylands Library* 35 (1952), 248–66, at 251–52; Baudouin de Gaiffier, "Miracles bibliques et

The role of this apocryphal anecdote as a shaping influence on medieval miracle stories becomes most apparent in saints' lives in which a wooden beam is eked out to its desired length through the same sort of stretching exercise in which Joseph and the young Jesus engage. A notable example appears in the *Life of Saint Erkenwald* compiled in the fourteenth century by John of Tynemouth, based on two eleventh- and twelfth-century legends (now erroneously printed under the name of Capgrave). In John of Tynemouth's version of the story, Saint Erkenwald and his sister Saint Ethelburga, who are jointly celebrated for founding the twin monasteries of Barking and Chertsey in the late seventh century, are overseeing construction of the abbey at Barking when it is discovered that one of the beams for the building is too short. Undaunted, Erkenwald and his sister roll up their sleeves, seize the ends of the beam, and tug until it lines up perfectly with the others:

> When the builders of the aforesaid house measured their timber, fitting it together in various places according to the fitness of the work, one of the beams that was necessary for their task was found to be considerably shorter than the others and was therefore unsuitable for the structure. But Erkenwald, the man of complete sanctity, and his sister Ethelburga, devoted to God, grasped the dry beam between their hands and stretched it until it was just as long as the others. This miracle was commonly acknowledged and publicly revealed.[28]

Vies des saints," *Nouvelle revue théologique* 88 (1966), 376–85, repr. in his *Études critiques d'hagiographie et d'iconologie*, Subsidia Hagiographica 43 (Brussels: Socii Bollandiani, 1967), 50–61; Amatus van den Bosch, "Le Christ, Dieu devenu imitable d'aprés S. Bernard," *Collectanea Cisterciensia* 22, no. 4 (1960–64), 341–55; and Gregorio Penco, "L'Imitazione di Cristo nell'agiografia monastica," *Collectanea Cisterciensia* 28 (1966), 17–34.

[28] *Epitome vitae et miraculorum s. Erkenwaldi* (*BHL*, no. 2602), ptd. *Acta Sanctorum*, Aprilis III, 781–87, at 781 (§3): "cum dictae domus artifices meremium suum mensurarent, diversis locis juxta decentiam operis coaptandum; inventa est trabs una, operi admodum necessaria, ceteris brevior, & ideo fabricae minus apta. Sed vir totius sanctitatis Erkonwaldus & soror sua Deo devota Ethelburga, aridam trabem inter manus arripientes, ipsam in longum traxerunt, quousque ceteris aequaretur: quod quidem miraculum communiter notum extitit & publice divulgatum"; quoted by de Gaiffier, "Le thème hagiographique," 20. Translations are mine unless otherwise indicated.

As Gordon Whatley has shown, this same episode recurs in the prose
Life and Miracles of Saint Erkenwald incorporated into a late fifteenth-
century recension of the Middle English *Gilte Legende* and became a
fixed feature of the later medieval English legend of Erkenwald.[29] A
second example from roughly the same period occurs in the fourteenth-
century *Life of Saint Sylvester* by Andreas Jacobi de Fabriano, in which
a beam is stretched to its desired length by Saint Sylvester in precisely
the same fashion. In this story, the carpenter hired to build a house for
Saint Sylvester is cautiously directed to measure each beam carefully,
"but the master carpenter was so sure of himself that he neglected to
measure the beam and carelessly cut off the end. He then carried it
back and intended to align it with the walls, but he was entirely unable
to do so because it was found to be lacking and had been improperly
measured too short."[30] At this point the despairing carpenter wanders

---

[29] Gordon Whatley, "A 'symple wrecche' at Work: The Life and Miracles of St. Erkenwald in the *Gilte Legende*, BL Add. 35298," in *Legenda Aurea: Sept siècles de diffusion*,
ed. Brenda Dunn-Lardeau, Actes du colloque international sur la *Legenda aurea*: texte
latin et branches vernaculaires à l'Université du Québec à Montréal 11–12 mai 1983
(Montreal: Éditions Bellarmin, 1986), 333–43, at 336; and Whatley, "Heathens and
Saints: *St. Erkenwald* in Its Legendary Context," *Speculum* 61 (1986), 330–63, at
354–55. As Whatley further notes ("A 'symple wrecche'," 336), this episode from the
life of Erkenwald was repeated later by Saint Thomas More as an illustration of the
veracity of what he termed "natural" miracles: More, *A Dialogue Concerning Heresies*
I.10, ed. Thomas M. C. Lawler et al., *The Complete Works of St. Thomas More*, 6.1
(New Haven and London: Yale University Press, 1981), 80–81. Earlier in the *Dialogue
Concerning Heresies* I.7, More discusses another example of the same miracle in which
a bishop stretches a beam for use in a church construction project (71), possibly an
allusion to the Lawrence story.

[30] *Vita s. Silvestri* (*BHL*, no. 7744), ed. Réginald Grégoire, *Agiographia Silvestrina
medievale*, Bibliotheca Montisfani 8 (Fabriano: Editiones Montisfani, 1983), 92: "Magis-
ter autem in seipso uilipendens uerbum siue ipsius consilium, de se confisus, trabem
immisuratam negligendo precidit. Quam sursum trahendo uoluit in parietibus collocare,
sed prorsus nequit, quia inuenta est minus habens, et breuior deficiente mensura." See
also de Gaiffier, "Le thème hagiographique," 24, who quotes from the older edition by
F. M. Pompei, "Andreae Iacobi tabellionis de Fabriano Vita sanctissimi Silvestri," *Inter
Fratres* 19 (1969), 7–69, at 37.

off to find Sylvester to alert him to the problem. When Sylvester arrives on the scene the situation appears hopeless:

> But the holy man [Saint Sylvester] placed his hands on the beam and said to the master carpenter, "You take hold of the beam at your end, and I will take hold of the other." Then something wonderful and completely amazing happened: the shortness of the beam was stretched out in length, so that no defect or inadequacy could be found in the beam; in fact, the excess length was of the same measure as the gap![31]

A third example, and one with more obvious ties to the apocryphal Infancy Gospel, comes from the Middle English stanzaic *Life of St. Anne*, which is, in part, a verse paraphrase of the *Gospel of Pseudo-Matthew* in which the beam-stretching episode is modified only in that the carpenter whom the young Jesus assists is not his father Joseph but a neighbor, and the object he is trying to build is not a couch but a house:

> Also befell yt in þat same ton
> Þer was a wryght þar gret renown
> Of a full gude werkman.
> A maister thakker of þe hus þat same tyde
> Was hys neghbur nere besyde.
> Unto hym spak he þan
> Ffor to make hym a sotyll warke.
> Þe wryght alsone had takyn hys m[a]rke
> On hys note fast began;
> When he hys werke togeder suld sett
> Ane tre was shorter þan þe fyrst mete.
> Þan gunne he curse and band
> & sayd, allas, þis werke ys loste;
> Now bred me paye all þat yt coste,

---

[31] *Vita s. Silvestri*, ed. Grégoire, 92–93: "At vir sanctus ad trabem manus suas apponens, ad magistrum sic inquid: Trahe capud trabis ad partem tuam, et ego ad partem alteram traham eum. Res mira et plena stupore, quod breuitas ligni est pertensa in longum, ut non defectus uel indigentia inueniretur in ligno, sed debitus excessus mensure!"; see also de Gaiffier, "Le théme hagiographique," 24.

Þat I may do full yll.
Ihesus come walkand hym allone
& harde þis wryght makand ys mone;
He sayd: gud man, be styll;
Wylke ys þat short tre my lefe brother?
Take þe ton ende, gyfe me þe tother,
& draw with gud wyll.
Ihesus hys ende a fote oyt drewe
& sayd, now es yt long enewe;
Go lay þi merke þer tyll.
At ihesus byddyng þat tre he drest,
Þan was hys worke wele of þe best.[32]

A cleverly inverted form of the miracle of the lengthened beam also works its way into a twelfth-century English version of the Holy Cross legend. Here the story goes that in the process of erecting his temple, King David orders his workers to cut down a tree that, unbeknownst to them, is in reality the tree of the wood of the Cross. From this tree he orders his workers to fashion beams that can be used for building the temple. Twice the workers measure and cut, and twice the wood proves either too long or too short for their task. In the end the workers are forced to find other materials, and the wood of the Cross is preserved intact inside David's temple until the time when it will be hewn into the Cross for the Crucifixion:

> When the tree had been brought into the temple, those same [workmen] went to it who had formerly measured it, and applied the same measure to it. When it was laid down there, it was two fathoms longer than the measure was. Then they were sorely afraid, and made it known to the king. And the king went thither in haste, wishing to know what of it [i.e., of their report] was true. When he saw it, he was stirred with exceeding wrath, and said that they were worthy of death for having, by their lying, brought him to this. Then he ordered it to be raised to the place where it was to go. When it was put there,

---

[32] *The Middle English Stanzaic Versions of the Life of Saint Anne*, ed. Roscoe E. Parker, EETS o.s. 174 (1928; Millwood, New York: Kraus, 1987), 60–61, lines 2305–30.

it was two fathoms shorter than the others. When he saw that, he was much afraid, and ordered them to bring it down and lay it in the temple, and he sorely repented having sinned so greatly with respect to the holy tree. He bade them then go out again, and try whether God Almighty would send them any other. And they did so. On the same day they soon found all that they wanted, and brought it to him, and they then took it where it was to be placed, and the holy tree lay always within the temple until the time came when our Lord would suffer.[33]

A variant form of the same story also occurs in the play on the "Beginning of the World" in the *Cornish Ordinalia*, in which two carpenters cut the Tree of Life to fashion the center beam of Solomon's temple. After carefully measuring and cutting, however, they discover that the beam is one and a half feet too short, so they tack on an extra piece of wood to extend it, only to find that it is now a foot and a half too long. The frustrated carpenters then take their problem to Solomon, who orders that the Tree be placed in the midst of the temple, "there to lie and to be scrupulously venerated by all on pain of death."[34]

---

[33] *History of the Holy Rood-Tree: A Twelfth-Century Version of the Cross-Legend,* ed. and trans. Arthur S. Napier, EETS o.s. 103 (London: EETS, 1894), 24–25: "þa ðe þæt treow in to þam temple ibroht wæs þa eoden þa ylcæ þerto þe hit ær imeten hæfdon ⁊ þæt ylce gemet þerto lægdon .þa ðe hit þær nyðer ilægd wæs þa wæs hit twam fæðmum længre þonne þæt imet were . Ða weron heo swiðe afyrhte ⁊ hit þam kinge cyddon ⁊ þe kyng ofstlice þider wende ⁊ wolde witæn hwæt his soðes wære . Ða he ða ðæt iseah þa wearð he mid swi licere hatheortnysse ástured ⁊ cwæð þæt heo dea þe scyldige wæræn þæt heo hine mid heoræ leasungæ on ðon ibroht hæfden . Het hit þa up ahebban ðær hit to sceolde . þa ðe hit ðerto ibroht wæs þa wæs hit twam fæðmæ sceortre þenne ða oðre . Ða þe he ðæt iseah þa wearð he swiðe geforht iworden ⁊ bæd þæt hit mon adun don sceolde ⁊ hit into þam temple lecgæn ⁊ he swiðlice bereowsode þæt he swa mucel agult hæfde þurh ðæt halig treow . Bead heom þa þæt heo ða gyt út wendon sceolden ⁊ fondian hwæðer heom god almihtig ænig oðer asendon wolde . ⁊ heo þa swa dyden . On ðone ylcæ dæg þa funden heo sonæ eall þæt heo wolden . ⁊ hit to him brohten . ⁊ heo ða hit brohten ðær hit beon sceolde ⁊ þæt halig treow innan þam tempel læg áá oð þeo tid com þe ure drihten þrowian wolde."

[34] *The Cornish Ordinalia: A Medieval Dramatic Trilogy,* trans. Markham Harris (Washington, D.C.: Catholic University of America Press, 1969), 68–70.

These and other medieval miracle tales[35] reproduce the beam-stretching exercise from the couch-building episode of the Infancy Gospels with such remarkable consistency that the parallels are unmistakable. The names of the saints and other characters change, of course, and the beam often is cut and stretched for different purposes, but the central details remain intact, so that each miracle story can be seen to

---

[35] See also the fifteenth- or sixteenth-century life of St. Augustine discussed by de Gaiffier, "Le thème hagiographique," 20; and see the miracles of St. Gerard, St. James of Tarentaise, and St. Wodoaldus summarized by E. Cobham Brewer, *A Dictionary of Miracles* (Philadelphia: Lippincott, 1894), 226, 228. Still another example is an episode in chap. 27 of the *Life of Saint Gall* (*BHL*, no. 3247) by Walahfrid Strabo (d. 849) in which a plank intended for use in the construction of a church by Saint Gall and his brothers is found to be shorter than the rest by a length of four palms. After Saint Gall breaks bread with the laborers (a gesture toward a re-enactment of the loaves and fishes miracle), they discover that the plank has grown so that it is longer than the others by one-half foot. Strabo, echoing Gregory of Tours' account of the Lawrence story, then explains that the plank was reported later to have brought about cures for toothache, "thus enhancing the glory of the original miracle by a succession of new ones," a comment that emphasizes the theme of proliferation associated with this miracle. See *The Life of St. Gall*, trans. Maud Joynt (London: Society for Promoting Christian Knowledge; New York and Toronto: Macmillan, 1927), 58–111, at 102; repr. with some abridgment and modernization by Mary-Ann Stouck, ed., *Medieval Saints: A Reader* (Peterborough, Ontario: Broadview, 1999), 223–49, at 244. In a footnote to her 1927 translation, Joynt quizzically remarks, "One cannot help wondering why the plank was not made the length required" (102). There is also an interesting negative formulation of this miracle, in which a pagan rather than a saint undertakes to lengthen a deficient beam by appealing to his pagan gods, who naturally fail to accomplish the miracle. This variation appears in the anonymous life of the seventh-century abbess Saint Eanswitha preserved by Capgrave (*BHL*, no. 2555), who relates that Eanswitha was courted by a pagan Northumbrian king or prince but resisted his advances by insisting that she would marry him only if he could harness the power of his pagan gods and induce them to lengthen a beam that had been set aside for use in the construction of her oratory but was three feet too short. The suitor's prayers prove ineffectual, and Eanswitha's virginity is preserved intact. See *Nova Legenda Anglie*, ed. Carl Horstmann, 2 vols. (Oxford: Clarendon Press, 1901), 1:296–99. This last example came to my attention via the summary of this episode by Rosalind C. Love, ed. and trans., *Three Eleventh-Century Anglo-Latin Saints' Lives: Vita S. Birini, Vita et Miracula S. Kenelmi and Vita S. Rumwoldi*, Oxford Medieval Texts (Oxford: Oxford University Press, 1996), clxviii.

re-enact the miracle performed by the child Jesus. As de Gaiffier observed, however, a fundamental aspect of hagiographic literature is its tendency to rework familiar patterns, and in addition to the texts just mentioned there are a number of medieval saints' lives in which the apocryphal anecdote is customized for a particular saint. Two distinct permutations of the miracle can be distinguished here: one in which the object stretched is not a beam but a piece of cloth, usually a garment; and the other, in which the object stretched is a coffin or sarcophagus. The first group is illustrated perhaps most clearly by the fifteenth-century *Life of Saint Coleta of Corbie*, in which Coleta one day calls on a monk named Brother Andrew, an expert in needlework, and asks him to fashion a habit for her out of a piece of cloth. Brother Andrew begins work on the habit but soon finds that the cloth Coleta has given him is at least an arm's length too short. He then takes the cloth back to Coleta and explains the problem, whereupon she smiles and says: "Go, brother, and pray to God, and then return. You will pull on one end of the cloth, and I will pull on the other, and we will see if it can be lengthened." When Brother Andrew returns from his prayer, they both take hold of the ends of the cloth as Coleta has instructed and stretch the cloth not just to the length required for making the habit but even further, so that Andrew ends up having to cut off a portion.[36] A similar event takes place in the *Life of Saint Vodoalus*, the eighth-century confessor of Soissons. By mistake, Vodoalus cuts a garment too short, but through divine intervention the cloth is restored to its original length.[37] In the *Life of Saint Brigit*, two paupers ask the saint for a garment to protect them from the cold. Saint Brigit has only one spare

---

[36] *Miracula s. Coletae* (*BHL*, no. 1871), ptd. *Acta Sanctorum*, Martii I, 539–89, at 553, col. 2: "Vade Frater, & ora Deum: & postmodum reueni: tu trahes ex vno latere pannum, ego autum ex alio latere, prouidendo si poterit elongari." See C. Grant Loomis, *White Magic: An Introduction to the Folklore of Christian Legend* (Cambridge, Mass.: Medieval Academy of America, 1948), 85.

[37] *Vita s. Vodoali* (*BHL*, no. 8728), ptd. *Acta Sanctorum*, Februarii I, 691–93, at 692, col. 2.

tunic but freely gives it to them, and when they take it from her they realize that it has increased in size so that both will fit inside it.[38] One of the exempla collected by Jacques de Vitry in the fifteenth century is the well-known story of Saint Martin, who, mindful of Christ's command to clothe the naked, exchanges his own coat for that of a poor man and subsequently performs mass while wearing the poor man's short, tattered tunic. In the midst of celebrating mass, Saint Martin raises his arms aloft, and the short sleeves of his coat are miraculously lengthened by the appearance of gold-embroidered sleeves, which spontaneously flow up his arms to his hands and thus prevent the assembled churchgoers from seeing his bare arms.[39]

---

[38] *Vita s. Brigidae* (*BHL*, no. 1460), ptd. *Acta Sanctorum*, Februarii I, 155–71, at 170, col. 1; see also Loomis, *White Magic*, 88. Similarly, a tenth-century Life of Saint Folcuinus (Fulquinus), the ninth-century abbot of Lobbes and bishop of Thérouanne, claims that whenever a woman in labor ate a portion of the stole in which Folcuinus was buried, she was relieved of her pains, and in order to make itself available to a larger number of women, the stole miraculously multiplied into three: *Vita s. Folcuini* (*BHL*, no. 3079), ptd. *Acta Sanctorum Ordinis S. Benedicti*, ed. Luc d'Achéry and Jean Mabillon, 2nd ed., 6 vols. in 9 (Venice: apud Sebastianum Coleti & Josephum Bettinelli, 1733–40), 4/1:589–93, at 593; also ptd. PL 137:533–42, at col. 542B; summarized by S. Baring-Gould, *The Lives of the Saints*, rev. ed., 16 vols. (Edinburgh: John Grant, 1914), 15:188; see also Loomis, *White Magic*, 88.

[39] *The Exempla or Illustrative Stories from the Sermones Vulgares of Jacques de Vitry*, ed. and trans. Thomas Frederick Crane (1890; New York: Burt Franklin, 1971), 42, 173 (no. 92). A second exemplum that appears to fall within this tradition is the bridal-quest narrative incorporated into the *Gesta Romanorum* and other collections in which a rich and powerful king sends forth his counselors to search for a wise and beautiful virgin whom he can take as his queen. When the counselors find a suitable candidate, the king tests her wisdom by assigning her the impossible task of making a shirt for him out of a piece of linen cloth only three inches square. When confronted with this task, the virgin protests: "'It is impossible to make a shirt of that; but bring me a vessel in which I may work, and I promise to make the shirt long enough for the body.' The messenger [who presented her with the cloth] returned with the reply of the virgin, and the king immediately sent a sumptuous vessel, by means of which she extended the cloth to the required size, and completed the shirt. Whereupon the wise king married her." The story concludes with a moralizing interpretation that explains, "the king is God; the virgin, the mother of Christ; who was also the chosen vessel. By the messenger is meant Gabriel; the cloth is the grace of God, which, by proper care and labour, is made

The second permutation is limited, so far as I have been able to discover, to a small group of Anglo-Saxon and Anglo-Norman saints' lives and appears to take its inception from Bede's account of the death and burial of King Sebbi, the seventh-century king of the East Saxons reputed to have built the first monastery at Westminster. When Sebbi's body is found to be too long for his stone sarcophagus, the workers interring him first try to squeeze him into the coffin by bending his knees and forcing the body to fit. But before the workers resort to violence, the sarcophagus miraculously lengthens itself to accommodate the body, with room to spare, and the sainted king receives an honorable burial:

> They had prepared a stone sarcophagus for his burial, but when they came to lay his body in it, they found that it was longer than the sarcophagus by a hand's breadth. So they chipped the stone so far as they could, adding about two inches' space. But still it would not take the body. So in view of the difficulty of burying him they debated whether they should look for another coffin or by bending the knees shorten the body so that it would fit the coffin. But an amazing thing happened, certainly the work of heaven which made both of these alternatives unnecessary. Suddenly, as the bishop stood by, together with Sigeheard (who reigned after Sebbi with his brother Swæfred and was the son of the royal monk) as well as a large crowd of men, the sarcophagus was found to be of the right length to fit the body, so that a pillow could even be put in behind the head while, at the feet, the coffin was four inches longer than the body.[40]

---

sufficient for man's salvation" (*Gesta Romanorum: Or, Entertaining Moral Stories*, trans. Charles Swan, rev. and corr. Wynnard Hooper [1876; New York: Dover, 1959], 114–15). This exemplum is indexed by Frederic C. Tubach, *Index Exemplorum: A Handbook of Medieval Religious Tales*, Folklore Fellows Communications 86, no. 204 (Helsinki: Akademia Scientiarum Fennica, 1969), no. 4337, who lists ten versions in Latin and English. In this story, however, the details of the garment-stretching miracle itself have been submerged through a transfer of emphasis to the virgin's identity as the vessel through which the miracle of Christ's Incarnation took place, and the garment miracle has been given a new spin through association with the commonplace metaphor of Christ's Incarnation as a donning of new clothes (see also, e.g., *Piers Plowman* C VII.130).

[40] Bede, *Historia ecclesiastica* IV.11, ed. and trans. Bertram Colgrave and R. A. B. Mynors, *Bede's Ecclesiastical History of the English People* (Oxford: Clarendon, 1969),

A strikingly similar account appears toward the close of Alcuin's prose *Life of St. Willibrord*, which is manifestly indebted to Bede for several details, including the miracle of the expanding sarcophagus:

> Willibrord's venerable body was enclosed in a marble sarcophagus which at first was found to be a half a foot shorter than the body of the servant of God. The brothers were exceedingly vexed by this and debated anxiously about what they should do, tugging repeatedly at the holy body to see if it would fit into the casket. But a wondrous event occurred through the gift of holy faith: the sarcophagus was suddenly discovered to be longer than the body of the man of God by the same amount that it earlier appeared too short. And so placing the body of the man of God in the sarcophagus with the accompaniment of hymns, Psalms, and highest honor, they buried it in the church before the monastery which this consummate priest of God had built and dedicated to the honor of the holy Trinity.[41]

367–69; also ptd. *Acta Sanctorum*, Augusti I, 517, col. 2: "Cuius corpori tumulando praeparauerant sarcofagum lapideum; sed cum huic corpus imponere coepissent, inuenerunt hoc mensura palmi longius esse sarcofago. Dolantes ergo lapidem in quantum ualebant, addiderunt longitudini sarcofagi quasi duorum mensuram digitorum; sed nec sic quidem corpus capiebat; unde facta difficultate tumulandi, cogitabant aut aliud quaerere loculum, aut ipsum corpus, si possent in genibus inflectendo, breuiare donec ipso loculo caperetur. Sed mira res et non nisi caelitus facta, ne aliquid horum fieri deberet, prohibuit. Nam subito adstante episcopo et filio regis eiusdem ac monachi Sighardo, qui post illum cum fratre Suefredo regnauit, et turba hominum non modica inuentum est sarcofagum illud congruae longitudinis ad mensuram corporis, adeo ut a parte capitis etiam ceruical posset interponi, a parte uero pedum mensura quattuor digitorum in sarcofago corpus excederet." To this episode may be compared the miracle associated with Saint Hugh of Cluny in which the balsam for embalming his body at first was found insufficient but then mysteriously was augmented: Hildebert of Lavardin, *Vita s. Hugonis abbatis Cluniacensis* (*BHL*, no. 4010), ptd. *Acta Sanctorum*, Aprilis III, 634–48, at 647, col. 2; also ptd. PL 159:857–94, at col. 890; see also Loomis, *White Magic*, 88.

[41] Alcuin, *Vita prosa s. Willibrordi* (*BHL*, no. 8935), ptd. *Acta Sanctorum*, Novembris III, 435–49, at 447 (chap. 25): "Conditum est venerabile corpus in sarcofago marmoreo, quod primum toto Dei famuli corpori quasi dimidium pedis brevius inventum est; fratribusque ob hoc valde contristatis et consilio suspensis quid agerent, et sepius tractantibus ubi aptum sancto corpori invenissent locellum. Sed miro modo, divina donante pietate, inventum est subito sarcofagum tanto Dei viri corpori longius, quanto brevius

A potentially comic variation of the same miracle is reported in Eadmer's *Life of St. Anselm*, where the problem is not that Anselm's body is too long but that he is too fat! After much unfruitful debate over how to accomplish the saint's burial, one of the more resourceful monks attending the service waves a bishop's crozier about like a magic wand, and the sarcophagus responds by miraculously deepening and makes room for the corpulent corpse:

> The next day, however, when he was committed for burial, the stone coffin which had been prepared for him many days earlier was found to be sufficient as to length and breadth, but too shallow for the most part. When we saw this we were at a loss, being determined not to allow him to be damaged in any way by the pressure of the stone lid. So there was much difference of opinion, some saying it could be arranged one way, and some another. Then one of the assembled multitude of brethren took the staff of the bishop of Rochester, who was then performing the burial service, and started to draw it along the top of the sarcophagus over the body of the Father. To our great astonishment he now found that the sarcophagus was higher than the recumbent body at every point, and so the venerable body of Father Anselm, archbishop of Canterbury and primate of all Britain, was shut in its sepulchre, a warning to all passersby to learn from its example the condition to which mankind is subject.[42]

---

ante apparuit. Et in eo viri Dei corpus cum ymnis, psalmodiis et omni honore condentes, sepelierunt illud in ecclesia praefati monasterii, quod ille summus Dei sacerdos in honorem sanctae Trinitatis aedificavit et dedicavit." The same miracle is more succinctly related in Alcuin's *Vita metrica s. Willibrordi* (*BHL*, no. 8938), ptd. *Acta Sanctorum*, Novembris III, 451–57, at 455. Alcuin's debt to Bede in the prose *Vita* is documented carefully by I Deug-Su, "L'opera agiografica di Alcuino: la 'Vita Willibrordi'," *Studi Medievali* 3rd ser. 21 (1980), 47–96, esp. 53, 62–63, 70–78, 83; however, Deug-Su says nothing of these two passages involving the miraculous lengthening of Sebbi's and Willibrord's coffins.

[42] *The Life of St. Anselm Archbishop of Canterbury* (*BHL*, no. 526a), ed. and trans. R. W. Southern (London, etc.: Thomas Nelson and Sons, 1962), 144–46: "In crastino autem cum sepulturae traderetur; sarcofagum quod illi fuerat pluribus retroactis diebus praeparatum, longitudine quidem et latitudine aptum, sed profunditate magna ex parte minus habens inventum est. Quod considerantes; animo deficiebamus, nulla scilicet ratione pati valentes, ut superiori lapide pressus, sua integritate aliquatenus laesus privaretur. Cum itaque in hoc plurimi fluctuarent, et alii sic, alii vero sic rem posse

An unusual variant of this coffin-stretching miracle is incorporated into the Miracles of Saint Erkenwald, compiled probably by a canon of Saint Paul's Cathedral named Arcoid in the early 1140s. Miracle 14 in this collection provides a brief but important record of the translation of Erkenwald's coffin from its temporary location in the crypt (where it was kept while the cathedral was being restored following the 1087 fire) to a more secure stone housing in the upper church on February 16, 1140. At first the cathedral priests attempt to conduct the rite of translation in secret without public interference, but a crowd of London citizens learns that the ceremony is in progress and storms the cathedral to catch sight of the holy body. The priests hurry to move the coffin to its new location before it is damaged by the crowd, but they then encounter an unexpected problem. As Arcoid explains:

> Since we could not withstand the onrush of the multitude any longer, we picked up the lead coffin in which the most holy body was resting, and tearfully we bore it to the new home that had been prepared for it. And lo, all our preparation appeared to be in vain, for the coffin was clearly too large both in length and breadth for the structure we had built to house it. But then a marvelous thing happened. For the sake of him who was being denied burial by the craftsman's ignorance, the opening in the stone was made larger by the right hand of him who extends the heavens. When the saint was being placed inside it, the hardness of the slabs became soft, the stone forgot its natural condition and submitted to the gaze of its creator. Truly I myself who write these things found our stone housing fitted the measurements of the lead coffin as well as if it had been constructed by rule and plumb-line to the exact size of the coffin. For I frequently checked it myself with my own hands, and, God be my witness, I could not fit my finger between coffin and stone at any point. Those present affirmed that the same thing happened once to the most holy Ethelberga, his sister. Nor is there any doubt that the wiser

---

componi dictitarent; quidam ex conferta multitudine fratrum acceptum baculum episcopi Rofensis qui funeris officium praesens agebat, per transversum sarcofagi super corpus patris ducere coepit, et jam illud omni ex parte corpori jacentis praeminere magna nobis exinde admiratione permotis invenit. Ita ergo venerabile corpus patris Anselmi Dorobernensis archiepiscopi ac primatis totius Britanniae sepulchro inclusum; quid conditio sortis humanae habeat in se, omnes qui pertranseunt sui exemplo monet attendere."

men present also called to mind what the venerable Bede, jewel among Englishmen, wrote concerning the holy king, Sebbe.[43]

The main difference here, of course, is not that Erkenwald's body is too large for his coffin, but rather that his coffin is too large for the stone shrine into which it is being deposited. The results are the same, however, and Arcoid's acknowledgment that this miracle should be compared with the one Bede reports about Sebbi is indication enough of the perceived similarity between these two stories.

And finally, a fifth passage that seems to have fallen under the influence of this same narrative pattern, even though the coffin-stretching itself is not realized fully, appears toward the end of the twelfth-century *Liber Eliensis* within a short account of the second translation of Saint Withburga, the daughter of King Anna of East Anglia and younger sister of Saint Etheldreda (Audrey). Following Withburga's death in 743, her body was disinterred and reburied twice, first in 974 by abbot Brithnoth of Ely and a second time in 1106 by abbot Richard. On this second occasion her translation was impeded by the discovery that her body was too long for the newly prepared sar-cophagus. The *Liber Eliensis* account, authored reputedly by Thomas of Ely about 1170, reads:

---

[43] *Miracula s. Erkenwaldi* (*BHL*, no. 2601), ed. and trans. E. Gordon Whatley, *The Saint of London: The Life and Miracles of St. Erkenwald: Text and Translation*, Medieval & Renaissance Texts & Studies 58 (Binghamton: Center for Medieval and Early Renaissance Studies, 1989), 152–55: "Impetum multitudinis ultra sustinere non ualentes, arrepto plumbeo sepulchro in quo corpus sanctissimum quiescebat, ad prepa-ratum habitaculum cum lacrimis illud ferebamus, et ecce omnis nostra preparatio irrita apparuit. Sarcina enim nostro edificio tam in longitudine quam in latitudine permultum amplior innotuit. Res miranda! Cui per ignorantiam artificis negatur sepultura, per celos extendentis dexteram amplior in lapide fit apertura. Vbi cum sanctus includitur, saxea duricies emollitur. Obliuiscitur lapis sue conditionis et paret obtutibus conditoris. Certe ego, qui hec scribo, ad mensuram plumbei sarcofagi lapideum edificium nostrum ita aptum et conueniens inueni, ac si regula et perpendiculo ad plumbi magnitudinem fuisset extructum; unde sepius propriis manibus attrectaui, deum testem inuoco, quod inter plumbum et lapidem in aliqua parte digitum figere nequiui."

Because the very brilliant Withburga's original sarcophagus, which had been constructed according to very precise measurements, had at some point become broken, the aforementioned Richard, rector of the church at Ely, prepared a new one so that the incorrupt virgin might be laid to rest in a new and incorrupt dwelling. But celestial Providence rendered that plan useless through a novel and extraordinary miracle. For when the new coffin which was about to receive the holy body was ready standing by, it was measured against the old one with the aid of a measuring rod and was found to be one foot shorter. Anyone who tried to remeasure each coffin found it to be no longer; the new one consistently fell short of the old one by the same disparity. Everyone stood about in shock and amazement, seeing their plan for the prepared shrine hindered by the greatness of the too-long body.[44]

At this point, however, the narrative takes a surprising turn: instead of the new sarcophagus miraculously stretching itself to fit the saint's body—as is generally the case in the stories about Sebbi, Willibrord, Anselm, and Erkenwald—Saint Withburga makes it known that she is perfectly satisfied with her old wooden sarcophagus, and she repairs the damage to it to make it functional once again. Her transfer to the new and "incorrupt" sarcophagus is thereby thwarted, and there is no need to alter the sarcophagus's size. This coffin-repair miracle has the salutary effect of promoting Withburga as an exemplar of saintly austerity and practicality, and the story ends much differently from the others I have just mentioned. But the first part of the story, with its focus on the careful and repeated measurements taken of the two sarcophagi,

---

[44] *Translatio ss. Etheldredae, Sexburgae, Ermenildae et Withburgae anno 1106* (*BHL*, no. 2637), ed. E. O. Blake, *Liber Eliensis*, Camden Third Series 92 (London: Royal Historical Society, 1962), 232 (§147): "Prefulgide autem Withburge ad certissimam mensuram veteris sarcofagi, quod iam dudum fuerat fractum, memoratus rector Eligensis aule Ricardus paraverat novum, quatinus in novo reposita incorrupta virgo incorruptum haberet hospitium, sed superna providentia id consilii novo et insolito miraculo evacuavit. Nam ubi nova tumba, que sacrum corpus exciperet, parata astitit, apposita prioris mensure virga, unius pedis quantitate brevior extitit. Quisquis iterare mensionem utriusque temptavit, non amplius invenit, semper nova a veteri prescripta brevitate defecit. Herebant omnes stupore et extasi, videntes suum propositum a parato locello productioris corporis maiestate arceri."

the excessive size of the saint's body, and the emphasis on human error in miscalculating the new sarcophagus's length, all set within the context of a burial or translation, is structured very much like the others, and I think it reasonable to suspect that the author of this account has come into contact with one or more of these coffin- or shrine-stretching anecdotes, with which it shares several distinctive features.

In the miracle stories involving Sebbi, Willibrord, and Anselm, the sarcophagus is explicitly said to either stretch or deepen itself *more* than it needs to in order to fit the body, and for this reason all three miracles fall under the classification of acts of supererogation, each case proving that the saint's power easily exceeds what is needed to set right human error. However, the version by Alcuin makes a special point of the fact that the excess growth is precisely equivalent to the original deficiency, an emphasis on balance and symmetry that places Alcuin's story directly in line with Fortunatus's poem about Saint Lawrence, Goscelin's story about Saint Augustine, and Andreas Jacobi de Fabriano's *Life of Saint Sylvester*.

Even in these two permutations of the miracle in which a cloth is stretched or a sarcophagus is enlarged, one can discern a common underlying pattern in which an object too small for its desired use is miraculously lengthened or deepened or augmented, and in this respect the examples I have cited share a uniform structure that permits only a small degree of redefinition among its constituent elements. Like many New Testament miracles, these stories "consist of recurring stereotyped narrative features"[45] that occur in a fixed sequence and reflect the formal integrity of members of a well-defined genre. Like a great many medieval miracles, they also encroach significantly on the territory of folklore and magic, since the motif of an object transformed in size is represented abundantly in medieval and modern folktales from around the globe.[46] To cite just one pertinent example, in many

---

[45] Theissen, *Miracle Stories*, 6.

[46] See Antti Aarne, *The Types of the Folktale: A Classification and Bibliography*, trans. and enlarged by Stith Thompson, 2nd ed., Folklore Fellows Communications 184

versions of the Noah legend there appears an episode in which Noah's attempt to build the ark is thwarted repeatedly by the devil, who succeeds in destroying the ark by either shattering the boards, turning himself into a mouse and gnawing through the side of the ark, or lengthening or shortening the beams so they will no longer fit together. In several examples of this tale from northern and eastern Europe, God then sends an angel to help Noah fend off the devil's attacks, and the angel helps Noah complete his work by stretching or shortening the beams in order to fit them back into place.[47] Most of these legends have been collected from oral tradition and are therefore essentially undatable, but written variants survive in thirteenth-century German and in fourteenth- and fifteenth-century English and were therefore in circulation already by the time most of the miracles mentioned in this essay were committed to writing. This transfer of an originally apocryphal

---

(1928; New York: Burt Franklin, 1964), 379–80 (no. 1244, "Trying to Stretch the Beam"); Hannjost Lixfeld, "Balkenstrecken (AaTh 1244)," in *Enzyklopädie des Märchens: Handwörterbuch zur historischen und vergleichenden Erzählforschung*, ed. Kurt Ranke (Berlin and New York: Walter de Gruyter, 1977–), vol. 1, cols. 1144–46. The most pertinent entry in Thompson's *Motif-Index* is no. D480.0.1: "Things miraculously stretched or shortened if needed by a saint" (Stith Thompson, *Motif-Index of Folk-Literature: A Classification of Narrative Elements in Folktales, Ballads, Myths, Fables, Mediaeval Romances, Exempla, Fabliaux, Jest-books, and Local Legends*, rev. ed., 6 vols. [Bloomington: Indiana University Press, 1955–58], 2:57, whose only supporting reference is to Loomis, *White Magic*, 89).

[47] Oskar Dähnhardt, *Natursagen: Eine Sammlung Naturdeutender Sagen Märchen Fabeln und Legenden*, 4 vols. (1907–12; New York: Burt Franklin, 1970), 1:269 ("Noah beim Holzfällen"); Francis Lee Utley, "The Devil in the Ark (AaTh 825)," in *The Flood Myth*, ed. Alan Dundes (Berkeley: University of California Press, 1988), 337–56, at 339–41; and Utley, "Noah, His Wife, and the Devil," in *Studies in Biblical and Jewish Folklore*, ed. Raphael Patai et al., Indiana University Folklore Series 13; American Folklore Society Memoir Series 51 (Bloomington: Indiana University Press, 1960), 59–91, at 72. Significantly, Utley, whose knowledge of this tale type was probably unsurpassed, made the connection between this episode and the Infancy Gospels when he observed that "in some cases, by the angel's help, the cut boards stretch out or diminish to fit their places by a miracle recalling the infant Jesus the Carpenter" ("Noah, His Wife, and the Devil," 340–41), but he appears never to have followed it up.

and hagiographic motif into the domain of folklore bears witness to the considerable overlap between these categories and is equally illuminating for the light it sheds on the role of oral transmission in the development of hagiographic literature. Borrowings from oral tradition into written saints' lives are certainly not unusual and have received increasing attention in recent years.[48] The fact that a similar process must be responsible for the proliferation of stories involving expanding beams, garments, and sarcophagi is apparent from the virtual lack of direct historical or textual connections among the various miracle tales cited in this paper. As de Gaiffier observed, no matter how closely the stories resemble one another structurally or thematically, they share few if any verbal correspondences that might indicate immediate borrowing on a textual level. Even the words for the most essential features of the story vary from example to example, so that, for instance, the terms used for "beam" range from *lignum* and *trabs* to *tabiculus*, *axis*, and *meremium*. Apart from Gregory's reliance on Fortunatus and Alcuin's reliance on Bede, few of the miracles I have cited can be identified as an immediate written source for another, which points toward the more realistic possibility that the majority of these stories were preserved and transmitted orally before they were written down in the form in which they now survive. The authors of these miracle tales, it would seem, were influenced less directly by written exemplars than by orally transmitted versions of a miracle traceable ultimately to the anecdotes of the apocryphal Infancy Gospels, which themselves point back to an ancient cycle of oral folklore.

---

[48] For some useful discussion of the oral sources that underlie written hagiographic texts see Friedrich Lotter, "Methodisches zur Gewinnung historischer Erkenntnisse aus hagiographischen Quellen," *Historisches Zeitschrift* 229 (1979), 298–365; Padraig O'Riain, "Towards a Methodology in Early Irish Hagiography," *Peritia* 1 (1982), 146–59; and Julia M. H. Smith, "Oral and Written: Saints, Miracles, and Relics in Brittany, c. 850–1250," *Speculum* 65 (1990), 309–43.

FALLING GIANTS AND FLOATING LEAD: SCHOLASTIC HISTORY IN THE MIDDLE ENGLISH *CLEANNESS*

MICHAEL W. TWOMEY

THE ABBEY SCHOOL OF ST. VICTOR in Paris led Christian biblical scholars in reintroducing the study of the literal level of the Bible in the twelfth century. One of its brightest lights was Peter Comestor, who lived at St. Victor while he wrote his *Historia scholastica* (completed in about 1173; henceforth *HS*) and was buried there, not far from Hugh of St. Victor. Comestor was influenced deeply by Andrew of St. Victor's commentary on the octateuch, one of the pioneer Latin works to introduce Hebrew learning into the study of the Bible at this time. The *HS* was the last of three great twelfth-century scholarly projects that changed biblical study for the rest of the Middle Ages. The *Glossa ordinaria* provided a fixed and standard commentary to go along with the biblical text. The *Sentences* of Peter Lombard provided a standardized theology. In the *HS*, Comestor combined scriptural and non-scriptural texts to make a variorum that went well beyond the historical account in the biblical text.

Comestor's work encouraged a new attitude toward the biblical text that licensed later medieval authors to recast biblical narratives. We can trace Comestor's influence on later medieval literature by numerous routes. The *HS* was taught in the universities, but it was disseminated widely among lay readers as well, in vernacular translations such as the French *Bible historiale* by Guiart des Moulins, from about the year 1295, and the Dutch *Rijmbijbel* by Jacob van Maerlant, from about the year 1271. For the present study, the most important are the Middle English adaptations of biblical history, some of which cite Comestor by name and some of which silently borrow from the *HS*, just as Comestor silently had lifted passages from Andrew of St. Victor's commentary on the octateuch in writing the *HS*.[1]

These Middle English biblical adaptations include the so-called *Genesis and Exodus*, written in about the year 1250, which is not only the earliest but also the most extensive adaptation of Comestor. As James Morey observes, in some places the text of *Genesis and Exodus* is "so close to the *Historia* that sense can be made of the Middle English only in consultation with the Latin."[2] *Cursor Mundi*, written in about 1300 and existing today in three versions, uses Comestor only occasionally

---

[1] In a recent study of Comestor's influence on Middle English biblical narratives, James H. Morey cites an Oxford statute of 1253 making study of the *HS* mandatory in the theology course: "Peter Comestor, Biblical Paraphrase, and the Medieval Popular Bible," *Speculum* 68 (1993), 6–7. More generally on Comestor see David Luscombe, "Peter Comestor," in *The Bible in the Medieval World: Essays in Memory of Beryl Smalley*, ed. Katharine Walsh and Diana Wood, Ecclesiastical History Society Studies in Church History, Subsidia 4 (Oxford: Blackwell, 1985), 109–29; and Esra Shereshevsky, "Hebrew Traditions in Peter Comestor's *Historia Scholastica*," *Jewish Quarterly Review* 59 (1968–69), 268–89 (against which see Samuel T. Lachs, "The Source of Hebrew Traditions in the *Historia Scholastica*," *Harvard Theological Review* 66 [1973], 385–86); and Saralyn R. Daly, "Peter Comestor: Master of Histories," *Speculum* 32 (1957), 62–73. On vernacular translations and adaptations see Morey, 8–9, 17–35; on Comestor's borrowing from Andrew of St. Victor see Beryl Smalley, *The Study of the Bible in the Middle Ages*, 3rd ed. (Oxford: Blackwell, 1983), 179. More generally on biblical adaptations in ME see Lawrence Muir, "Translations and Paraphrases of the Bible, and Commentaries," *A Manual of the Writings in Middle English: 1050–1500*, ed. J. Burke Severs and Albert E. Hartung, 10 vols. to date (New Haven: Connecticut Academy of Arts and Sciences, 1967–), 2:381–409, 534–52; and on *Cursor Mundi* see R. Ramo, "Works of Religious and Philosophical Instruction," *Manual* 7:2276–78 and 2503–07.

[2] Morey, "Peter Comestor," 28.

but seems to draw on many other sources, which it has integrated into a fairly seamless, if rambling, history of both biblical testaments. *The Middle English Metrical Paraphrase of the Old Testament* from about the year 1400 is indebted heavily to Comestor's *HS*.[3] The Vernon manuscript contains an Old Testament history and an *Estoire del Evangelie* that both take details from Comestor. The *Northern Passion* and *Stanzaic Life of Christ* also make use of Comestor.[4]

Although it has not been considered part of this group, *Cleanness*, a fourteenth-century alliterative poem in British Library MS Cotton Nero A.x, where it shares a home (and probably an author) with *Sir Gawain and the Green Knight*, employs the methods of scholastic history in its use of biblical narratives. To explain the fifth Beatitude, "Beati mundo corde, quoniam ipsi Deum videbunt" [Blessed are the clean of heart, for they shall see God; Matt. 5:8], the poem relates a series of scriptural examples that demonstrate God's anger at uncleanness. First is the Parable of the Marriage Feast, one of the so-called Parables of the Kingdom that illustrate God's judgment. The Parables of the Kingdom are proleptic, demonstrating how things will be at the moment of death when the soul is judged. But a parable is only an edifying fiction. The *Cleanness* poet is more interested in historical proof, which comes from the Old Testament stories of the Flood and of Sodom. When he has finished with these stories, the poet takes up another problem, that of the person who has cleansed his soul and then returns to his sin. This problem, too, requires historical proof, this time from the story of Baltassar and the Handwriting on the Wall.

Cleanness sometimes has been regarded as a poetic sermon or homily because of its use of biblical narratives to illustrate a biblical

---

[3] See the edition by Herbert Kalén and Urban T. Ohlander: vol. 1, Göteborgs Högskolas Årsskrift 28.5 (Gothenburg: Elanders, 1923); vols. 2–3, Göteborgs Högskolas Årsskrift 61.2, 66.7 (Gothenburg: Elanders, 1955, 1960), also published as Gothenburg Studies in English 5, 11 (Stockholm: Almquist & Wiksell, 1955, 1960); and vols. 4–5, Gothenburg Studies in English 16, 24 (Stockholm: Almquist & Wiksell, 1963, 1972).

[4] See Morey, "Peter Comestor," 26–35.

verse;[5] however, unlike sermons and homilies it skillfully augments biblical narrative with apocryphal and original material. In this respect it resembles the Middle English popular bibles inspired by Comestor's *HS*. *Cleanness* may be said to resemble the *HS* insofar as it reconciles historical materials from outside the Bible with biblical narrative. Like biblical history, the motive of *Cleanness* could be called eschatological, because its concern is to explain the significance of history from a perspective that can only be anticipated—that of the Last Judgment. There are, of course, important differences between *Cleanness* on the one hand and the *HS* and its Middle English followers on the other. *Cleanness* retells only selected episodes of the Bible, whereas the *HS* includes the historical books of Scripture, from Genesis on. The poet of *Cleanness* abandoned the practice of citation, focused on select biblical narratives, and invented dialogue and action out of his own imagination. But when we look at individual episodes of *Cleanness*, the influence of Comestor's method—the scholastic method of assembling various historical accounts into an expanded biblical narrative—is striking. In important respects, *Cleanness* handles biblical history as do other Middle English biblical adaptations that are indebted to Comestor and that often cite him as a source. Like *Cursor Mundi*, *Cleanness* intersperses canonical stories with legends, typologies, moralities, and *exempla*. For example, *Cleanness* uses apocryphal material in the Flood episode and in the Sodom episode, material that the poet of *Cleanness* would have found in Comestor and in *Cursor Mundi*. This essay will focus on how these two episodes in *Cleanness* employ the materials and methods of scholastic history seen in *HS* and in its followers.

---

[5] Monica Brzezinski, "Conscience and Covenant: The Sermon Structure of *Cleanness*," *Journal of English and Germanic Philology* 89 (1990), 166–80; Doris E. Kittendorf, "*Cleanness* and the Fourteenth Century *Artes Praedicandi*," *Michigan Academician* 11 (1979), 319–30; Michael H. Means, "The Homiletic Structure of *Cleanness*," *Studies in Medieval Culture* 5 (1975), 165–72; and Dorothy Everett, *Essays on Middle English Literature* (Oxford: Clarendon Press, 1955), 69–74.

Because it focused on history rather than theology, scholastic history had considerable freedom. As Beryl Smalley has observed:

> Old Testament history differed from theology in that a scholar could select and reject his sources at pleasure without involving himself in heresy. But the habit of respect for authority was strong even here. Since there was no urgent need in matters of historical fact, as there was in matters of faith, to decide between "Yes" and "No," exegetes had evolved a system of "Either, Or." They would string together a list of alternative explanations connected by *vel* or *aliter*. In this way they satisfied curiosity and shifted responsibility to the reader.[6]

Comestor's method in the *HS* is to paraphrase the biblical account first, bringing in related material from elsewhere in the Bible, then to follow that with supplemental information from various patristic and medieval sources. As befits his reputation for digesting the scriptures, Comestor was acquainted with Latin, Greek, and Hebrew authors. For example, in his chapter on the causes of the Flood (*HS* Genesis, chap. 31, PL 198:1081–82), Comestor combines extracts from Genesis 6:1–2 with commentary about the sons of God and the daughters of men. Then he offers accounts from the Jewish historian Flavius Josephus and from the Latin version of the Syriac apocalypse of Pseudo-Methodius. By placing non-biblical authorities after Scripture in narrative sequence, Comestor privileges Scripture and leaves it to his reader to decide what to make of the other material. Nevertheless, non-scriptural sources are to be taken seriously. In his first reference to Methodius, for example, Comestor notes that Methodius was divinely inspired: "When he was in prison, the martyr Methodius prayed, and he received a revelation from the Spirit concerning the beginning and the end of the world."[7] In the same section, Comestor implicitly compares Methodius to Scripture,

---

[6] Smalley, *Study of the Bible*, 128. On the later Middle Ages' interest in historical information for understanding the literal level of scripture see Smalley, 214–42.

[7] "Sed Methodius martyr oravit, dum esset in carcere, et revelatum est ei a Spiritu de principio, et fine mundi" (*HS* Genesis, chap. 25, PL 198:1076).

considering Scripture an abbreviated account of a larger history, by saying, "But yet let us return to the brevity of Genesis."[8]

The poet of *Cleanness* employs these strategies for reshaping biblical narrative. He combines passages from different parts of the Bible into a new narrative while citing only one as a source. For example, towards the beginning of *Cleanness* the poet inserts the Parable of the Marriage Feast as a warning against uncleanness. Although he identifies the gospel of Matthew as the source, the parable is, in fact, a composite of the versions in Matthew 22:2–14 and Luke 14:16–24. From Matthew he draws the basic outline of the story, but from Luke he draws the excuses given by the guests who refuse to come to the feast (lines 61–72) and the ensuing command the lord gives to his servants to go out into the highways and round up the poor, the maimed, the halt, and the blind (lines 73–124). From Matthew comes the incident of the guest without a wedding garment who is thrown outside where there is weeping and gnashing of teeth. The poet suppresses a crucial detail in Matthew—how the lord sends out his army to slay the guests who refused to come. And the poet changes the offense of the man expelled from the wedding: in Matthew the man violates decorum by wearing street clothing instead of a wedding garment; in *Cleanness* he violates decorum by wearing dirty clothing. In this example, the poet makes one continuous narrative out of two gospels, citing only one of the gospels as a source. Later on, the poet uses the same strategy in narrating the Fall of Jerusalem, the Captivity of the Jews, and Baltassar's feast. This later section claims only the book of Daniel as its source (line 1157), when, in fact, the narrative depends on other biblical books as well, such as Hieremias, 1 Samuel, and Exodus.[9]

---

[8] "Sed tamen redeamus ad brevitatem Genesis" (*HS* Genesis, chap. 25, PL 198:1076).

[9] For example see the notes to lines 1269–80 and 1272–73 in the edition of J. J. Anderson, *Cleanness*, Old and Middle English Texts (Manchester: Manchester University Press, 1977). All citations from the text of *Cleanness* will be from this edition.

Comestor put the gospels in a single section called *In evangelia*. Rather than recount all four separately, Comestor re-wrote the gospels into one synoptic narrative, a gospel harmony divided into chapters composed of gospel extracts, paraphrases, and commentaries. For instance, chapter 86, on the transfiguration of Christ, makes use of Matthew 17, Mark 9, and Luke 9, and cites Augustine's commentary on Galatians (PL 198:1581–82). Throughout, Comestor privileges the gospel of Matthew, quoting from Matthew when a given narrative is echoed in other gospels. As it happens, Comestor's telling of the Parable of the Marriage Feast (*In evangelia*, chap. 128, PL 198:1605–06) is a bare epitome of the Matthean version with an eschatological gloss—so it is not a source for the version of the parable in *Cleanness*. However, Comestor's Matthean bias recurs in *Cleanness*, which attributes the parable only to Matthew: "As Maþew meleȝ in his masse" (line 51). Similarly, *Cleanness* provides an eschatological moral ("Thus comparisuneȝ Kryst þe kyndom of heuen / To þis frelych feste þat fele arn to called," etc., lines 161–62, etc.).

The poet also enriches biblical narratives with non-biblical details. In Genesis 8:7, Noah sends out a raven to see if the waters of the Deluge have begun to subside, but for reasons unstated, the raven does not return. So the *Cleanness* poet provides an explanation for this failure to return: the raven in *Cleanness* finds corpses on which it feasts, and glutted with rotted flesh, it ignores Noah's command to return, whereupon Noah curses it (453–68). This non-biblical story comes from a Jewish tradition that is recorded by Christian writers from about the fifth century onwards.[10] The version of this legend in *Cleanness* is not repeated verbatim from a source. Throughout, *Cleanness* follows no

---

[10] The tradition is summarized neatly in the edition of Robert J. Menner, *Purity: A Middle English Poem*, Yale Studies in English, 61 (New Haven: Yale University Press, 1920), note to line 459. Further on this episode see my essay, "The Sin of *Untrawþe* in *Cleanness*," in *Text and Matter: New Critical Perspectives of the Pearl-Poet*, ed. Robert J. Blanch, Miriam Youngerman Miller, and Julian N. Wasserman (Troy, N.Y.: Whitston, 1991), 132–33.

source closely for more than a line or so at a time. Comestor's account of the Flood in the *HS* (Genesis, chap. 34, PL 198:1085) is the precedent for *Cleanness*'s use of the same legend.

As the legend of the raven suggests, when it supplements biblical narrative, scholastic history can be a vehicle for the themes of the monstrous and marvelous. *Cleanness*'s interest in the monstrous and the marvelous has been noted in connection with its use of *Mandeville's Travels*, by all accounts the most popular travelogue produced in England before the Renaissance.[11] I would suggest that we now may see that interest as an aspect of its larger program of scholastic history. Consider, in comparison with the corresponding passage in Genesis, the poet's account of the origin and sin of the giants before the Flood:

> So ferly fowled her flesch þat þe fende loked
> How þe deȝter of þe douþe wern derelych fayre,
> And fallen in felaȝschyp with hem on folken wyse,
> And engendered on hem ieaunteȝ with her japeȝ ille.
>
> Þose wern men meþeleȝ and maȝty on vrþe,
> Þat for her lodlych laykeȝ alosed þay were;
> He watȝ famed for fre þat feȝt loued best,
> And ay þe bigest in bale þe best watȝ halden.

---

[11] See *Cleanness*, ed. Anderson, 6–7, n. 10, and notes to lines 1013–51, 1405–12, and 1469–72; also Liam O. Purdon, "Sodom and Gomorrah: The Use of *Mandeville's Travels* in *Cleanness*," *Journal of the Rocky Mountain Medieval and Renaissance Association* 9 (1988), 63–69, and earlier scholarship cited therein, especially Carleton Brown, "Note on the Dependence of *Cleanness* and the Book of *Mandeville*," *Publications of the Modern Language Association* 19 (1904), 149–53. The Mandeville literature in English is surveyed by Ralph Hanna III, "Mandeville," in *Middle English Prose: A Critical Guide to Major Authors and Genres*, ed. A. S. G. Edwards (New Brunswick: Rutgers University Press, 1984), 121–32. A more exhaustive study of manuscripts, sources, and influences is Christiane Deluz, *Le Livre de Jehan de Mandeville: Une "géographie" au XIVe siècle*, Publications de l'Institut d'Études Médiévales / Textes, Études, Congrès, 8 (Louvain-la Neuve: Université Catholique de Louvain, 1988).

And þenne euele₃ on erþe ernestly grewen,
And multyplyed monyfolde inmonge₃ mankynde,
For þat þe ma₃ty on molde so marre þise oþer
Þat the wy₃e þat al wro₃t ful wroþly bygynne₃.

When he knew vche contre coruppte in hitseluen,
And vch freke forloyned from þe ry₃t waye₃,
Felle temptande tene towched his hert;
As wy₃e wo hym wythinne werp to hymseluen:

'Me forþynke₃ ful much þat euer I mon made;
Bot I schal delyuer and do away þat doten on þis molde,
And fleme out of þe folde al þat flesch were₃,
Fro þe burne to þe best, fro brydde₃ to fysche₃.

Al schal doun and be ded and dryuen out of erþe
Þat euer I sette saule inne, and sore hit me rwe₃
Þat euer I made hem myself; bot if I may herafter,
I schal wayte to be war her wrenche₃ to kepe.' (ll. 269–92)[12]

In comparison, Jerome's Vulgate reads:

And when men began to multiply over the earth and they produced daughters, the sons of God seeing that their daughters were fair, they took wives
for themselves from among them. And the Lord said, My spirit will not
remain in man eternally because he is flesh, and his days will be a hundred

---

[12] "Those were merciless men and mighty on earth, / Who were famed for their hateful behavior. / He who best loved fighting was famed for being noble, / And the biggest in evil was considered the best. / And then evils on earth grew in earnest, / And multiplyed manyfold among mankind, / Inasmuch as the mighty on earth so corrupted these others / That the Man who made all began to be very angry. / When he knew that each country was corrupt in itself, / And each man strayed from the right ways, / Fierce, tempting anger touched his heart, / As a man sorry at heart, he said to himself: / 'I repent greatly that ever I made man, / But I shall destroy and do away those who act foolishly on this earth, / And drive out of the earth everything that wears flesh, / From the man to the beast, from birds to fishes; / Everything shall be downed and dead and driven out of earth / That ever I set soul in; and it grieves me sorely / That ever I made them; but if I may hereafter, / I shall look to be careful to notice their deeds'."

and twenty years. Now giants were upon the earth in those days, after the sons of God went into the daughters of men, and they bore children. These were the mighty men of old, men of renown. And God seeing that the wickedness of men was great on the earth, and that all the thought of their heart was bent upon evil, it repented him that he had made man on the earth. And being touched inwardly with sorrow of heart, he said: I will destroy man, whom I have created, from the face of the earth, from man even to beasts, from the creeping thing even to fowls of the air, for it repenteth me that I have made them (Gen. 6:1–7).[13]

In only a few places does the *Cleanness* poet render Genesis at all closely into Middle English. Most obvious, perhaps, is what the poet has suppressed. Verse 3, for instance, in which God shortens the lifespan of mankind to 120 years, has been removed. In line 273 "potentes a saeculo" becomes "maȝty on urþe," and it is rendered again in line 279 by "maȝty on molde." In line 275 "famosi viri" is translated by "alosed" (274), and in line 275 it is translated again by "famed." However, "multa malitia hominum" is split across lines 277 and 278, where it is rendered by "evelez on erþe" that "multiplyed monyfolde inmongez mankynde." "Tactus dolore cordis intrinsecus" becomes line 283, "Felle temptande teen towched his hert." Genesis 6:6 is conflated with the following verse and assigned to lines 283–92. The poet deletes the second half of Genesis 6:5, "cuncta cogitatio cordis intenta esset ad malum omni tempore," as well as Genesis 6:3, "Dixitque Dominus," etc.

---

[13] "Cumque coepissent homines multiplicari super terram et filias procreassent / videntes filii Dei filias eorum quod essent pulchrae / acceperunt uxores sibi ex omnibus quas elegerant / dixitque Deus non permanebit spiritus meus in homine in aeternum quia caro est / eruntque dies illius centum viginti annorum / gigantes autem erant super terram in diebus illis / postquam enim ingressi sunt filii Dei ad filias hominum illaeque genuerunt / isti sunt potentes a saeculo viri famosi / videns autem Deus quod multa malitia hominum esset in terra / et cuncta cogitatio cordis intenta esset ad malum omni tempore / paenituit eum quod hominem fecisset in terra / et tactus dolore cordis intrinsecus / delebo inquit hominem quem creavi a facie terrae / ab homine usque ad animantia / a reptili usque ad volucres caeli / paenitet enim me fecisse eos." Citation to the Vulgate is to *Biblia Sacra iuxta Vulgatam Versionem*, ed. Robert Weber, 3rd ed. Bonifatius Fischer et al. (Stuttgart: Deutsche Bibelgesellschaft, 1983); all translations are my own.

The genealogy of the giants in lines 269–72, which says that "the fiend" produced the giants by fornicating with "the daughters of [the race of] men," is taken not from the Bible but from an apocryphal legend found in Comestor's *HS*. Genesis 6:4 attributes the birth of the giants to the union of the sons of God and daughters of men, the standard medieval exegesis of which was that males from the line of Seth inter-married with females from the line of Cain. Scholars and editors of *Cleanness* believed that this interpretation lay behind lines 269–72, until Edward Wilson cited the apocryphal tradition, mentioned as early as Augustine, that the fallen angels (or demons) sired the giants.[14] One of the most important vehicles for this tradition in the later Middle Ages is the *HS*:

> It could have been that incubi (or) demons begat the giants—named for the huge-ness of their bodies, so-called from *geos*, which means "earth"—because incubi or demons have the custom of assaulting women at night. For indeed the hugeness of their souls corresponded to the hugeness of their bodies.[15]

---

[14] This exegesis is found as early as Julius Africanus (3rd c.) but was disseminated through Jerome and Augustine. See the sources cited in my article, "*Cleanness*, Peter Comestor, and the *Revelationes Sancti Methodii*," *Mediaevalia* 11 (1985), 213, n. 2; for a summary of the entire tradition see Jack P. Lewis, *A Study of the Interpretation of Noah and the Flood in Jewish and Christian Literature* (Leiden: Brill, 1968). This tradition was connected to *Cleanness* by Oliver F. Emerson, "Legends of Cain, Espe-cially in Old and Middle English," *Publications of the Modern Language Association* 21 (1906), 901; see also Edward Wilson in *The Gawain-Poet*, Medieval and Renais-sance Authors (Leiden: Brill, 1976), 90–92. Wilson cites examples of the apocryphal tradition of the fallen angels in Augustine, Comestor, Higden, and Andrew of Wynton.

[15] "Potuit etiam esse, ut incubi [vel] daemones genuisset gigantes, a magnitudine corporum denominatos, sic dicti a geos, quod est terra, quia incubi vel daemones solent in nocte opprimere mulieres; sed etiam immanitati corporum respondebat immanitas animorum" (*HS* Gen. 31, PL 198:1081). See Menner's note to lines 251 ff. (in *Purity*); and Wilson, *The Gawain-Poet*, 90–92. Compare Andrew of St. Victor, *Andreae de Sancto Victore Opera* I: *Expositio super Heptateuchum*, CCCM 53 (Turnhout: Brepols, 1986), 45, which considers the sons of God to be angels. This story ultimately derives from the apocryphal texts Enoch and Jubilees. The idea of the giants that they present is found, even in faint traces, in the canonical texts, in exegesis, and in the rabbinic

In the manner of scholastic history, the poet of *Cleanness* further opens out his account of the giants by supplementing Scripture. In classical and Christian tradition alike, giants are violent, they sin against nature, and they rebel against God. The Latin word *gigas* was derived etymologically from the Greek word *ge* meaning 'earth.' We find this etymology in the all-important *Etymologiae* of Isidore of Seville. In discussing the monstrous races, Isidore says, "*Gigantes* are named from a Greek etymology, for the Greeks called them *gegeneis*, that is to say, born from the earth."[16] The popular *Magnae derivationes* of Huguccio of Pisa (late 12th c.) adds to this an allusion to the assault of the mythical giants against Olympus, to which Dante also alludes via the giants Ephialtes and Briareus in canto 31 of the *Inferno*.[17]

---

commentaries that became available to Christians via Andrew of St. Victor and his followers. On Andrew of St. Victor see Smalley, *Study of the Bible*, 112–95, esp. 149–55. Sources such as the Midrash Rabbah (Palestine, 6th c.) document how men turned away from the natural order before the Flood: "Hitherto, they were created in [the] likeness and image [of God], but from then onward Centaurs were created. Four things changed in the days of Enosh [i.e., Enoch]: The mountains became [barren] rocks, the dead began to feel [the worms], men's faces became ape-like, and they became vulnerable . . . to demons. Said R. Isaac: They were themselves responsible for becoming vulnerable to demons, [for they argued]: what is the difference whether one worships an image or worships man? Hence, 'Then man became degraded to call upon the name of the Lord' (Gen. 4:26)" (Midrash Rabbah, Genesis, 24.6; in *Midrash Rabbah*, trans. Harry Freedman and Maurice Simon, 10 vols. [London: Soncino, 1939, repr. 1961], 1:203; cp. 23.6 at 1:196–97). Other sins include bestiality (26.4–5, at 1:212–13), miscegenation (28.8, at 1:228), robbery, violence, incest and idolatry (31.1, 6, at 1:239, 241). Both Midrash Rabbah and the Babylonian Talmud compare the generation of the Flood with Sodom: see Midrash Rabbah 27.3 (trans. Freedman and Simon, 1:221) and Sanhedrin 107b–108a in *Babylonian Talmud, Seder Nezikin*, gen. ed. Isidore Epstein, *Sanhedrin*, trans. Harry Freedman, 2 vols. (London: Soncino, 1935), 2:737–40. For a general discussion see Lewis, *Noah and the Flood*, 127–28.

[16] *Etimologías* 11.3.13, ed. José Oroz Reta, with an introduction by Manuel C. Díaz y Díaz, 2 vols., Biblioteca de Autores Cristianos 433, 434 (Madrid: BAC, 1982–83), 2:48.

[17] *Magnae derivationes*, Oxford, MS Bodl. e Mus. 96 (3582), fol. 187: "Videlicet gigantes vel gegantes id est terrigene quia filii terre dicuntur. fuisse. ge terra geneis gens dicitur. unde giganteus -a, -um, et composita cum machia quod est pugna et dum giganthomachia est igitur pungna [sic] gigantum contra deos" [Namely *gigantes* or

The biblical giants were wiped out in the Flood, but other races of giants emerged. Like the pre-Flood giants, these new races were regarded by commentators as a symbol of the return of sinfulness to the world. Hence Nemrod was taken to be a giant. The passage in which he is named, Genesis 10:8, was considered to be an allusion back to the antediluvian giants, since it identified him in a formula similar to Genesis 6:4 "potens in terra": "Now Chus begot Nemrod: he began to be mighty on the earth" [Porro Chus genuit Nemrod / ipse coepit esse potens in terra]. According to the interlinear gloss that formed part of the *Glossa ordinaria*, the standard biblical commentary after the twelfth century, to be mighty or powerful in the earth (Gen. 6:4 *potentes a saeculo*) is to be a giant: "potens in terra vel gigas."[18] Nemrod becomes the progenitor of new races of giants. These include the Rafaim (Gen. 14:5, 15:20; 2 Sam. 5:18, 23:13), the Enacim (Num. 13:34; Deut. 2:10), Og of Basan (Num. 21:33–35; Deut. 1:4, 3:11; Josh. 12:4, 13:12), the Emim (Deut. 2:10–11), Goliath (1 Sam. 17), and the four sons of Arafa in Geth (2 Sam. 21:15–22).[19]

Commonly, these post-diluvial giants are seen in the light of the same controlling sins we have observed in the generation of the Flood.

---

gegantes that is "people of earth," because they are said to have been sons of earth. *Ge* means 'earth,' *geneis* means 'people,' whence *giganteus -a, -um*; and compounded with *machia* which is 'battle' it thus makes *giganthomachia*, thus battle against the gods].

[18] Citation to the *Glossa ordinaria* is to *Biblia sacra cum glossis interlineari et ordinaria, Nicolai Lyrani postilla, ac moralitatibus, Burgensis additionibus, et Thoringi replicis*, 6 vols. (Venice, 1588), 1:58G.

[19] The Rafaim are not singled out as giants in Scripture; but on the basis of his Hebrew sources Jerome confidently identified them as such in the *Liber interpretationis hebraicorum nominum*, CCSL 72 (Turnhout: Brepols, 1959), 70, 87, 92. He is echoed in, for example, the *Glossa ordinaria*, the interlinear gloss, and Nicholas of Lyra's postill on Gen. 14:5. *Glossa ordinaria*: "*percusseruntque Raphaim*: Alia editio habet, et ceciderunt gigantes in Astaroch, et Carnaim, et gentes, fortes cum eis, et homines in Sabae ciuitate antequam Sodomam peruenirent. Quatuor reges profecti de Babilone interfecerunt gigantes, hoc est Raphaim" (1:63C). Interlinear gloss: "*Raphaim*: Gigantes, id est de se presumentes" (1:63B). Nicholas of Lyra: "*percusseruntque Raphaim*: Id est gigantes" (1:63D).

Allegorized as the devil or as the adversaries of God generally, the giants live in an unclean, forbidden land. They must be opposed, as a trial of the faith of God's people. Man is like a giant when he sins. Thus Proverbs 21:16: "The man who strays from the way of doctrine shall abide in the company of giants" [Vir qui erraverit a via doctrinae / in coetu gigantum commorabitur].

The giant races are regarded as a single race, a genus, despite the apparent diversity of Old Testament giants and their appearance as isolated families or individuals at different times and in different places. In biblical commentary the giants are the products of their birth. We have seen that there were two stories about their origin before the Flood: either they were produced by the line of Seth and the line of Cain, or they were produced by *incubi* and human women. What these two traditions share is the underlying idea of species corruption. Fornication between discrete groups implies the corruption of a spiritually pure group by a spiritually impure group. As John Block Friedman has shown in his book *The Monstrous Races in Medieval Art and Thought*, in the medieval popular tradition species corruption is one of the chief causes of monstrosities, which as *monstra* or *portenta* were incarnate, inverse revelations of divine law.[20] Giants are the unnatural offspring of an unnatural union.

We see this in *Cleanness* in a number of ways. As the poet notes in line 272, the demons and the human women fornicate "in the human way," since there is no other way for divine and formerly divine beings

---

[20] See John Block Friedman, *The Monstrous Races in Medieval Art and Thought* (Cambridge, Mass.: Harvard University Press, 1981), 108–30. As an example of this belief, Friedman cites the Old French verse translation, done ca. 1290 by the "Clerk of Enghien," of "De monstrosis hominibus," the influential third book of Thomas of Cantimpré's *De naturis rerum* (ca. 1240). The Onocentaurs and another, unnamed, tribe are produced by bestial intercourse between man and animals. "The verbal similarity between adultery and adulteration may have led him to believe that the one was appropriate reward for the other. Bearing this out are the neighbors of the above tribes, 'inverted' Cynocephali, whose nature develops from the imaginative implications of their sexual crime" (129).

to engage in sexual contact. They thus violate their own natures and precipitate the corruption of human nature. The moral consequences of species corruption are reflected in the giants' behavior. In line 273 the poet associates the giants' might with mercilessness, and in line 274 he attributes their fame to their crimes, thereby unifying his moral portrait of the giants around the "multa malitia hominum" in Genesis 6:5.

The rise of the giants in *Cleanness* thus is presented from the pre-humanist viewpoint of medieval Christian tradition, in which, owing to their genealogy, the giants are known for rebellion against the divinity and for violence against each other and against men.[21] In the Vulgate, Baruch 3:26–28 represents this tradition, laying heavy emphasis on the giants' lack of wisdom: "There were the giants, those renowned men that were from the beginning, of great stature, expert in war. God did not choose them; neither did he give them the way of knowledge. And they perished because they did not have wisdom; they perished through their folly."[22] In a similar fashion, in lines 273–76 the *Cleanness* poet reduces the giants' might and their love of fighting to the mere folly of those who "doten on þis molde."

Like the giants in medieval romance and in collections of marvels called *mirabilia*, the giants in *Cleanness* hold to a code that is a perversion of chivalry. In lines 275–76, these merciless men pervert the chivalric ideal of *fredom* through their battlefield exploits, for among the giants, to be *fre* is only to love and excel in fighting. By contrast,

---

[21] Emerson, "Legends of Cain," 905–16, discusses the tendency to equate the pagan gods with the Genesis giants. See also R. E. Kaske, "The *Eotenas* in *Beowulf*," in *Old English Poetry: Fifteen Essays*, ed. Robert P. Creed (Providence: Brown University Press, 1967), 290–92, 296–99, et passim; and Kaske, "*Sapientia et Fortitudo* as the Controlling Theme of *Beowulf*," *Studies in Philology* 55 (1958), 438–40.

[22] "ibi fuerunt gigantes nominati illi qui ab initio fuerunt / statura magna scientes bellum / non hos elegit Deus / neque viam disciplinae dedit illis / et perierunt eo quod non haberent sapientiam / et perierunt propter insipientiam suam." This passage is cited by Augustine in his discussion of the giants in *De civitate dei* 15.23, CCSL 48 (Turnhout: Brepols, 1955), 492.

in *Sir Gawain and the Green Knight*, for example, *fredom* summarizes
the socio-ethical virtues of Arthur's court (line 101), of Bertilak (lines
803, 847, and 1156), and of Gawain's spiritual models Adam, David,
and Samson, whom Gawain invokes when he is caught with the green
girdle (line 2422).[23] Chaucer's Knight loved "trouthe and honour, fredom
and curtesie" (I.46). In *Cleanness* the biblical "multa malitia hominum"
is poetically expanded into an ironic code of arms in which the words
fre and *best* are drained of ethical meaning and defined solely by violence and by the suffering the giants cause to others. In the giants'
code, *fredom* is unrestrained desire for fighting. In line 275, the word
loved emphasizes this reversal of values, for among the giants love is
merely appetite. Likewise, in line 276, "bigest in bale" distorts a potentially positive quality into a negative one. Middle English *bale* has
active and passive senses: "evil done" and "evil suffered" (see OED
bale sb. I). To be "bigest in bale" could refer to the ability to cause suffering or to the ability to endure suffering: the one would be an attribute
of the giants, the other an attribute of questing knights, pilgrims, and
martyrs. The very description of the giants' behavior locates them
morally within the sphere of romance by implicitly contrasting them
with chivalric example. Even in this most theologically rigorous poem,
the poet shows, as he does in the other three poems of Cotton Nero
A.x, his awareness of the ambiguity of ideals and the language that
describes them.

The giants in *Cleanness* also were inspired by onomastic tradition,
which in turn derives from the Midrashic commentary of the Jews.
Onomastics was a central part of biblical study, since etymology was
regarded as a valid means of recovering the original language of Adam,
which had been obscured by the confusion of tongues at the tower of

---

[23] Note that among the perils Gawain faces on his way to Hautdesert are "etaynez, þat
hym anelede of þe heȝe felle" (723). Bertilak is himself "half etayn on erde" (140).
Citation is to the text of J. R. R. Tolkien and E. V. Gordon, 2nd ed., rev. Norman Davis
(Oxford: Clarendon, 1967).

Babel. In this ur-language, linguistic signifiers and their signifieds were matched logically to reveal the intrinsic nature of the signifieds.[24] Hebrew words were of great interest to Christian biblical scholars because they were older than Latin words and, therefore, believed to be closer to the language of Adam, if not the very language itself. In the Hebrew Old Testament, the giants of Genesis 6:4 are called *nefilim* [falling ones]. The Midrash Rabbah says: "*Nefilim* denotes that they hurled [*hippilu*] the world down, themselves fell [*naflu*] from the world, and filled the world with abortions [*nefilim*] through their immorality."[25]

The Hebrew gloss from the Midrash Rabbah conveys the idea of symbolic retribution: the giants fell from the world because they fell on others. This idea is reflected in the Vulgate in passages concerning giants. In Job 16:15 the devil falls on Job "like a giant": "He strikes me wound upon wound; he *falls* on me like a giant" [Concidit me vulnere super vulnus / irruit in me quasi gigans]. In 1 Samuel 17:49 Goliath falls by virtue of David's sling: "and the stone sank into his forehead, and he *fell* on his face on the earth" [et infixus est lapis in fronte eius / et cecidit in faciem suam super terram]. In 2 Samuel 21:22 the four

---

[24] See Ernst Robert Curtius, "Etymology as a Category of Thought," Excursus no. XIV in *European Literature and the Latin Middle Ages*, trans. Willard R. Trask (New York: Pantheon, 1953), 495–500. On onomastics, a special branch of etymology, see Franz Wutz, *Onomastica Sacra: Untersuchungen zum Liber Interpretationis nominum Hebraicorum des hl. Hieronymus*, Texte und Untersuchungen zur Geschichte der altchristlichen Literatur, Reihe 3, Bd. 11.1–2 (Leipzig: J. C. Hinrichs, 1914–15). Richard H. Rouse and Mary Rouse have observed that although it "enjoyed only a limited circulation before 1200, [the *Liber*] was thoroughly revised around the turn of the century to become part of the biblical canon, appearing in virtually all Bibles thereafter" ("*Statim invenire*: Schools, Preachers, and New Attitudes to the Page," in *Renaissance and Renewal in the Twelfth Century*, ed. Robert L. Benson and Giles Constable, with Carol D. Lanham [Cambridge, Mass.: Harvard University Press, 1982], 221). In its revised form, the *Liber* was organized alphabetically and was, thus, easily searchable. Yet it received close attention even before the twelfth century from OE authors: see Fred C. Robinson, "The Significance of Names in Old English Literature," *Anglia* 86 (1968), 14–58. A similar study is needed for ME literature.

[25] Midrash Rabbah 26.7, trans. Freedman and Simon, 1:218.

giant sons of Arafa in Geth *"fell* at the hand of David and his servants" [ceciderunt in manu David et servorum eius]. The Hebrew onomastic gloss that explained the moral character of the giants was adopted by Jerome. In his *Hebrew Questions on the Book of Genesis*, which notes, "In Hebrew it says, 'the falling ones were in the earth in those days,' that is *nefilim*" [In hebraeo ita habet 'cadentes erant in terra in diebus illis,' id est *nefilim*].[26] In the *Commentary on Isaiah* Jerome interprets the word *gigantes* to mean *irruentes*, "falling [on others]."[27]

These onomastic glosses are reflected in the procreation, behavior, and punishment of the giants in *Cleanness*. In line 271, *incubi* "fallen in fela3schyp" with the daughters of men to beget the race of giants, who fall on each other and on others in lines 273–76. When God resolves to punish the giants He says: "'Al schal doun [reflecting *cadentes*] and be ded and dryven out of erþe'" (line 289). In the Flood episode of *Cleanness*, falling is a central theme, expressing the derangement in nature brought about by the antediluvians and by God's radical punishment of their sin, which typologically re-enacts the Fall of Lucifer and the Fall of Man, to which the *Cleanness* poet explicitly compares the Flood in lines 205–52. It is important to emphasize that the theme of falling is not found in the text of Genesis 6:4—the poet found it in name-etymologies like Jerome's.

---

[26] Jerome, *Hebraicae quaestiones in libro Geneseos*, CCSL 72 (Turnhout: Brepols, 1959), 10. The onomastic gloss *cadentes* 'falling ones' is repeated by, e.g., Bede, *Quaestiones super Genesim* (PL 93:293); Rupert of Deutz, *De Trinitate et operibus eius—in Genesis*, 4.4 (PL 167:339); the interlinear gloss to Gen. 6:4 (*Biblia sacra*, Venice ed., 1588, 1:50E); and Andrew of St. Victor, *Expositio super Heptateuchum*, CCCM 53 (Turnhout: Brepols, 1986), 46.

[27] "Geneseos quoque narrat liber, quod postquam coeperunt homines multi fieri, . . . et filae eis natae sunt, acceperunt eas, non angeli, sed filii Dei, de quibus orti sunt gigantes, sive ut in Hebraeo [*sic*; i.e., Graece] scriptum est epiptontes, id est, irruentes" [Also the book of Genesis relates that after men became numerous, . . .and daughters were born to them, not angels, but sons of God took them, from which were born giants, or as it says in Hebrew (that is, Greek) *epiptontes*, that is *irruentes*]. *Commentariorum in Isaiam prophetam*, book 18, on Isa. 66:7 (PL 24:658).

The Flood episode shows the *Cleanness* poet re-imagining biblical history out of Scripture and the scholarship surrounding it. One further aspect of scholastic history found in *Cleanness* is the way in which the poet divides biblical narratives. Since Comestor wrote his *HS* before the modern chapter divisions of the Bible were devised by his student Stephen Langton, the *HS* separates the Bible into original narrative units.[28] Comestor's division of biblical texts influenced Middle English authors to divide the Bible similarly. For example, in the Middle English *Genesis and Exodus* the manuscript capitals correspond neatly with the chapter divisions of the *HS*.[29]

The destruction of Sodom in *Cleanness* is divided in a manner quite similar to that of the *HS*, but in order to recognize this we must acknowledge the poet's famous description of the Dead Sea in lines 1015–48 as an intrinsic part of the Sodom narrative as given by Comestor, whose chapter 53 in Genesis adds an account of the Dead Sea. Although a version of *Mandeville's Travels* is agreed to be the immediate source of this passage in *Cleanness*, the main outline of the passage, and its placement after God's punishment of Sodom in Genesis, derives from the *HS*. As a comparison of the *HS* with *Cleanness* shows, Comestor establishes major details picked up later in *Cleanness* together with the order in which these are presented: what sinks and what floats in it; substances found in it; and the "apples of Sodom" growing along its banks:

> Þere fyue citees wern set nov is a see called,
> Þat ay is drouy and dym, and ded in hit kynde;

---

[28] See Ralph Loewe, "The Medieval History of the Latin Vulgate," *Cambridge History of the Bible*, vol. 2, ed. G. W. H. Lampe (Cambridge: Cambridge University Press, 1969), 147–48.

[29] See Arthur Fritzsche, "Ist die a.e. 'Story of Genesis and Exodus' das Werk eines Verfassers?" *Anglia* 5 (1882), 43–90, esp. 47–48 and table on 88–90.

Blo, blubrande, and blak, vnblyþe to neȝe,
As a stynkande stanc þat stryed synne,
Þat euer of synne and of smach smart is to fele.
Forþy þe derk dede see hit is demed euermore.

For hit dedeȝ of deþe duren þere ȝet;
For hit is brod and boþemleȝ, and bitter as þe galle,
And noȝt may lenge in þat lake þat any lyf bereȝ,
And alle þe costeȝ of kynde hit combreȝ vchone.

For lay þeron a lump of led and hit on loft fleteȝ,
And folde þeron a lyȝt fyþer and hit to founs synkkeȝ.
And þer water may walter to wete any erþe,
Schal neuer grene þeron growe, gresse ne wod nawþer.

If any schalke to be schent wer schowued þerinne,
Þaȝ he bode in þat boþem broþely a monyth,
He most ay lyue in þat loȝe, in losyng euermore,
And neuer dryȝe no dethe to dayes of ende.

And as hit is corsed of kynde, and hit coosteȝ als,
Þe clay þat clenges þerby arn corsyes strong,
As alum and alkaran, þat angre arn boþe,
Soufre sour and saundyuer and oþer such mony;

And þer walteȝ of þat water, in waxlokes grete,
Þe spumande aspaltoun þat spysereȝ sellen.
And suche is alle þe soyle by þat se halues,
Þat fel fretes þe flesch and festres bones.

And þer ar tres by þat terne of traytoures,
And þay borgouneȝ and beres blomeȝ ful fayre,
And þe fayrest fryt þat may on folde growe,
As orenge and oþer fryt and apple-garnade,

Al so red and so ripe and rychely hwed
As any dom myȝt deuice, of dayntyeȝ oute;

Bot quen hit is brused oþer broken oþer byten in twynne,
No worldeȝ goud hit wythinne, bot wyndowande askes.[30]

Regarding the same, Comestor writes:

The region became a salt—and sterile—lake that is called the Sea of the
Dead, since neither fish nor birds live in it, as they do in others. It sustains
neither ship nor any other material—though indeed perhaps everything floats
on it—unless it is sealed with pitch, on account of the living men inside. For
what is wholly lacking life sinks to the depths. If something living is in some
fashion put under, it springs back up. A burning lamp floats, but an extin-
guished one sinks. In many places the lake spews forth black lumps of pitch,
and therefore it is called the Asphalt Lake, or Asphaltidis. It is still said of
the apples growing in orchards all about it, which remain green until maturity,
that if you cut the ripe ones open, inside you find ashes.[31]

---

[30] "Where once were five cities is now called a sea / That is always murky and dim, and
dead in its nature; / Livid, bubbling, and black, unpleasant to approach, / As a stinking
pool that destroyed sin, / Which in its sin and its savor is always bitter to taste, / Therefore the dark Dead Sea it is called evermore. / For its deeds of death persist there yet;
/ For it is broad and bottomless, and bitter as the gall, / And nothing alive may stay in
that lake, / And it destroys every one of the qualities of nature. / For lay a lump of lead
on it and it will stay afloat, / And place a light feather on it and it sinks to the bottom.
/ And wherever its water flows and wets the earth / No green will ever grow there, nor
grass nor wood either. / If any man were pushed into it in order to be killed, / Even if
he stayed in that deep place for a month, / He must always live in the loch, evermore
in perdition, / And never suffer death, to the end of time. / And as it is cursed in nature,
and its coasts also, / The clay that clings there is strong corrosives, / Such as alum and
bitumen, which are both caustic, / Bitter sulfur and glass-gall, and many other such. /
And there flows from that water, in big wax lumps / The foaming asphalt that spicers
sell. / And such is all the soil by the shores of that sea / That cruelly eats flesh and rots
bones. / And there are trees by that tarn of traitors, / And they bud and bear very fair
blooms, / And the fairest fruit that may grow on the earth, / Such as oranges and other
fruit and pomegranates, / As red and ripe and richly hued / As any imagination might
devise out of delicacies; / But when it is bruised or broken or bitten in two, / There is
no worldly good within, but powdery ashes."

[31] "Verso est ergo regio in lacum salis, et sterilem, qui dicitur Mare Mortuum, quia nec
pisces, nec aves, in eo vivunt, ut in aliis. Navem quoque non patitur, nec ullam sustinet
materiam, quin tota forsitan supernatet, nisi bituminatam, propter homines intus viventes.
Nam omne carens vita in profundum mergitur. Si quid vivum aliqua arte immersis,

As J. J. Anderson observes in his edition's note to these lines in *Cleanness*,

> a description of the properties of the Dead Sea became a traditional part of the story of the destruction of Sodom and Gomorrah. The most relevant parallels for *Cleanness* are in passages from *Mandeville's Travels* [and] *Cursor Mundi* 2861 ff. . . . The traditional descriptions go back to Josephus, *De Bello Judaico*, IV.8.4, but the poet of *Cleanness* is clearly influenced particularly by the description in *Mandeville's Travels*.[32]

In Mandeville the *Cleanness* poet found many of the details seen here, and even some of the language. For example, lines 1025–48 have the floating lead from this essay's title, the sinking feather, submerged bodies that never die, various pollutants, and apples that have nothing but ashes inside. It is not clear which version of *Mandeville's Travels* the *Cleanness* poet knew. The word *foundered* in line 1014 recalls the Old French *fondirent* in the Egerton MS (Insular version) of *Mandeville*, and line 1026 "hit to founs synkkez" recalls the Old French "elle irroit au founz."[33] Since the Middle English translations of Mandeville cited by scholars who have studied *Cleanness*'s use of Mandeville (see note 11) render the Old French differently in these two places, a French version rather than an English version may have been the poet's source. Another possible influence is a text such as *Cursor Mundi*. The *Cleanness* poet's emphasis on the unnaturalness of the Dead Sea is found in

---

superexsilit. Lucerna ardens superenatat, exstincta mergitur. Multis in locis nigras glebas bituminis vomit, et ideo Lacus Asphalti, vel Asphaltidis dicitur. Dicitur etiam quod poma nata in arboribus circumpositis, usque ad maturitatem coloris sunt viridis, matura si incidas, favillas intus invenies" (*HS* Gen., chap. 53, PL 198:1101).

[32] *The Buke of John Mandevill*, ed. George F. Warner, Roxburghe Club (London: Nichols & Sons, 1889), 73–74; *Cursor Mundi*, ed. Richard W. Morris, EETS 57 (London: Trübner, 1874), lines 2861–80; and *The Jewish War*, trans. G. A. Williamson, rev. Mary Smallwood, Penguin Classics (London: Penguin, 1981), 271–73. On Mandeville see also note 11 above.

[33] *Buke of John Mandevill*, ed. Warner, 51, 50.

Mandeville, but *Cursor Mundi* draws an explicit moral about it, as *Cleanness* does in lines 1049–52. Like *Cleanness*, *Cursor Mundi* (lines 2881–2912) considers the homosexuality of Sodom a particularly serious sin.

The Dead Sea is part of the standard tour through the Holy Land in travel literature. But if the *Cleanness* poet was inspired by details in *Mandeville's Travels*, the practice of describing the Dead Sea after narrating the destruction of Sodom was established by the *HS*. Comestor's account of the destruction of Sodom does not follow the biblical chapter divisions, which separate God's encounter with Abraham at Mambre in chapter 18 from the angels' encounter with Lot at Sodom in chapter 19. Comestor divides the Sodom narrative between two chapters, 52 and 53 in the Genesis section of the *HS*. Chapter 52 begins with a combined quotation from Genesis 18:16 and 20, where God begins to speak with Abraham about punishing Sodom. *Cleanness* lines 677–84 come at this point, but this section of *Cleanness* is closer to Genesis 18:16–19 than it is to Comestor, since it renders verses 18 and 19, which Comestor suppressed. However, *Cleanness* has a large manuscript capital at line 689, "The grete soun of Sodamas . . . ," which begins the very next sentence in Comestor's chapter 52, "Et ait ad illum, 'Clamor Sodomorum.' . . ." Chapter 53 in the *HS* begins at Genesis 19:16, where the two angels physically lead Lot and his family out of Sodom, which corresponds to *Cleanness* lines 893–946, "Ruddon of þe day-rawe ros vpon vȝten. . . ." This second section in *Cleanness* begins with a large manuscript capital that sets it apart from the rest of the Sodom narrative. Chapter 53 concludes, like this section of *Cleanness*, with a description of the Dead Sea.

A few caveats are in order, however. If the *Cleanness* poet indeed was inspired by Comestor's chapter divisions, it is hard to say whether he knew of them directly from the *HS* or from the popular French translation, the *Bible historiale*, which circulated widely in fourteenth-century England. A more serious problem is that the contents of Comestor's chapters 52 and 53 do not match exactly the contents of these two sections of *Cleanness*. The difference is that *Cleanness* is a dramatic narrative with speeches, and it contains additional apocryphal lore not found even in Comestor. For example, when Lot invites the angels into his house, he orders his wife to prepare a meal without leaven or salt. She goes off to her kitchen grumbling to herself about her finicky guests, and puts salt in the food anyway. This may be a version of a Hebrew legend explaining Genesis 19:3, which says that Lot served his guests unleavened bread,[34] but no one has been able to identify its source. Likewise, the *Cleanness* poet replaces Comestor's description of the Dead Sea in chapter 53 with Mandeville's. Finally, the MS capitals in *Cleanness* may not have been indicated by the author, and, instead, may have been scribally determined. There have been a number of reasonable attempts at explaining the MS capitals in *Cleanness*, but it is not at all certain that they represent the intentions of the author.[35]

The methods of scholastic history allowed the *Cleanness* poet to pick and choose his narrative details. Unlike Comestor, the poet does not offer the reader alternatives, having arranged narrative details of his own choosing into a unified account of the events leading up to the Flood. We should not be surprised if *Cleanness* differs from Comestor. The *Cleanness* poet characteristically does not copy verbatim from a source text, nor does he paraphrase often. Like Chaucer in his mature tales, his practice is to re-invent his sources, whatever they may be, as in the Flood episode. Although *Cleanness* is not a retelling of the Bible from the beginning onwards, *Cleanness* re-tells biblical narratives in ways similar to other Middle English biblical adaptations such as *Cursor Mundi*, all of which are indebted to Comestor and often cite him as a source. *Cursor Mundi*, for example, narrates most of the Bible, and it intersperses canonical stories with legends, typologies, moralities, and

---

[34] Oliver F. Emerson, "A Note on Middle English 'Cleanness'," *Modern Language Review* 10 (1915), 374.

[35] See R. J. Spendal, "The Manuscript Capitals in *Cleanness*," *Notes and Queries* 221 (1976), 240–41.

exempla. Like *Cleanness*, it uses the non-canonical stories of the raven from the Flood episode, which I mentioned earlier, and of the Dead Sea at the end of the Sodom episode, both legends that *Cursor Mundi* found in Comestor. Even if the manuscript capitals are not authorial and are not directly inspired by Comestor or the French *Bible historiale*, they do show that whoever decided to break up the text in this way took the authorial liberty to divide the narrative in places other than the chapter divisions in Genesis. The ultimate origin of this practice is Comestor.[36]

[36] I wish to thank Alasdair MacDonald for inviting me to the Rijksuniversiteit Groningen, The Netherlands, in May, 1993, where I presented an earlier version of this article as a lecture to the Anglistisch Instituut. I am grateful to Thomas D. Hill, Carol V. Kaske, and Sachi Shimomura for their suggestions on the present version.

FROM MONSTER TO MARTYR:
THE OLD ENGLISH
LEGEND OF SAINT CHRISTOPHER

JOYCE TALLY LIONARONS

THE LEGEND OF SAINT CHRISTOPHER was known in Anglo-Saxon England in a variety of different forms: there is a fragmentary Old English *Passion of Saint Christopher* in British Library MS Cotton Vitellius A.xv, better known as the *Beowulf* manuscript;[1] there is a complete but much shorter *Life* of the saint included in two of four extant manuscripts containing the ninth-century *Old English Martyrology*;[2] and Wanley's catalogue preserves the *incipit* and *explicit* of a vernacular homily concerning Christopher from BL MS Cotton Otho B.x, a manuscript unfortunately almost totally destroyed in the 1731 Cotton library fire.[3] In addition to the Old English versions, a Latin *Vita Sancti Christophori* survives in Anglo-Saxon manuscripts, and

---

[1] The standard edition is that of Stanley Rypins, *Three Old English Prose Texts in MS Cotton Vitellius A.xv* (London: Oxford University Press, 1924), but the text also has been edited by Andy Orchard in his *Pride and Prodigies: Studies in the Monsters of the Beowulf Manuscript* (Cambridge: D. S. Brewer, 1995). Citations in this essay are to Rypins's edition.

[2] *An Old English Martyrology*, ed. George Herzfeld (London: Oxford University Press, 1900). The manuscripts containing the *Life of Saint Christopher* are British Library MS Cotton Julius A.x and Cambridge, Corpus Christi College MS 196.

[3] Orchard, *Pride and Prodigies*, 12.

there is an Old Irish analogue in the *Leabhar Breacc*,[4] although it is unclear whether or not the Irish book was known in England. None of these texts are outstanding in sheer literary value, but they are interesting in that all of them are in agreement concerning the saint's most distinctive attribute: Christopher is portrayed here as "healf-hundisces manncynnes,"[5] a *cynocephalus*, that is, a man with the head of a dog. This fact is stated explicitly in each version except the fragmentary *Passion*, which is missing the beginning of the legend where such a characteristic customarily would have been mentioned. There is general scholarly consensus, however, that the idea is implicit throughout the extant two-thirds of the Old English text, both because the text is based on Latin sources in which the saint's canine nature is made explicit and because the Old English hagiographer includes details implying that Christopher is physically anomalous. Not only is he described by the narrator as "twelve fathoms tall" [twelf fædma lang][6] but also the emperor Dagnus refers to him as if he were an animal, calling him "the worst of wild beasts" [wyrresta wilddeor].[7]

The idea of a dog-headed saint probably was less strange to a literate Anglo-Saxon audience than it is to a modern one, since the educated Anglo-Saxon would have come across dog-headed humans in numerous other texts: John Block Friedman calls the *cynocephali* "among the most popular" of the so-called "Plinian" or "monstrous" races, while David Gordon White refers to them more whimsically as "Christianity's favorite fairyland monsters."[8] The Old English *Wonders of the East* and *Letter of Alexander to Aristotle*, both of which are

---

[4] J. Fraser, "The Passion of Saint Christopher," *Revue Celtique* 34 (1913), 307–25.

[5] Cotton Otho B.x, cited in Orchard, *Pride and Prodigies*, 12.

[6] Rypins, *Three Old English Prose Texts*, 68.

[7] Ibid., 70.

[8] John Block Friedman, *The Monstrous Races in Medieval Art and Thought* (Cambridge, Mass.: Harvard University Press, 1981), 15; David Gordon White, *Myths of the Dog-Man* (Chicago: University of Chicago Press, 1991), 30.

preserved along with the *Saint Christopher* fragment in Cotton Vitellius A.xv, each describe a race of dog-headed humans.[9] Additional material about the *cynocephali* could be found in the Anglo-Latin *Liber Monstrorum*[10] or in the works of Isidore of Seville. Medieval authorities in general relied on Pliny's *Historia Naturalis* for information concerning such exotic creatures; however, the ultimate source for the idea seems to have been Ktesias's *Indika*, written 398–97 B.C.E.[11]

Ktesias locates the *cynocephali* in the mountains of India and describes them as having a mixture of human and animal characteristics: like men they hunt using weapons such as javelins or bows, but like animals they eat raw, and often human, flesh. Like human beings they wear animal skins as clothing, but like animals they lack the ability to speak and communicate only by barking. Later writers embellish Ktesias's account. The Alexander cycle gives the dog-heads enormous teeth and the ability to breathe flames,[12] a tradition represented in Old English by the description of the *cynocephali* in *Wonders of the East*: "They have horses' manes and boars' tusks and dogs' heads and their breath is like a fiery flame" [Hi habbað horses mana & eoferes tuxas & hunda heafdu & heora oroð byð swylce fyres leg].[13] The thirteenth-century Dominican encyclopedist Vincent of Beauvais even describes a hermaphroditic *cynocephalus* said to have visited the French court in his *Speculum Naturale* (31.126).[14]

Along with the other "monstrous" races believed to inhabit the East, the *cynocephali* function in the European Middle Ages as a sort of collective Other for medieval Christian culture—they seem almost, but not quite, human; they are alien, yet in some way still the same.

---

[9] See Rypins, *Three Old English Prose Texts*, 33 and 54.

[10] *Liber Monstrorum de Diversis Generibus*, ed. Franco Porsia (Bari: Dedalo, 1976).

[11] See Friedman, *Monstrous Races*, for the best full history of the *cynocephali*.

[12] Ibid., 15.

[13] Rypins, *Three Old English Prose Texts*, 54.

[14] Vincent of Beauvais, *Speculum Naturale Vincenti* (H. Liechtenstein, Venetjis, 1494).

Their differences provide a necessary foil, a seemingly binary opposition against which medieval Western society can construct a cultural identity, while the resemblances simultaneously make them a ready receptacle for the repressed fears, anxieties, fantasies, and desires of Christian culture. As Jeffrey Jerome Cohen points out in his "Seven Theses" about monsters, the cultural construction of monstrosity produces "an incorporation of the Outside, the Beyond—of all those loci that are rhetorically placed as distant and distinct but originate Within."[15] The same can, of course, be said of Otherness that is based on such non-monstrous traits as gender, race, religion, or sexuality. But because the Plinian races are specifically monstrous Others, that is, hybrids between the human and bestial like the *cynocephali* or human beings with decidedly non-natural physical characteristics like the one-legged *sciapods*, they reveal most clearly what Michael Uebel calls the two paradoxes of imagined Otherness, first that "alterity is never radical, because the terms of any binarism interdepend, interanimate," and second that the boundary between self and other necessarily has a "double status," being at the same time a "marker of separation and line of commonality."[16] When the monstrous races are considered seriously, the paradoxes inherent in Otherness and made manifest in monstrous hybrids like the *cynocephali* destroy all illusion of the Other as incorporating a truly binary opposition: there is difference, but not antithesis. And once differences are looked at as variants within a single classificatory system rather than as polar opposites, the designations of Self and Other break down, instigating "category crisis," that is, a disintegration of culturally constructed identity described by Marjorie Garber as arising from:

[15] Jeffrey Jerome Cohen, "Monster Culture: Seven Theses," in *Monster Theory: Reading Culture*, ed. Jeffrey Jerome Cohen (Minneapolis: University of Minnesota Press, 1996), 7.

[16] Michael Uebel, "Unthinking the Monster: Twelfth Century Responses to Saracen Alterity," in *Monster Theory*, ed. Cohen, 265.

a failure of definitional distinction, a borderline that becomes permeable, that permits of border crossings from one (apparently distinct) category to another. . . ." [What crosses the border] will always function as a mechanism of overdetermination—a mechanism of displacement from one blurred boundary to another.[17]

Moreover, as psychologist Arnold I. Davidson points out, "monsters that seem to call into question, to problematize, the boundary between humans and other animals . . . operate [as a] major locus of the experience of horror."[18] The category crisis and concomitant horror produced by the *cynocephali* are particularly acute, for as semiotic indicators dogs are singularly rich and ambiguous in meaning, embodying concepts as diverse as loyalty and perfidy. Not only do they participate in proverbs, *exempla*, and legends of all kinds, but they also are always already hybrids in themselves, cousins to the wolf yet at the same time part of human culture, "dwell[ing] on the boundary between domestication and savagery."[19]

It was, perhaps, the universal familiarity of the dog as a cultural image in combination with the alterity of the *cynocephalus*'s monstrous form that made the dog-heads particularly popular in Western cultural imaginings of the East. Edward Said argues that the European viewpoint of the East that he terms "orientalism" generally allows for only "a restricted number of typical encapsulations"[20] of Eastern experience, encapsulations that serve to normalize the alien phenomena of the East either by incorporating elements already familiar to European society or by familiarizing unfamiliar elements by dint of constant repetition in European sources. In this way:

---

[17] Marjorie Garber, *Vested Interests: Cross-Dressing and Cultural Anxiety* (New York: Routledge, 1992), 16.

[18] Arnold I. Davidson, "The Horror of Monsters," in *The Boundaries of Humanity: Humans, Animals, Machines*, ed. James J. Sheehan and Morton Sosna (Berkeley and Los Angeles: University of California Press, 1991), 36.

[19] White, *Myths*, 15.

[20] Edward Said, *Orientalism* (London: Routledge & Kegan Paul, 1978), 58.

[s]omething patently foreign and distant acquires . . . a status more rather than less familiar. One tends to stop judging things either as completely novel or as completely well known; a new median category emerges, a category that allows one to see new things, things seen for the first time, as versions of a previously known thing.[21]

The orientalist view of the East in general therefore embodies the same sort of vacillation between difference and identity leading to category crisis as the European view of the monstrous races and the *cynocephali* in particular. As Said points out, this vacillation between categories characterizes and explains the widespread and wildly incorrect medieval Christian idea that Islam is a binary opposite to Christianity: "Mohammed is always the imposter (familiar, because he pretends to be like the Jesus we know) and always the Oriental (alien, because although he is in some ways 'like' Jesus, he is after all not like him)."[22]

Because they serve the same cultural function of abjected Other, it is no wonder that orientalized conceptions of religious difference and the monstrous races merged in the medieval European identification of heretics and other religious dissidents with dogs. Friedman points out that "dog" was a common Christian epithet for Muslims;[23] and he adds that in:

Psalm 21:17 David cries out in despair that "dogs have compassed me: the assembly of the wicked have enclosed me: they pierced my hands and my feet." This passage was naturally connected with the passion of Christ, and Hugh of St. Cher, following Cassiodorus, explained that allegorically the dogs were the Jews, who were called dogs because just as a dog barks at what is strange to him, so the Jews rejected the new doctrines of Jesus and barked against them. Dogs also stood for heretics who knowingly rejected the truth.[24]

---

[21] Ibid., 58.

[22] Ibid., 72.

[23] Friedman, *Monstrous Races*, 67.

[24] Ibid., 61.

It was a short step from the conception of the religious Other as a dog to the idea of dog-headed monsters as heretics, cannibals, or even, as we have seen, hermaphrodites. After all, to cite Cohen once again, "[a]ny kind of alterity can be inscribed across (constructed through) the monstrous body."[25]

Literary portrayals of the *cynocephali* tend to stress either the bestiality or the humanity within the hybrid. In the Alexander tradition as well as in the larger context of medieval orientalist writings like the *Wonders of the East*, the *cynocephali* are primarily distinguished by their animal natures and their enmity towards Europeans. As noted above, the author of the Old English *Wonders of the East* emphasizes the bestial characteristics by adding horses' manes and boars' tusks to the canine heads; the *Letter of Alexander to Aristotle* also stresses the dog-heads' hostility to human beings:

> we saw amongst the wooded groves and trees a great multitude of cyno-cephali who came because they wished to wound us, and we shot them with arrows, and they soon fled away and went back into the woods.[26]

> [gesawon we betweoh þa wudu bearwas & þa treo healfhundiga micle mængeo . ða cwoman to þon þ[aet] hie woldon us wundigan & we þa mid strælum hie scotodon . & hie sona onweg aflymdon ða hie eft on þone wudu gewiton]

Likewise, the description in the *Liber Monstrorum* emphasizes the animal rather than the human characteristics of the *cynocephali*, stating explicitly that "in eating raw flesh they do not imitate human beings, but rather the beasts themselves" [non homines, quidem crudam carnem manducando, sed ipsas bestias imitantur] (I.16).[27]

---

[25] Cohen, "Monster Culture," 7.

[26] Rypins, *Three Old English Prose Texts*, 33.

[27] Porsia, *Liber Monstrorum*, 166.

Despite such literary representations, however, neither the Plinian races in general nor the *cynocephali* in particular could be dismissed as mere animals, and for the Middle Ages the most important category distinction was whether or not such creatures could be considered fully human and, thus, to possess souls in need of Christian redemption. Although both Augustine in *The City of God* (XVI.8) and Isidore in his *Etymologiae* (XI.iii.15) express doubts as to the essential humanity of the monstrous races, each finally accepts them as human, albeit with sometimes frightening and perhaps portentous differences from the rest of humanity. Augustine considers them the inheritors of Cain's curse and, thus, descendants of the biblical Ham. Isidore explains their existence by comparing them to the individual "monstrous" births that occur among human beings: "Just as in individual races there are certain monstrous men, so in the entire human species there are certain monstrous races, like Giants, Cynocephali, Cyclops, and others . . ." [Sicut autem in singulis gentibus quaedam monstra sunt hominum, ita in universo genere humano quaedam monstra sunt gentium, ut Gigantes, Cynocephali, Cyclopes, et cetera . . .].[28]

Among medieval theologians a generally positive opinion, called by Friedman the "proselytizing missionary view," prevails. Here, "[t]he monstrous races were neither an accident in the Creation nor indicative of a failure in God's plan. They were a part of His creation whose meaning and purposes were, if unclear, still regarded in a positive light."[29] This also seems to be the viewpoint represented in most pictorial depictions of *cynocephali*. These are more common in Eastern iconography than in Western, but art historian Venetia Newall has been able to document several Western examples, including a "kynocephalate join[ing] in the song of praise on Serbian icons illustrating the psalm, 'All creatures praise the Lord'," and Burgundian examples of "dog-heads spreading the word of God at the furthest borders of the earth." In a

---

[28] *Etymologiae* XI.iii.12–14, cited in Orchard, *Pride and Prodigies*, 104.

[29] Friedman, *Monstrous Races*, 89.

particularly ecumenical representation, "on an ivory relief in the Louvre, dated 850 A.D., dog-heads are [shown] in Paradise in the company of satyrs, centaurs, and sirens."[30]

Literary representations emphasizing the human side of the *cynocephali* focus on their conversion to Christianity. One conversion narrative important for its resemblance to the Saint Christopher story survives in the Ethiopian *Gadla Hawâryât*, or "Contendings of the Apostles," extant in a fourteenth-century manuscript but traceable to fourth- and fifth-century apocrypha.[31] The "Contendings" tells the story of a cannibalistic *cynocephalus* who is converted by an angel in order to give aid to the apostles Andrew and Bartholomew in their attempt to convert a society of human cannibals. The *cynocephalus* is described as "exceedingly terrible" in appearance, being "four cubits in height" and having not only the head of a dog but also burning eyes "like lamps of fire," a boar's tusks, and a lion's claws and mane (173–74). He seems more bestial than human in all respects until his conversion, which is represented as if it were as much a conversion to humanity as to Christianity, when the angel promises, "God will give unto thee the nature of the children of men, and He will restrain in thee the nature of the beasts" (173). Then the angel makes the sign of the cross over the *cynocephalus*, and "straightway did the nature of the beast go forth out of him, and he became as gentle as a lamb" (173). He also gains the power of human speech and reveals that his name is *Hasûm*, "Abominable," although the apostles immediately rename him "Christian" in honor of his conversion (175). Christian/Abominable helps the apostles mainly by terrifying and slaughtering unrepentant pagans until, the conversion of the cannibals completed, he once again becomes "gentle as a lamb" (179).

---

[30] Venetia Newall, "The Dog-Headed Saint Christopher," in *Folklore on Two Continents: Essays in Honor of Linda Degh*, ed. Nikolai Burlakoff, Carl Lindahl, et al. (Bloomington, Ind.: Trickster Press, 1980), 245.

[31] E. A. Wallis Budge, ed., *The Contendings of the Apostles* (Oxford: Oxford University Press, 1935).

Latin versions of the *Passio Sancti Christophori Martyris* tell a strikingly similar story.[32] The saint is originally a giant cynocephalic cannibal with flowing hair and burning eyes that shine like the morning star ("sicut stella matutina"). Like the *cynocephali* of the Alexander cycle, he barks but cannot speak. His name suits his behavior: he is *Reprobus*, "the Condemned." He is converted by an angel, who strikes him and blows on his mouth, thereby giving him the capacity for human speech. Much like Abominable/Christian in the "Contendings of the Apostles," his major service to Christianity is initially as a warrior against pagan armies. When he is baptized he is given the name Christopher, and his appearance changes so that his dark face becomes white as milk ("vultus . . . per sacri chrismatus inunctionem candidior lacte resplenduit"). He is taken prisoner by the pagan Roman Emperor Decius (called Dagnus in the Old English *Passion*), who tries to lure him away from Christianity through bribery; when that fails the emperor resorts to torture and finally to murder. Christopher's martyrdom is celebrated in the Western Church on July 25, and in the Eastern Churches on May 9.

In the Old English versions of the Saint Christopher legend the necessity of distinguishing between identity categories—animal or human, believer or heretic, God or idol—is problematized for both characters and readers. The first, and ultimately the easiest, distinction to be made is that between human and animal, or perhaps human and monster. Christopher is described in the *Old English Martyrology* as coming "from the nation where men have the head of a dog and from the country where men eat each other" [of þære þeode þær men habbað hunda heafod *ond* of þære eorðan on þære æton men hi selfe] (67). His canine features and his cannibalistic past alone would seem to render Christopher monstrous, but like the *cynocephali* in other Old English

---

[32] *Der hl. Christophorus, seine Verehrung und seine Legende*, ed. Hans-Friedrich Rosenfeld, Acta Academiae Aboensis, Humaniora X:3 (Åbo: Acta Academeiae Aboensis, 1937).

orientalist texts, his appearance is made more frightening by his similarity to a lion or boar and by the uncanny light of his eyes: "his locks were exceedingly thick, his eyes shone like the light of the morning-star, and his teeth were as sharp as a boar's tusk" [his loccas wæron ofer gemet side, *ond* his eagan scinon swa leohte swa morgensteorra, *ond* his teð wæron swa scearpe swa eofores tuxas] (67). Christopher is, initially at least, terrifying, and terror modulates into horror as the ambivalence of his features threatens the readers of the *Life* with category crisis in their attempts to decide whether he is fully a human being or fully an alien monster. Resolution of the crisis is critical, for if failure to adhere to ontological category distinctions in appearance makes the *cynocephali* into literal monsters, failure to make comparable distinctions in eating habits makes human beings into cannibals and, therefore, into metaphorical monsters, since at base cannibalism is a failure to make distinctions between Self and Other, human and animal. It is therefore only by constructing impermeable boundaries between categories within the legend that the readers can distinguish themselves from both the *cynocephali* and the cannibals. Moreover, although Christopher's canine inability to communicate except by barking—"he could not speak like a man" [he ne mihte sprecan swa mon] (66)—may be less horrifying than his society's cannibalism, it indicates yet another problem of category distinction, in this case between meaningful and non-meaningful sounds. As the word's etymological meaning indicates, a monster may signify, "show forth" (L. *monstrare*), but only a human being can create linguistic signs or distinguish among them.

As in the case of Abominable/Christian, Christopher's essential humanity is linked to his belief in the Christian God, which can be revealed only when he becomes fully human by learning to speak. The resolution of one part of the category crisis thus synecdochically resolves the whole: Christopher's hybrid nature is disambiguated and the horror of his monstrosity dispelled when he acquires language. The *Martyrology* represents Christopher's attainment of speech as a divine gift:

> He believed in God in his heart, but he could not speak like a man. When he prayed to God to give him human speech, a certain man in a white robe stood by him and breathed into his mouth; afterwards he could speak like a man.

> [he wæs gode geleaffull on his heortan, ac he ne mihte sprecan swa mon. Þa bæd he god þæt he him sealde monnes gesprec; þa stod him æt sum wer on hwitum gegirelan ond eðode him on þone muð; þa mihte he siððan sprecan swa mon] (67)

Unlike Abominable/Christian, whose dark skin turned white as milk at his conversion, Christopher undergoes no physical change; nonetheless, his acquisition of language effects a metaphorical transformation that allows the readers of the *Life* to resolve the category crisis and to regard him henceforth as fully human.

Christopher's linguistic and by extension ontological transformation allows the narrative to progress from the question of distinguishing human from monster to the more difficult and important problem of discerning the divine. In the Latin and Irish versions of the legend, the saint exercises his new ability to speak by preaching the Word of God, and this brings him to the attention of the pagan emperor Decius, who has him arrested and tortured. In the Old English *Martyrology*, however, Decius seems unaware of the saint's Christianity; he merely wants to see Christopher's head, "so that he might see what it was like" [þæt he gesege hulic þæt wære] (66). The pagan emperor's inability to perceive Christopher's Christianity or the essential humanity it signifies is emblematic of his inability to distinguish the true God from idols or demons. When Christopher is brought before him, Decius is so astonished by the sight of the *cynocephalus* that, in a symbolically appropriate action that is equally comic, "he fell off his royal throne" [he feoll of his þrymsetle] (68). Then, upon learning that Christopher is not only a dog-head but also a Christian, Decius proceeds to have him tortured and orders his execution when he refuses to abjure Christianity. Thus the pagan emperor fails to resolve the twin category crises which the Christian readers of the *Life* have already negotiated: he categorizes neither the human nor the divine correctly, mistaking Christopher for a monster and pagan idols for gods.

Although the *Martyrology* account does not describe the encounter between the emperor and the saint at length, the extant portion of the fragmentary *Passion of Saint Christopher* begins on the first day of the saint's torture and proceeds to detail his three-day passion and final martyrdom. Because the beginning of the text is missing, it is impossible to say how the author of the *Passion* handled Christopher's conversion or gift of speech; as the text stands, however, the confrontation between Christopher and the emperor, here named Dagnus, creates the same two category crises for the readers and characters as does the *Martyrology* account: what constitutes the boundary between humanity and monstrosity? how is the divine to be recognized? Christopher, the cynocephalic monster, bears the sign of the Other in his non-European race and his symbolically heretical, i.e., dog-like, appearance, yet he is explicitly a Christian and, therefore, the same as the Anglo-Saxon reader in what medieval culture would regard as his most important characteristic. Dagnus looks human, but his paganism and hostility to Christianity align him with the metaphorical "dogs" of Judaism and Islam, barking against truths that are strange to them. Moreover, as Jill Frederick points out in one of the few published discussions of this work, "by virtue of his pagan beliefs, his separation from the true God, [Dagnus] is monstrous."[33]

The text rapidly becomes an exercise in discerning the underlying reality beneath surface appearances. In the *Passion of Saint Christopher*, as in most medieval saint's lives, that reality is obvious to everyone except Dagnus, who, in the typical fashion of a hagiographic villain, exhibits extraordinary blindness and stubbornness in the face of Christopher's teachings, which are just as typically reinforced by the saint's

---

[33] Jill Frederick, "'*His ansyn wæs swylce rosan blostma*': A Reading of the Old English Life of St. Christopher," *Proceedings of the Patristic, Medieval, and Renaissance Conference* 12–13 (1989), 139.

miraculous ability to withstand torture unharmed. Even Dagnus' own men recognize the truth of Christopher's faith, but when they tell the emperor that "blessed would you have been, Dagnus, if you had never been born, you who with grim slaughter have ordered such a champion of God to be tortured" [eadig wær ðu dagnus gif þu næfre geboren nære þu ðe þus wæl grimlice hetst tintregian þillicne godes cempan] (68), they are killed for their trouble. Christopher is beaten with iron rods, placed in a fire to burn, and drenched in boiling oil, all to no avail. His passion recalls Christ's in its length of three days and in the nature of his torments: on the first day he is enthroned on an iron seat over a massive fire and crowned with a burning helm in a grim parody of Christ's authority,[34] while on the second he is fastened to a *treow*, 'tree,' in front of the emperor's hall in parody of the crucifixion. The saint triumphs over every torment. The fire does not burn him but, rather, allows the beauty of his faith to shine forth through the "monstrosity" of his face: "his face was like a rose in blossom" [his ansyn wæs swylce rosan blostma] (69). Although Dagnus' men spend the entire second day, "from the earliest part of the day until evening" [fram þære ærestan tide þæs dæges oð æfen] (71), shooting arrows at the saint tied to the tree, their arrows miraculously stop in the air to float a few inches from his body—we are told that "God's power was hanging in the wind at the holy man's left side" [godes mægen wæs on ðam winde hangigende æt þæs halgan mannes swyðran healfe] (71). Finally, on the third day of Christopher's passion, when Dagnus examines the hovering arrows and, in the face of what would seem irrefutable evidence to the contrary, refuses to see or admit the power of the Christian God, the emperor's spiritual blindness is made literal: "two of the arrows shot into the king's eyes and he was blinded by them" [twa flana of þam strælum scuton on þas cyninges eagan & he þurh þ[æt] wæs ablend] (72). Dagnus' spiritual blindness can be cured only by conversion; his eyes are healed after Christopher's death by the

---

[34] Orchard, *Pride and Prodigies*, 17.

application of a mixture of the martyred saint's blood and the earth on which he was killed.

The Old English hagiographer revels in the paradoxes of his text throughout: not only is the "monstrous" *cynocephalus* the true saint and the "human" emperor the true monster but also the logic underlying Christopher's martyrdom in general reverses ordinary human experience:[35] for Christopher the torments are "sweeter than the bee-bread of honey" [swettran þonne huniges beobread] (68); he knows that his martyrdom is in reality "victory" [sigor], not defeat, and that through his physical death he will be "brought to life" [geliffæsted]. The medieval Christian audience easily would have followed such inverse logic, since it is the familiar fare of hagiography, and the reader's recognition that a cynocephalic "monster" could also be a saint coincides neatly with the discursive paradoxes of the martyrologies in general.

But even though the trauma of category crisis is mitigated here by the fact that from the beginning the reader knows that Christopher, however monstrous in appearance, is the saint and that Dagnus, however human he might seem, is the monster, the anxiety of the crisis never entirely dissipates. The boundary between human and monster has been shown to be permeable, and the reader necessarily remains conscious of how easy it would be, in the absence of direct textual pointers to the contrary, to mistake the saint for the monster and the monster for the saint. Even more anxiety-producing for a medieval reader would be the consciousness of how easy it could be, in a world in which miracles are rare or seem to belong to the distant past, to reject out of hand that which seems monstrous and Other but which actually shows forth, *demonstr*ates the divine.

Arnold Davidson asserts that "Our horror at . . . monsters reflects back to us a horror at, or of, humanity."[36] That horror is rooted in our certain knowledge that human beings can and do act "monstrously,"

---

[35] Orchard calls the logic "topsy-turvy" and cites some of the same examples (*Pride and Prodigies*, 17).

[36] Davidson, "Horror of Monsters," 36.

that the boundary between human and monster is always blurred, the distinction between categories always culturally constructed and never absolute. The *cynocephali* of the medieval orientalist narratives are horrifying because they are, in fact, human, but at the same time they fail to make certain fundamental distinctions and, by so doing, are doomed to remain speechless and cannibalistic. Dagnus is horrifying because, while he is capable of inflicting inhuman torture on innocent human beings, he is incapable of distinguishing between appearance and reality, saint and monster, pagan idols and the true God. The legend of Saint Christopher opens for its readers the disturbing possibility that we too could fail to distinguish properly between categories, that we too could become monstrous. If the Old English versions of the Saint Christopher legend do not truly horrify us, it is only in part because we no longer believe in the existence of the Plinian races. In large part it is also because the legend did not find a medieval author capable of realizing its literary potential as a narrative of category crisis. That it survives in as many forms as it does, however, indicates that the potential for horror was there and was recognized, if not fully exploited, by the Anglo-Saxon hagiographers.

FIGHTING MEN, FIGHTING MONSTERS: OUTLAWRY, MASCULINITY, AND IDENTITY IN THE *GESTA HEREWARDI*

TIMOTHY S. JONES

THE *GESTA HEREWARDI* is an unusual text, a Latin prose narrative composed by a monk at Ely, probably early in the twelfth century, about a Saxon rebel who resisted the Norman conquerors in the fens of Cambridgeshire in the 1070s.[1] In his preface, the author reports that he

---

[1] The *Gesta* survives in a single manuscript (Peterborough Cathedral MS 1, fols. 320–39, now in the Cambridge University Library) copied at Peterborough by Robert Swaffham late in the thirteenth century. Ernest O. Blake (*Liber Eliensis*, Camden Society Third Series 92 [London, 1962], 36, n.8) suggests a date of composition early in the twelfth century, following the arguments of Joost de Lange in *The Relation and Development of English and Icelandic Outlaw Traditions* (Haarlem: H. D. Tjeenk Willink & Zoon, 1935) and Felix Liebermann in "Über ostenglische Geschichtsquellen," *Neues Archiv* 18 (1893), 225–67. The sole dissident is Ingrid Benecke, who argues for a date of composition between 1227 and 1250 based on references to Robert de Horepol and Bedford Castle in the concluding episode of the text (*Der Gute Outlaw* [Tübingen: Niemeyer, 1973], 13–21).

The most satisfactory edition is that appended by Thomas D. Hardy and G. T. Martin to their edition of Geoffrey Gaimar's *Lestorie des Engles*, Rerum Britannicarum Medii Aevi Scriptores 91, 2 vols. [London, 1888–89], 1:339–404. Citations are from this edition; translations are from Michael Swanton, "The Deeds of Hereward" in *Medieval Outlaws: Ten Tales in Modern English*, Thomas H. Ohlgren, ed. (Stroud: Sutton, 1998), 18–60, unless otherwise indicated.

has assembled his story from written and oral materials available in Peterborough, Ely, and the surrounding area, including the tales of men who had fought alongside the hero. Some of these materials may be extant in the Peterborough manuscript of the *Anglo-Saxon Chronicle* and the *Liber Eliensis*. For the most part, these texts describe the events of Hereward's life, which we accept as historical, the sack of Peterborough, and the siege of Ely.[2] The author of the *Gesta*, however, claims to have discovered some of the early exploits of the hero in "a few loose pages, partly rotten with damp and decayed and partly damaged by tearing" [pauca et dispersa folia, partim stillicidio putrefactis et abolitis et partim abscissione divisis] (19; 339). This material has seen little critical comment, yet this portion of the *Gesta* distinguishes it from other narratives of outlawry in medieval England.

Those scholars who have commented on the *Gesta* have done so by reading it in the context of these other accounts of outlawry: the Anglo-Norman *Fouke le fitz Waryn* and *Witasse le Moine*, Blind Hary's *Wallace*, ballads of Robin Hood, and *Gamelyn*.[3] As a result, they have concentrated on Hereward's struggle with the Normans, regarding him, for instance, as an expression of Saxon antipathy toward the invaders. Viewed in this way, the *Gesta* appears to represent Hereward in the typical English fashion. Like Fouke fitz Waryn, Gamelyn, William

---

[2] The entry for 1070 in the Peterborough version of the *Anglo-Saxon Chronicle* reports that "Hereward and his gang" attacked Peterborough and plundered the church. Domesday records that a Hereward held twelve bovates of land near Witham from St. Peter's at Peterborough and four bovates at Laughton from Odger the Breton. In addition, the claims for Kesteven report that: "The Wapentake states that Hereward did not have Asforther's land in BARHOLM hundred on the day he fled"; and that Abbot Ulfketill assigned land at Rippingale to Hereward but repossessed it "before Hereward fled from the country" (*Lincolnshire*, ed. Philip Morgan and Caroline Thorn, 2 vols., *Domesday Book*, ed. John Morris, vol. 31 [Chichester: Phillimore, 1986], items 8.34, 42.9, CK 4, CK 48).

[3] See Benecke, *Der Gute Outlaw*; de Lange, *Icelandic Outlaw Traditions*; Maurice Keen, *The Outlaws of Medieval Legend*, rev. ed. (London: Routledge and Kegan Paul, 1977); and John C. Holt, *Robin Hood*, rev. ed. (New York: Thames & Hudson, 1989).

Wallace, William of Cloudisley, and many historical outlaws, Hereward appears as an adult who chooses outlawry in desperate circumstances as a form of self-help when faced with injustice or irreconcilable obligations. Such a context invites a reading that emphasizes the historical and social impetus for outlawry and the creation and preservation of outlaw narratives, but it neglects the psychological dimension of the outlaw, which the writer of the *Gesta* has created by giving Hereward something no other legendary English outlaw enjoys: a youth. In fact, attention to Hereward's youth foregrounds an additional historical dimension of the text and its production, viz., the presence of a peculiarly Scandinavian tradition of representing the character and actions of the outlaw.

With the exception of stories that arose concerning the early years of the Anglo-Saxon Earl Godwin, the *Gesta*'s interest in the protagonist's youth is unique among English outlaw narratives.[4] Even the Anglo-Norman romance *Fouke le fitz Waryn*, which is obsessed with family history, has little to say about its protagonist's early years.[5] But the first third of the *Gesta* does more than merely show an interest in a young hero: it imagines that hero as characteristically rebellious,

---

[4] For Godwin's youth see, in particular, Walter Map, *De Nugis Curialium: Courtier's Trifles*, ed. and trans. M. R. James, rev. C. N. L. Brooke and R. A. B. Mynors (Oxford: Clarendon, 1983), 414–16; and *Knýtlinga saga*, ed. Bjarni Guðnason, in *Danakonunga sögur*, Íslenzk fornrit 35 (Reykjavik: Hið Íslenzk fornritafélag, 1982), 192–93.

[5] *Fouke le fitz Waryn*, ed. E. J. Hathaway et al., Anglo-Norman Text Society 26–28 (Oxford: Blackwell, 1975). The text attempts to account for the enmity between the outlaw hero and King John by citing a childhood argument between the two that resulted in Fouke hitting the future monarch over the head with a chessboard, a scene borrowed from the French romance *Renaud de Montaubon* (*Les Quatre Fils Aymoun*). Benecke, in contrasting the *Gesta* with *Fouke le fitz Waryn*, rightly observes that the context of family history in the latter embodies the Anglo-Norman desire for a politically authenticating history, but she has little to say about the youthful adventures of Hereward, noting only that they confirm his military prowess (*Der Gute Outlaw*, 32, 33). See also Susan Crane, *Insular Romance* (Los Angeles and Berkeley: University of California Press, 1986), on *Fouke le fitz Waryn* and family romance.

asocial, and strong-willed from childhood. As a youth, Hereward is thrown out of his father's house for disturbing the peace and then outlawed for usurping his father's property and authority. Fleeing to Northumberland, he preserves his uncle's household by killing a monstrous bear but makes enemies as well and must move on. Arriving in Cornwall, he repeats the episode by killing the berserk suitor of the princess but, once more, provokes antipathy among members of the court. Setting out yet again, he finally finds military success and acceptance in the army of the prince of Ireland.

In this representation of the outlaw's psychology, the *Gesta* reveals a complex debt to the cultural traditions of medieval Scandinavia. The youthful character of Hereward resembles nothing so much as the early development of the protagonists of the Old Norse and Icelandic outlaw narratives, especially *Grettis saga* and *Egils saga*.[6] Although this relationship has been noted by literary scholars, they generally have sought to identify sources and analogues to expose either a common Germanic heritage or cultural transmissions between England and Scandinavia. None have considered in detail the radically different psychology of outlawry constructed by the Scandinavian culture in contrast to the English. This tradition introduces an elaborate construction of the

---

[6] *Egils saga Skalla-Grímssonar*, ed. Sigurður Nordal, Íslenzk fornrit 2 (Reykjavik: Hið Íslenzka fornritafélag, 1933); *Egil's Saga*, trans. Hermann Pálsson and Paul Edwards (Harmondsworth: Penguin, 1976); *Grettis saga Ásmundarsonar*, ed. Guðni Jónsson, Íslenzk fornrit 7 (Reykjavik: Hið Íslenzka fornritafélag, 1936); and *Grettir's Saga*, trans. Denton Fox and Hermann Pálsson (Toronto: University of Toronto Press, 1974).

In their present form these sagas are too late to have influenced the composition of the *Gesta Herewardi* in any direct manner. Both typically are numbered among the five greatest of the sagas written in Iceland during the thirteenth and fourteenth centuries. *Egils saga* was probably written about 1230, possibly by Snorri Sturluson, while *Grettis saga* was written a century later, the last of the great sagas (Pálsson and Edwards, 7; Fox and Pálsson, vii). The events described in these sagas, however, took place during the early years of Icelandic settlement. Egil, according to Sigurður Nordal's reconstruction, was born ca. 910 and died ca. 990, and the action of *Grettis saga* takes place in the early eleventh century, following the introduction of Christianity to Iceland (Fox and Pálsson, 248).

outlaw as a young man working his way through rituals of maturity, undergoing a liminal period of adolescent testing, and developing the skills and values necessary for the assertion of an adult male identity.[7] In particular, the narrative of Hereward's youth in the *Gesta* reveals a young man shifting between poles of paternal authority and transgression, the former embodied in a series of father figures and the latter by corresponding monsters.[8]

The young hero of the *Gesta* possesses exceptional abilities, but he provokes a series of conflicts with male authorities, beginning with his own father, Leofric of Bourne. According to the *Gesta*, Hereward:

> was remarkable for his figure and handsome in his features, very fine with his long blond hair, open face and large grey eyes—the right one slightly different from the left. However, he was formidable in his appearance and rather stout because of the great sturdiness of his limbs.

> [spectabilis forma et vultu decorus, valde decoratus ex flavente caesarie et prolixa facie, oculisque magnis, dextro ab alio variante, modicum glaucus, unde severus aspectu fuit; et ex nimia densitate membrorum admodum rotundus] (20; 341)

Despite his musculature he was very agile and graceful, and from childhood he was exceptionally courageous and generous. But these virtues,

---

[7] Hermann Pálsson and Paul Edwards, *Legendary Fiction in Medieval Iceland*, Studia Islandica 30 (Reykjavík, 1970), describe a related variety of the legendary saga hero typified by Arrow-Odd.

[8] The conflict between the outlaw and his father is absent almost entirely in other narratives of outlawry, many of which, in fact, depend on a deceased or absent father. The notable exception is Thomas Malory's "Book of Sir Tristram." When Trystram begs for his father to spare the life of his wife, even though she had tried to poison her stepson, King Melodyas reluctantly agrees, and "the kynge and hir accorded." However, the incident appears to create a conflict between father and son, and "than the kynge wolde nat suffir yonge Trystrams to abyde but a lytyll in his courte." Thomas Malory, *The Works of Sir Thomas Malory*, vol. 1, ed. Eugene Vinaver, rev. P. J. C. Field (Oxford: Oxford University Press, 1990), 375.3, 4.

in excess, proved to be vices for the young Saxon. As a youth (*juven-culus*) Hereward challenged anyone "whom he thought to be in any way a rival in courage or fighting" [quem vel in fortitudine aliquantum rebellem suae virtuti cognoscebat seu in certamine] (20; 342), and he was too generous in distributing his father's property to the needy. Thus provoked by his son's generosity and the anger of the community, Leofric drove Hereward out of the house. Hereward, however, remained in the area and continued to support himself and his companions from the produce of his father's property. Frustrated by Hereward's persistent provocation, Leofric finally asked King Edward to banish his son from the kingdom, and he was sent into exile at age eighteen.

Henry Goddard Leach has noted that in provoking his father to wrath, Hereward sets out on the same path as the Icelandic outlaws Egil Skallagrímsson and Grettir Ásmundarson.[9] Egil takes after his father, Skallagrim, in appearance (dark-haired and ugly) and in temperament (sharp-tongued and easily moved to anger)—characteristics that lead to alienation from the family and the human community.[10] As a boy, Egil is strong for his age and especially adept at games, but he is a sore loser, "so everyone took care that their sons knew when to give in to him" [en allir kunnu þat at kenna sonum sínum, at þeir vægði fyrir Agli] (93; 99). Still, at age six Egil becomes enraged and kills an older

---

[9] *Angevin Britain and Scandinavia* (Cambridge, Mass.: Harvard University Press, 1921), 343–47.

[10] The characterization of Egil has been compared to that of Starkaðr by Kaaren Grimstad, "The Giant as Heroic Model: The Case of Egill and Starkaðr," *Scandinavian Studies* 48 (1976), 284–98. Like Starkaðr, Egil is an alien, constantly wandering, and hence the structure of *Egils saga* is one of episodic adventures like the Eddic stories of Oðinn and Þorr, the *fornaldarsögur* and courtly romance, rather than that of the other *Íslendingasögur* (293).

On the similarities between Grettir Ásmundarson and Starkað see Marlene Chiklamini, "Grettir and Ketill Hængr, the Giant Killers," *Arv: Journal of Scandinavian Folklore* 22 (1966), 136–55; Richard Harris, "The Deaths of Grettir and Grendel: A New Parallel," *Scripta Islandica* 24 (1973), 25–53; and Pálsson and Edwards, *Legendary Fiction*, 48, 67.

boy who treats him roughly in a ball game. At twelve, when his father kills his friend Þord while playing too roughly with the boys, Egil responds by killing one of Skallagrim's favorite farm hands at the evening meal, and "for the rest of the winter father and son spoke not a single word to each other, for good or ill" [en þeir feðgar roeddusk þá ekki við, hvárki goot né illt, ok fór svá fram þann vetr] (102; 95).[11] In spring Egil forces his brother to take him to Norway, where his quick temper and acid tongue continue to provoke trouble.

Grettis saga is even more detailed in its development of the conflict between father and son. Unlike Egil, Grettir Ásmundarson is a good looking child, but he is similarly "self-willed, taciturn and harsh, sardonic, and mischievous" [mjok ódæll í uppvexti sínum, fátalaðr ok óþyðr, bellin bæði í orðum ok tiltekðum] (24; 36). When his father gives him work to do around the farm at age ten, Grettir rebels against jobs he considers mundane or unmanly. In succession, he kills un-manageable geese and goslings, rakes his father's back with a wool comb when he tires of massaging it, and flays one of Ásmundr's favorite horses in order to avoid herding it in the cold weather. When Grettir kills Skeggi a short time later and is outlawed by the Alþing, Ásmundr proves unsupportive, sending his son off on a boat to Norway with only provisions for the voyage.

As in the Icelandic sagas, the conflicts in role playing that instigate outlawry in the *Gesta Herewardi* are located in family relationships, not in social and political ones. In his study of Middle High German literature, James Schultz catalogs many examples of what he terms

---

[11] A similar scene takes place in *Gunnlaugs saga ormstungu*, when young Gunnlaugr asks his father to outfit a ship for him at age twelve (ed. Peter Foote and Randolph Quirk [London: Viking Society for Northern Research, 1953]). The young fellow is big, strong, and generally handsome, but he has an ugly nose and is "obstreperous by nature, and ambitious . . . utterly unyielding and ruthless" [havaðamaðr mikill i ollu skaplyndi ok framgjarn snemmendis ok við allt avægninn ok harðr] (322). Like Grettir and Egil he is "a good though somewhat scurrilous poet" [skald mikit ok heldr niðskar] (322). One day his father finds him dragging supplies from the barn for a voyage and angrily puts a stop to his plans. Six years later, he finally lets Gunnlaugr go abroad.

exfiliation, the separation of child from parent, observing that "[a]l-though exfiliation offers many opportunities for intergenerational conflict . . . it is remarkable how seldom conflict actually materializes."[12] More often, this separation is the result of death, maturation, outside intervention, or chance. In the case of Hereward and the Icelandic outlaws, however, the exfiliation clearly is active and the result of intergenerational conflict. Because he is a youth of prodigious strength and courage, Hereward is capable of leading a band of men before he has the material means of supporting them. Generational conflict results as Hereward must usurp the economic power of his father in order to define himself as mature and masculine according to the community standards. Though this action is one of rebellion against his father, it is also one approved by Anglo-Saxon culture, as evidenced by the gnomic comment in *Beowulf*: "So a young man, by doing good deeds and giving valuable gifts while still in his father's house, ought to make sure that in the future the people, his beloved companions, stand by him when war comes" [Swa sceal (geong g)uma gode gewyrcean, fromum feohgiftum on fæder (bea)rme þæt hine on ylde eft gewunigen wilgesiþas, þonne wig cume, leode gelæsten].[13]

Leaving home, Hereward spends several years wandering through the countries of the North, earning respect and admiration from his military skills but unable to settle anywhere because of jealousy and his confrontational temperament. His first stop is Northumberland and the household of his godfather, Gisebert of Ghent, where he encounters

---

[12] James Schultz, *The Knowledge of Childhood in the German Middle Ages, 1100–1350* (Philadelphia: University of Pennsylvania Press, 1995), 129.

[13] *Beowulf and the Fight at Finnsburg*, ed. Friedrich Klaeber, 3rd ed. (Lexington, Mass.: D. C. Heath, 1950), lines 20–24. In *Jómsvíkinga saga*, similar behavior is attributed to King Svein Forkbeard of Denmark in his youth. Svein raids his father's kingdom for three years in an attempt to get Harold to acknowledge his paternity. The most he receives, however, is the concession, "You are a difficult man to deal with . . . and your ways show that you are of no mean birth" (*The Saga of the Jómsvíkings*, trans. Lee M. Hollander [Austin: University of Texas Press, 1955], 54). Hollander translates from the version of the saga in Stockholm, Royal Library MS 7 4to.

his first monster, a giant bear.[14] This bear's monstrosity lies in its pedigree, its indiscriminate violence, and its sexual appetite. It reputedly is the offspring of a "Norwegian bear which had the head and feet of a man and human intelligence, which understood the speech of men and was cunning in battle" [quem inclyti ursi Norweyae fuisse filium, ac formatum secundum pedes illius et caput . . . sensum humanum habentem, et loquelam hominis intelligentem ac doctum ad bellum] (21; 343). The sexual transgression implicit in this mixed heritage is compounded by the observation that the bear's father raped a girl in the forest and thus begot King Beorn of Norway.[15] When the bear breaks loose from its cage, it rampages through the house "tearing to pieces and killing every living thing it could reach" [omne dilanians et interficiens vivum quod consequi potuit] (21; 343). This violent and apparently vengeful behavior is atypical of natural bears but characteristic

---

[14] An encounter with a bear is a common rite of passage for young men in Icelandic literature, often occurring at the home of the foster father. See Mary Danielli, "Initiation Ceremonial from Norse Literature," *Folklore* 56 (1945), 229–45.

[15] The name *Biernus* in the Latin text is clearly derived from *bjorn*, "bear" in Old Norse and a common surname in the Scandinavian world, but it is not the name of any historical Norwegian king. The same claim, however, is made for Earl Siward of Northumbria in a chronicle composed at Crowland Abbey, *De Comitibus Huntendum et Northampton*, ed. Jacobus Langebek, Scriptores Rerum Danicarum Medii Aevi, vol. 3 (Copenhagen, 1774), 287–302. See Axel Olrik, "Sivard den digre, en vikingesaga fra de danske i Norengland," *Arkiv för nordisk filologi* 19 (1903), 199–223. The parallel with the *Gesta Herewardi* is noted by Edward A. Freeman, *The History of the Norman Conquest of England, its Causes and its Results*, vol. 3 (Oxford, 1873), 520–21, and Max Deutschbein, *Studien zur Sagengeschichte Englands*, vol. 1 (Cöthen: Otto Schulze, 1906), 249–51. The story also is reminiscent of the account of Boðvarr Bjarki's origins in *Hrólfs saga kraka*. Such stories of sexual union between woman and bear are common in the mythologies of all regions inhabited by bears. See Stith Thompson, *Motif-Index of Folk Literature* (Bloomington: Indiana University Press, 1955–58), B601.1, R13.1.6, R45.3.1, for general lists; and H. R. Ellis Davidson, "Shape-changing in the Old Norse Sagas," in *A Lycanthropy Reader*, ed. Charlotte Otten (Syracuse: Syracuse University Press, 1986), 142–60, for an account of other examples of the Bear Mother motif in Scandinavian folklore.

of a variety of monsters.[16] Moreover, Hereward encounters the bear "proceeding to the lord's chamber where his wife and daughters and the women had fled in fright" [ad thalamum domini . . . ubi uxor illius et filiae ac mulieres timide confugerant] (21; 343). In combination with the bear's family history, this action reintroduces a sexual threat to the scene of chaotic violence. By running his sword through the beast's head in a single, directed action, Hereward imposes order on the situation, ending the transgressive sexuality and the uncontrolled violence.

Though he strikes this blow for the forces of order, Hereward remains in a liminal adolescent state. First, he refuses to accept the official token of maturity: knighthood. The *Gesta* tells us that this adventure earned him the title but that he refused it, "saying that he ought to make a better trial of his courage and spirit" [dicens melius se virtutem et animum suum probare debere] (21; 344). Through this action, Hereward indicates that his own expectations exceed those of the community; and although this is appropriately heroic, it is at the same time a criticism of the other men in the household. Later, when her own sickly son dies, Gisebert's wife suggests that Hereward could become their adopted son, but he declines. These refusals are necessitated by the antipathy of the rest of the household, which has been embarrassed by Hereward's success and, perhaps, feels threatened by his prowess. His success has both affirmed his own masculine prowess and challenged that of the other men of the house, so, like David, Hereward is praised by the women as they sing and dance. Like Saul, the men of the house become jealous and angry and attempt to kill the young man by

---

[16] On the sexual danger of giants see Claude Lecouteux, "Harpin de la montaigne (*Yvain*, v. 3770 et ss.)," *Cahiers de Civilisation Médiévale* 30 (1987), 219–25; Emmanuèle Baumgartner, "Géants et Chevaliers," in *The Spirit of the Court: Selected Proceedings of the Fourth Congress of the International Courtly Literature Society*, ed. Glyn S. Burgess and Robert A. Taylor (Woodbridge: Boydell & Brewer, 1985), 9–22; and Jeffrey Jerome Cohen, "Decapitation and Coming of Age: Constructing Masculinity and the Monstrous," *The Arthurian Yearbook* 3 (1993), 171–90.

hurling a javelin at him.[17] Gisebert is either incapable or uninterested in supporting his godson, and Hereward leaves for Cornwall.

So too, Grettir's accomplishment earns him the enmity of the brothers Bjorn and Hjarrandi, and his inability to make peace with them causes further trouble. In another example, the protagonist of *Vilmundar saga viðutan* kills a bear at the end of a day's competition with Hjarrandi, and the two become sworn brothers. But like Grettir and Hereward, Vilmundar finds it difficult to live in the company of others and retreats to the forest, thus earning his nickname, *viðutan*, "the outsider."[18] Commenting on the response of Hagen to Sigfried's defeat of the dragon in the *Niebelungenlied*, Albrecht Classen notes that in such situations the hero "has not only defeated [the monster], but he has also assumed its power and strength, its wealth and super-human force."[19] The hero, paradoxically, is most monstrous when he has killed a monster. So Hereward, like the monstrous bear itself, challenges the carefully constructed certainties and identities of the community, provoking its fear and hatred.

Arriving at the court of the Cornish prince Alef, Hereward discovers another sexual threat, Ulcus Ferreus, "the strongest warrior among the two nations of the Scots and Picts" [in duabus gentibus Scottorum et Pictorum ex illorum cognatione bellator fortissimus] (22; 345). This arrogant brute hopes to marry the daughter of Prince Alef and entertains the household with his boastful tales. At one point he begins to insult the English nation, claiming that he could kill three English warriors with one blow. The Cornish crowd is willing to listen uncritically to his boast, but Hereward responds with a worm-tongued challenge: "Since those men you say you killed were conceived in your

---

[17] Compare 1 Sam. 18:6–7 and 19:10.

[18] *Vilmundar saga viðutan*, ed. Agnete Loth, *Late Medieval Icelandic Romances*, vol. 4, Bibliothecae Arnamagnæanæ (Copenhagen: Munksgaard, 1965).

[19] "Monsters, Devils, Giants, and other Creatures," in *Canon and Canon Transgression in Medieval German Literature*, ed. Albrecht Classen (Göppingen: Kümmerle Verlag, 1993), 94.

own mind, begotten of your heart and not of a mother, it is appropriate that they should be slain by one blow of your mouth!" [Quoniam illos viros quos a te dicis interfectos in mente tua concepisti, et ex corde tuo illos non a matre natos genuisti, dignum est ut uno ictu oris interfecti sint] (22; 345).

This sharpness of tongue and a craftiness of mind predominate when Ulcus meets the young man in the woods a few days later. After his initial retort, Hereward had offered to fight Ulcus at any time, but when Ulcus surprises him unarmed, he immediately plots a way to acquire a weapon. "There's no glory," he argues, "in a famous man so well supplied with weapons and strength putting down an unarmed man" [Nudum opprimere, armis et viribus valde constitu, inclito gloria non est] (23; 346). He begs Ulcus to allow him an hour to bequeath his possessions to a priest to be distributed among the poor. The request appeals to Ulcus' vanity and certainty of victory, but Hereward plans only to retrieve a weapon. When they finally come to blows, Hereward's are "unexpected and covert" [improvisos et occultus], and when Ulcus feels his death blow, he laments that he has been overthrown by a "cunning lad" [puero prudente] (23; 346). The household retainers agree and drag Hereward before the prince "declaring that their toughest man had been killed by treachery" [robustissimum illorum dolo fuisse interfectum asserentes] (23; 347). The prince is reluctant to act, and his daughter rescues Hereward by sending him as a messenger to her true lover, the son of the Irish king.

This episode clearly is related to confrontations with berserk suitors in medieval Scandinavian literature.[20] Such incidents are common in the sagas, although elements here are incomplete or corrupted. Typically,

---

[20] The similarity has been noted by both de Lange, *Icelandic Outlaw Traditions*, and Deutschbein, *Studien zur Sagengeschichte Englands*. The latter suggests that the fight between Boðvarr Bjarki and Agnarr recorded by Saxo is a source for the episode in the *Gesta* (250–53), while the former claims only a generic similarity. My own argument, rather than attempting to assert a specific source, in fact depends on illustrating the popularity and ubiquity of the motif.

according to Gerd Sieg, the episode falls into four parts: a *berserkr* demands the wife, daughter, or sister of a farmer; if denied he challenges the farmer or his champion to a duel; he is confident of winning because either his skin is invulnerable to conventional weapons or he can dull sword blades with his evil eye; and he is defeated by a special sword, sometimes kept hidden, which often is used to amputate a leg.[21] Saxo Grammaticus, for instance, records the story of Starkaðr's fight with Wisin, who was able to blunt the edge of every weapon with his evil eye and "was made so bold in consequence, by having lost all fear of wounds, that he used to carry off the wives of distinguished men and drag them to outrage before the eyes of their husbands" [Quamobrem tantum viribus eius audaciam peperit exclusus vulnerum metus, ut etiam illustrium virorum coniuges, maritis spectantibus, raptas ad stuprum pertraheret].[22] In order to thwart this magical defense, Starkaðr

---

[21] Gerd Sieg, "Die Zweikämpfe der Islandersagas," *Zeitschrift für deutsches Altertum* 95 (1966), 1–27. Benjamin Blaney, "The Berserk Suitor: The Literary Application of a Stereotyped Theme," *Scandinavian Studies* 54 (1982), 279–94, gives a list of thirty-three of these confrontations in Icelandic literature.

[22] *Saxonis Gesta Danorum*, ed. Jørgen Olrik and Hans Raeder, vol. 2 (Copenhagen: Munksgaard, 1931), 155. Translation from Oliver Elton, *The First Nine Books of the Danish History of Saxo Grammaticus*, Publications of the Folk-Lore Society 33 (London, 1893), 230. On Saxo's presentation of Starkaðr see Marlene Chiklamini, "The Problem of Starkadr," *Scandinavian Studies* 43 (1971), 169–88, who argues that Saxo humanizes Starkaðr by rationalizing and reinterpreting his giantish qualities as "an effective means in relating the feats and character of a warrior who championed the values of heroic tradition" (188). In contrast, Grimstad argues that the author of *Egils saga* chose to model the hero on Starkaðr in order to "enlarge his stature" ("The Giant as Heroic Model," 295).

Also on Starkaðr see Axel Olrik, *Sakses Oldhistorie: Norröne Sagœr og Danske Sagn* (Copenhagen, 1894), 76–80, 222–29, and *Danmarks Heltedigtning*, II (Copenhagen, 1910); Paul Hermann, *Erläuterungen zu den ersten neun Büchern der dänischen Geschichte des Saxo Grammaticus* (Leipzig: Wilhelm Engelmann, 1922), 410–67, 557–681; Herman Schneider, *Germanische Heldensage* (Berlin, 1933), vol. 2, part 1, pp. 125–83; Wilhelm Ranisch, "Die Dichtung von Starkad," *Zeitschrift für deutsches Altertums* 72 (1935), 113–28; Jan de Vries, "Die Starkadsage," *Germanisch-*

covered his sword with a fine skin to hide it from view and, thus, killed the bully.

These scenes occur repeatedly in Old Norse and Icelandic litera-ture, especially in the lives of outlaws. In fact, both Egil and Grettir confront multiple berserk suitors. In *Egils saga*, for instance, the *ber-serkr* Ljot demands that Fridgeir of Blindheim give him his sister or fight a duel. The young farmer is ill suited for battle, but he is the nephew of Egil's friend Arinbjorn, and so Egil takes up the *hólmganga* for him. Ljot approaches the combat in typical berserk fashion, howl-ing and biting his shield. Likewise, Egil takes two swords to the duel, although he only uses one in the lopsided contest.[23] Similarly, *Grettis saga* informs us that "At that time it happened in many parts of Norway that outlaws and criminals would come suddenly out of the forests and challenge farmers to duels for their women, or take posses-sions by force wherever there were few men to protect them" [Þat var þá víða í Nóregi, at markamenn ok illvirkjar hlópu ofan af morkum ok skoruðu á menn til kvenna eða tóku á brott fé manna með ofríki, þar sem eigi var liðsfjolði fyrir] (87; 175). This happens to the farmer Einarr at Christmas one year while Grettir is visiting him. The *berserkr* Snaekoll rides up to the farm and demands that Einarr hand over his daughter Gyrid or fight for her. When the aging farmer stalls and Grettir pretends to be uninterested in fighting, Snaekoll begins to rage, howling and biting the rim of his shield. Suddenly, Grettir kicks the bottom edge of the shield, driving the upper edge into Snaekoll's

---

Romanische Monatschrift 36 (1955), 281–97; and Georges Dumézil, "Les trois péchés de Starcatherus," *Aspects de la fonction guerrière chez les Indo-Européens*, Sections des Sciences religieuses 68 (Paris, 1956), 80–93.

[23] In the following chapter, Egil duels with Atli the Short over the possession of property at Ask. Atli is never explicitly identified as a *berserkr*, but Egil is unable to break his flesh with a sword and resorts to wrestling and tearing Atli's throat out with his teeth. The two scenes, argues Blaney, are set parallel in order to juxtapose the two sides of Egil's character, his bravery and loyalty against his greed and vindictiveness ("The Berserk Suitor," 290).

mouth and splitting his jaws. He then yanks the *berserkr* off his horse and beheads him.[24]

At first glance, perhaps, it is not clear how the Cornwall episode in the *Gesta Herewardi* conforms to this pattern. Ulcus does not ride up and demand Prince Alef's daughter, but he does appear to rule the court by inspiring fear. Alef has little to say about the arrogant suitor, but his refusal to prosecute Hereward for his death suggests that he was not an eager supporter of the suitor. Certainly the young woman found a match with Ulcus repugnant, for "she dreaded that terrifying man with misshapen limbs" [formidolosum hominem et incompositum membris] and was already in love with the prince of Ireland (23; 347). Although he is not identified as a *berserkr*, his stature and arrogance lend Ulcus the qualities of the saga suitors. Moreover, his racial heritage probably is meant to enhance his barbarism.[25]

It is the matter of the sword which best suggests a parallel with the Norse tradition, although the story surviving in the *Gesta* is badly corrupted. When he finds himself defeated and dying, Ulcus complains, "Ah, if only I had the blade which just now I handed to my future wife" [O utinam spatam prae manibus, quam sero meae sponsae futurae tradidi] (23; 346). This statement comes as a total surprise, as there has been no previous mention of this sword. However, when the princess sends Hereward off to the prince of Ireland, she gives him the sword almost as an afterthought. It makes sense to see in these details the corruption of a story that more fully corresponds to the berserk suitor pattern. Imagine the overconfident Ulcus giving up his special sword as a gift, or perhaps the resourceful princess tricking him into giving it to her.[26] The princess then gives the sword to Hereward, which he retrieves under the guise of donating his belongings to the priest. This

---

[24] Grettir also dispatches a band of *berserkir* led by Thorir Paunch and Ogmund the Evil, who attack the farm of his host, Thorfinn Karsson (38–44).

[25] Blaney notes that unwelcome suitors may include giants, monsters, and foreign princes as well as *berserkir* ("The Berserk Suitor," 280).

[26] De Lange suggests the latter (*Icelandic Outlaw Traditions*, 17).

weapon proves capable of killing Ulcus, and the duplicity involved earns Hereward the reproach of his adversary and men of court. Ulcus himself shows some suspicion when he comments to Hereward that the young woman "earlier delighted in the obstinacy of your words, praised your long hair, your features and the insolence of your reply" [quae olim ex verborum tuorum pertinacia gavisa, caesariem tuam laudabat et faciem et responsionis arrogantiam] (23; 345,6). Such a reconstruction has precedents in the Norse and Icelandic literature. In *Hrólfs saga Gautrekssonar* the Irish princess secretly gives her berserk father's sword to Hrólf. Similarly, when the *berserkr* Moldi demands the daughter of Jarl Herrodr in *Svarfdæla saga*, Þorsteinn Þorgnysson agrees to take up the duel. Before the contest, the Jarl gives him a sword that belonged to Moldi's brother, Ljotr the Black. Þorsteinn keeps this weapon hidden from Moldi's evil eye and then kills him with it. Likewise, in *Þorsteins saga Víkingssonar*, when the *berserkr* Harekr demands King Hring's daughter, Vikingr agrees to fight in her defense. Before the duel, however, his father presents him with the sword Angrvaðill, forged by Harekr's father Kolr to be the only weapon capable of killing his offspring. Harekr is dismayed at the sight of the weapon and is quickly killed.[27]

---

[27] *Hrólfs saga Gautrekssonar*, ed. Guðni Jónsson, Fornaldur sögur Norðurlanda 4 (Reykjavik: Íslendingasagnaútgáfan, 1954); *Svarfdæla saga*, ed. Jonas Kristjansson, Íslenzk fornrit 9 (1956), 142–47; and *Þorsteins saga Víkingssonar*, ed. Guðni Jónsson, Fornaldur sögur Norðurlanda 3 (Reykjavik: Íslendingasagnaútgáfan, 1954). Both of these examples are cited by Blaney ("The Berserk Suitor," 281–84).

    Grettir also uses a special weapon, the barrow sword, to kill the *berserkir* Þorir and Ogmundr. Inger Boberg lists ten sagas in which a giant or troll is killed with his own sword (*Motif-Index of Early Icelandic Literature*, Bibliotheca Arnamagnæanæ 27 [Copenhagen: Munksgaard, 1966], Z312.2.) Most notable of these is *Hrólfs saga Gautrekssonar*, where Hrólf and his men come upon the house of the giant Grimnir. Because Hrólf has killed Grimnir's brother Grimar, the giant intends to hold the hero prisoner until he can think of a suitably painful death. While the giant sleeps, Hrólf stabs him with his own sword as one of his companions pokes out his eyes with a burning log. In the following chapter, Hrólf uses the giant sword to kill the twelve *berserkir* of King Halfdan.

A final element of the undesirable suitor episode—common to many of the sagas but notably absent in *Egils saga*, *Grettis saga*, Saxo's story of Starkaðr, and Hereward's Cornwall adventure—is the marriage between the hero and the woman he preserves. For most of those who engage in duels with *berserkir*, the hand of the woman is, if not a primary motivation, a substantial reward. Egil, of course, already is married, and he fights on account of his friendship for Arinbjorn. Grettir fights in order to help his host: it is an act of noble kindness in a life full of turmoil and bad luck where such good deeds often go awry. Grettir's restless, proud, vindictive, and unbending nature prevents him from living at peace in human society. Marriage is a symbol for what he can never hope to have, so it never figures as a possibility here. Likewise, marriage represents a prohibited space for Starkaðr. Several of his duels are fought to preserve the sanctity of marriage, but the *Gautreks saga* account of his life explains that he has been cursed by Þorr "to have neither a son nor a daughter, and his family line will end with him" [skal hvórki eiga son né dóttur ok enda svó ætt sina].[28] Similarly, Hereward still is learning the boundaries of sexuality and masculinity. Once again he has preserved order by destroying the sexual threat, but his own presence continues to destabilize the community.

Sent to Ireland with a message for the prince of that land, he becomes involved in a war and for the first time wins general acclaim and acceptance into the military community. He joins the prince of Ireland in a war against the duke of Munster, and on account of his success, noble men begin sending their sons to train with him. Soon he and the prince have gathered a substantial band of followers and subdue all the king's enemies.[29] But in his preoccupation with his new

---

[28] *Die Gautrekssaga in zwei Fassungen*, ed. Wilhelm Ranisch, Palaestra 11 (Berlin: Mayer and Müller, 1900), 29. Translation from Hermann Pálsson and Paul Edwards, *Gautrek's Saga and Other Medieval Tales* (New York: New York University Press, 1968), 39.

[29] De Lange observes that some of the details of the battle against the duke of Munster correspond to accounts of the Battle of Clontarf in *The War of the Gædhil with the*

brothers in arms, Hereward forgets his errand until the princess of
Cornwall sends a letter complaining of the delay and announcing that
yet another suitor is threatening to abduct her. Returning to Cornwall
in disguise, Hereward finds himself at a wedding banquet. In a scene
reminiscent of *King Horn*, the hero makes himself known to the princess
and defeats the second undesired suitor.[30] This time Hereward fights no
monster, but the confrontation with the second suitor is in some ways
a confrontation with one side of himself. Structurally speaking, both
Hereward and the suitor have filled the same role in preventing the
marriage of the princess to the prince of Ireland. The suitor has attempted to take the princess for his own wife, while Hereward has
drawn the prince away into the homosocial atmosphere of the war
band, making him forget the princess. Compelled by the princess's
letter to rescue her, Hereward goes beyond the suppression of uncontrolled or inappropriate desire in the two preceding episodes and
actively affirms the heterosexual order of marriage.

   This peripatetic life comprises an essential feature of Hereward's
youth and his characterization as an outlaw. Although he eventually
will marry, he is as yet unprepared for the maturity demanded by marriage. Like the spurned knighthood, it is a symbol of a conformity he
is unwilling to embrace. These youthful adventures characterize a
space that Victor Turner would identify as liminal, a region where the
standard structures of culture do not apply, yet a place where they are
learned.[31] In navigating the strait between cliffs of paternal law and

---

Gaill, ed. J. H. Todd (London, 1867), *Brennu-Njáls saga*, ed. Finnur Jónsson, Alt-
nordische Saga-Bibliothek 13 (Halle, 1908), and *Þorsteins saga Síðuhallssonar*, ed.
Alfred Jakobsen in *Austfirðinga sögur* (Copenhagen, 1902–03) (*Icelandic Outlaw
Traditions*, 18, 19).

[30] *King Horn: A Middle English Romance*, ed. Joseph Hall, Early English Text Society,
o.s. 14 (Oxford: Clarendon Press, 1901), lines 1035–1270.

[31] See Victor Turner, *The Ritual Process: Structure and Anti-Structure* (1969; Ithaca:
Cornell University Press, 1977), and *Drama, Fields, and Metaphors: Symbolic Action
in Human Society* (Ithaca: Cornell University Press, 1974).

berserk lawlessness, the young hero learns the border between culture and chaos. Thus Hereward must learn to submit those qualities in himself which partake of the berserk to the order that grants stability to the community. One of the great institutions of order was, of course, the patrilineal descent of property, which becomes the cause of conflict between Hereward and the Norman conquerors.[32] When Hereward returns to Bourne, it is the sight of Norman knights in his father's house and his brother's body swinging from the gate that prompts his insurgence, not any abstract ideal of Anglo-Saxon patriotism.

So prepared, Hereward enters the major phase of his life, his battle with William the Conqueror. But more than that, the *Gesta Herewardi* and the popular traditions that underlie it have created a biography that makes sense of the historical fragments of Hereward's life. Borrowing themes and episodes circulating in the Scandinavian world, it conforms the life of a rebellious warrior to a set of heroic ideals that make him sympathetic to the population of northeastern England. As a result, his rebellion against William becomes a logical step in the life of a powerful and determined man: such characters cannot avoid the jealousies that they provoke, nor turn aside from affront to their pride. If their luck is bad, they die tragically like Grettir, Gisli, and Brennu-Njal; if it is good, they endure like Egil. According to the *Gesta*, Hereward's luck is good: he is reconciled with the king and restored to his inheritance. Although he is presented as one of those heroic outsiders who patrol the border of civilization, ultimately his character, unlike that of Grettir and Starkaðr, is reconcilable with life in the human community.[33]

---

[32] Tim Lundgren notes that when Hereward is shipwrecked in Flanders on his way home, he aids the local lords in retaining their rightful property and privileges ("The Robin Hood Ballads and the English Outlaw Tradition," *Southern Folklore* 53 [1996], 233).

[33] An early version of this paper was presented at the 29th International Congress on Medieval Studies at Western Michigan University in May of 1994. My thanks to John B. Friedman, Marianne E. Kalinke, and Charles D. Wright for their critical input.

Monsters of Misogyny: Bigorne and Chicheface— Suite et Fin?

Malcolm Jones

THE VARIOUS MONSTERS spawned by medieval misogyny included the unholy pair of the painfully thin *Chicheface*, starved for want of faithful obedient wives, its only diet, and the swollen-bellied *Bigorne*, glutted on a surfeit of complaisant husbands ruled by their wives.[1] The earliest mention of *Chichevache* in English literature is a sarcastic reference in Chaucer's Envoy to The Clerk's Tale (ca. 1386):

> O noble wyves, ful of heigh prudence,
> Lat noon humylitee youre tonge naille,
> . . . .
> Lest Chichevache yow swelwe in hire entreille! (1183–84, 1188)

There is no corresponding mention of *Bigorne*, however.

---

[1] I find I have happened on the same title as Steven M. Taylor, "Monsters of misogyny: The Medieval French *Dit de Chincheface and Dit de Bigorne*," *Allegorica* 5 (1980), 98–124, but having, as it were, arrived at it independently, I let it stand. An earlier iconographic survey is Francesco Novati, "Bigorne e Chichface; ricerche d'iconografia popolare," in *Mélanges offerts à M. Emil Picot par ses amis et ses élèves*, 2 vols. (Paris: E. Rahir, 1913), 2:67–87.

Chaucer's final phrase about Chichevache was echoed in one of Lydgate's early fifteenth-century "minor" verses:

Or Chychevache ne wol not fayle
You for to swalowe in hir entrayle (76–77)

One of the welcome shorter pieces of the "voluminous, prosaick and driveling monk" of Bury—in Ritson's memorable and not wholly undeserved characterization—*Bycorne and Chichevache* is an important piece that marks the first record of the canonical pairing in English, introduced in one manuscript as the text of "the deuise of a peynted or desteyned clothe for an halle a parlour or a chaumbre deuysed by Iohan Lidegate at the request of a werthy citeseyn of London."[2] It is unfortunate that we are left to infer the appearance of this painted cloth from the verses and the accompanying rubrics; painted cloths rarely survive from this date, being in essence *ersatz* tapestries but much cheaper than their more pretentious relations, and, accordingly, less valued and less likely to be preserved.[3] It is clear, however, that Lydgate's verses

---

[2] Henry N. MacCracken, *The Minor Poems of John Lydgate*, EETS o.s. 192 (London, 1934), 433–38.

[3] The existing literature on painted cloths is inadequate; I hope, in due course, to remedy this deficiency. The following will give some idea of the range of iconography in this medium, culled mainly from wills (dates): Coronation of the Virgin (1463); Seven Ages of Man (1463); King Robert of Sicily (1463); joust of Anthony Woodville and the Bastard of Burgundy (late 15th c.); Virgin Mary and the Three Kings of Cologne (1468); St. Margaret (1487); Life of Job (1477); rest on the Flight to Egypt (1523); St. Nicholas (15th c.); Daniel (1490, suite of three); St. John the Baptist (1501); *kalendars* [Labors of the Months] (1500); Robyn Hod (1492) (what a loss, since it predates any of the woodcut images!); Triumph of Absolon (1538); Triumph of Judith (1538); Woman of Canaan (1538); the Good Samaritan (1538); and a gentlewoman spinning (1536). A rare survival is Hercules slaying the hydra reproduced in H. A. Feldman, *The Ancient House* (Ipswich: Ancient House Press, n.d. [ca.1980]), as are the four scenes from the *Acts of the Apostles* still at Hardwick Hall, where they were executed ca. 1600 and about which Anthony Wells-Cole has written so informatively in his recent ground-breaking book, *Art and Decoration in Elizabethan and Jacobean England: The Influence of Continental Prints, 1558–1625* (New Haven: Yale University Press, 1997),

accompanied the sort of unified presentation of the monsters and their human prey that does not otherwise survive in the visual record until the late sixteenth century (see below). Thus we may be sure that his *device* certainly is dependent on the French tradition of these monsters.

The colloquial name *chicheface*, meaning literally 'skinny face,' is found both as a common noun meaning 'skinny person, starveling, bag-of-bones,' e.g., in the fourteenth-century *Lamentations de Matheolus*— ". . . comme une chicheface, / Maigre par dessoubs ma peaucelle."[4] It also is found as a nickname, e.g., in one of Coquillart's late fifteenth-century verses which refers to one *Laurence la grant Chicheface*.[5] There were also taverns so called, presumably from their painted signs, e.g., one in fifteenth-century Amiens and another in contemporary Paris.[6]

R. J. Menner notes that *bigorne* derives from Latin *bicornis*, i.e., a two-horned beast.[7] Early examples of the word used as a name are hard to find. Its appearance as the sobriquet of one *Perrin Bicorne* in the fifteenth-century *Le Pardonneur, Le Triacleur et La Taverniere*, though seen by some editors as a reference to the satirical monster, seems more likely to allude to the widely satirized female fashion of wearing horned headdresses.[8]

275–89, though they are probably of abnormally high quality for this medium.

Other recent articles are Denys Sutton, "English Medieval Paintings Newly Discovered in Norfolk," *Apollo* 111 (June 1980), 464–65; and F. Pomarede, "Les 'toiles peintes' du Musée de Reims," *Mémoires de la société d'agriculture, commerces, sciences et arts du département de la Maine* 91 (1976), 229–4.

[4] Edition of *Lamentations de Matheolus* 3:3220–21; quoted in Eleanor Prescott Hammond, *English Verse between Chaucer and Surrey* (Durham: Duke University Press, 1927), 113.

[5] *Guillaume Coquillart, Oeuvres*, ed. M. J. Freeman (Geneva: Droz, 1975), 92, line 607.

[6] A. A. Dubois, *Les Rues et Enseignes d'Amiens* (Amiens: A. Douillet et Cie., 1889); and Edouard Fournier, *Histoire des enseignes de Paris* (E. Dentu, 1884).

[7] Robert J. Menner, "Bycorne-Bygorne, Husband of Chichevache," *Modern Language Notes* 44 (1929), 456.

[8] André Tissier, *Recueil de farces (1450–1550)*, tome 5 (Geneva: Droz, 1989), 247, no. 29, line 35 and note.

Lydgate's verses are, importantly, the earliest attestation of the tradition of *graphic* representation of these marital monsters, but from later in the century we learn from Coquillart's poem *Les Droits Nouveaux* of 1480 that "on vent [chichefaces] tous les jours au Palays," i.e., that Chicheface prints, doubtless accompanied by explanatory verses, were on sale near the Palais de Justice in Paris.[9] Furthermore, he mentions the mythical monster in the context of a new young mother's desire not to see her *tetons* become *tetasses*, hanging down [*pensues*] like those of a *Chicheface*—exactly as the monster's pendent dugs are shown in the earliest prints, which seems to confirm that the poet was familiar with precisely the same type. Ferdinand Geldner published the earliest known such print (discovered in the binding of a book published in 1527), which he dated ca. 1495 and attributed to the Parisian printer, Guy Marchand.[10]

From ca. 1537 survive unique copies of separate but companion sheets entitled *Chicheface qui mange toutes les bonnes femmes*, and *Bigorne qui mange tous les hommes qui font le contentement de leurs femmes*,[11] probably printed in Lyon.[12] The ca. 1537 *Chicheface* woodcut and text are both clearly copied from that of ca. 1495. The probability that its companion was similarly derived from a no longer extant late fifteenth-century print is strengthened by wall-paintings of both beasts in the chateau at Villeneuve-Lembron (Puy-de-Dôme), which are assigned to the first decade of the sixteenth century.[13]

---

[9] Freeman, *Guillaume Coquillart*, p. 150, line 433.

[10] Ferdinand Geldner, "Chicheface. Ein unbekannter französischer Einblattdruck," *Gutenberg Jahrbuch* (1959), 41–44.

[11] Printed in Anatole de Montaiglon and James, Baron de Rothschild, *Recueil de poésies françoises des XVe et XVIe siècles, morales, facétieuses, historiques*, vol. 11 (Paris: P. Jannet, 1876), 277–92, and vol. 2 (Paris: P. Jannet, 1855), 187–203, respectively.

[12] Both woodcuts are reproduced in Justin Fanil, "L'origine de la facétie *Bigorne et Chicheface*," *Aesculape* 5 (1954), 115–19.

[13] Conveniently reproduced in Roger Sherman Loomis, *A Mirror of Chaucer's World* (Princeton: Princeton University Press, 1965), 161, 162. Johannes Bolte, "Bigorne und

Annie Regond notes that a rather similar Chicheface is painted on one of the panels of a coffered ceiling in the chateau at Plessis-Bourré near Angers, dated 1500X06.[14] Above the beast, the Plessis-Bourré text, according to the only published transcription, reads:

> MOY L'ON APPELLE ACHARIACE [*sic*]
> MAIGRE DE CORPS ET DE FACE
> JE SUYS, ET BIEN Y A RAISON.
> JE NE MENGUS PAS A FOISON
> QUE FAMES QUI FONT LE COMMANT
> DE LEURS MARIS ENTIEREMENT
> DES ANS Y A PRES DE DEUX CENZ
> QUE CESTE CY JE TIENS AUX DENS.

The text above the woman reads:

> PAR AVOIR FAIT ET ACOMPLI
> TOUS LES COMMANS DE MON MARI
> SOUFFRIR ME CONVIENT GRAND TOURMENT
> VOUS QUI VOYEZ LE DEMOURANT
> NE VEUILLEZ COMME MOI FAIRE;
> ENFANCE LI [*MA FAIT*] FEIRE.[15]

Except for four lines missing from above the beast, the text is identical to that at Villeneuve-Lembrun. Furthermore, it seems likely that the Plessis-Bourré beast's name should read *Chicheface* rather than *Achariace* although it was not so recognized by the transcriber.

Chicheface," *Archiv für das Studium der neueren Sprachen und Literaturen* 106 (1901), 1–18, esp. 13, noted a mid-seventeenth-century description of a wall-painting of both beasts on a house in the Swiss village of Wyl in Thurgau.

[14] Annie Regond, *La peinture murale du XVIe siècle dans la région d'Auvergne* (Clermont-Ferrand: Institut d'Etudes du Massif Central, 1983), 45–53, esp. 52.

[15] Charles Urseau, *Les peintures du plafond de la salle des gardes au Château du Plessis-Bourré* (Paris: Typographie Plon Noirret et Fils, 1909), 5.

Comparison of the verse texts that accompany the Chicheface painting at Villeneuve-Lembron shows that they are related to those of the ca. 1495 print, as are the portraits of the monsters. Both, for example, are depicted with two cloven and two clawed feet. If the ca. 1537 cut can be accepted as representing the lost prototype for the Villeneuve Bigorne painting, the visual similarities are, if anything, even closer. It should be noted, however, that the text which accompanies the Villeneuve Chicheface painting is not especially close to that of the printed texts of ca. 1495 and ca. 1537. The wall-painting inscription has been considerably abbreviated, from the ten nine-line stanzas of the former (and nine of the latter) to just two. The Villeneuve Bigorne inscription, in contrast, extends to six *nonains*, four of which are practically identical with the unique Bigorne printed text of ca. 1537, which presumably reprints that of the lost companion print to the ca. 1495 Chicheface.

If we accept that the ca. 1537 texts do, in fact, faithfully represent a fifteenth-century French textual tradition, do Lydgate's verses from the first half of that century show any evidence of being translated from this French type? In 1927 Hammond concluded:

> There are some verbal resemblances between his lines and the surviving French poems . . . but structurally the English is quite different. In Lydgate the two monsters are represented, in the same poem, as husband and wife, and the text is arranged to suit a series of pictures.[16]

Although the ca. 1537 Bigorne text opens with the beast introducing itself ("Bigorne suis en Bigornoys") and Lydgate's beast similarly presents itself ("Of Bycornoys I am Bycorne"), it would appear that the English poet otherwise has recast his French source totally, while adhering to the outline. An interesting difference from the tradition represented by the ca. 1537 texts is that the beast also gives a speech—in the words of the manuscript rubric—"to a companye of men comyng

---

[16] Hammond, *English Verse between Chaucer and Surrey*, 114.

towardes this beest Bicorne," but such a company indeed is depicted in the standardized Northern European prints of ca. 1600, which unite the two beasts into a single composition. Maybe Lydgate had access to an already unified presentation of this type which has not survived.

By 1586 the paired woodcuts (plainly derived from the French tradition) appear side by side at the head of a single German illustrated broadsheet, but still only in an adjacent presentation rather than a unified composition.[17] The decades around the year 1600 saw the pair of hitherto separate images evolve into a single picture unified by its landscape setting, which became standard throughout Northern Europe. Versions in French, German, Flemish, and English also are known. The English sheets are of interest for the history of early seventeenth-century English popular culture, as the woodcut version is presumably a copy—cheaper, of course—of the engraving of the same year. The woodcut sheet printed by Edward Allde for Henry Gosson in 1620[18] is entitled *Fill Gut, & Pinch belly: One being Fat with eating good Men, the other Leane for want of good Women*. The engraved version, surviving only in a later seventeenth-century impression, styles the monsters *Bulchin and Thingut* and was executed by Renold Elstrack for William Butler.[19]

It seems likely that the etymologically two-horned monster, *Bigorne*, whose diet is complaisant husbands who allow themselves to be ruled by their wives, is related in some way to the notion that the cuckolded husband grew horns (see verses to *Bulchin and Thingut* in Appendix 1). None of the extant representations of Bigorne, however, shows the monster as bearing two horns. Curiously, the rubric to the verses

---

[17] The images are reproduced in Bolte, "Bigorne und Chicheface," 1.

[18] A. W. Pollard and G. R. Redgrave, *A Short Title Catalog of books printed in England, Scotland and Ireland and of English books printed abroad 1475–1640*, 2nd ed., rev. and enl. W. A. Jackson and F. S. Ferguson, 2 vols. (Oxford: Oxford University Press, 1986), 23757 (hereafter *STC*).

[19] For full details see Arthur M. Hind, *Engraving in England in the Sixteenth & Seventeenth Centuries. Part II The Reign of James I* (Cambridge: Cambridge University Press, 1955), 210–13.

spoken by Lydgate's *Chychevache* describes it as "a longe horned beest sklendre and lene with sharpe teethe and on his body no thing saue skyn and boone," perhaps, as Hammond suggests, on account of a popular etymological association of the second element of its name with French *vache*, 'cow.'

Iconographically the representations of Chicheface bear a strong resemblance to the drawing of the *Cocodryllus* (i.e., crocodile) in a late twelfth-century bestiary manuscript in Cambridge University Library (MS Ii.4.26). Although the text of the bestiary makes no mention of horns, singling out the animal instead for its horrible teeth and claws, the artist gave the animal what probably were intended as long thin curved ears that stand upright, and these closely resemble horns. The fact that it grips an unfortunate man in its jaws increases the resemblance to Chicheface. Perhaps Lydgate's description of *Chychevache* as "a longe horned beest" ultimately derives from such a bestiary *Cocodryllus* illustration.

In 1971 the iconographer Mary D. Anderson suggested that carved images of a monster swallowing a man on misericords and elsewhere, customarily described as "Judas in the jaws of Satan," represent instead the Bigorne.[20] The original misericord examples she cites are those at Carlisle (ca. 1410) and St. Davids in Dyfed (ca. 1500), though two years earlier, in her Iconographical Index to George Remnant's *Catalogue of Misericords in Great Britain*, she also had listed an example at Worcester (late fourteenth century).[21] While chronologically this suggestion chimes well with the date of Lydgate's verses, there are no corresponding Chichevache misericords, and all the signs are that when only one monster is present it is more likely to be the earlier independently attested Chicheface.

---

[20] Mary D. Anderson, *History and Imagery in British Churches* (Newton Abbot: John Murray, 1971), 154–55.

[21] George L. Remnant, *A Catalogue of Misericords in Great Britain* (Oxford: Clarendon Press, 1969), 210.

In contrast to the shadowy *independent* existence of the overfed Bigorne, the lean Chicheface type is well evidenced in French literature: Achille Jubinal printed a poem from an early fourteenth-century manuscript that describes the *chinchefache*,[22] and Jean Avalon pointed out that *Dame Tigre* in the second part of *Le Roman de Renard le Contrefait* [40,013–019], composed between 1328 and 1342, is clearly the same beast.[23]

In England, as we have seen, references to the pair are not found as such before the date of Lydgate's painted cloth. Extant depictions begin only with the sudden appearance in 1620 of two versions of the unified composition: a woodcut with verses by the Water Poet, John Taylor, which survives uniquely in the collection of the Society of Antiquaries of London (fig. 1); and a representation by the engraver Reynold Elstrack, which was "missing" until Sheila O'Connell of the British Museum discovered it in 1997 in the collection of the Pierpont Morgan Library[24] and which we thus are able to publish here in full for the first time (fig. 2). The texts of both sheets are given in Appendix 1.

The names given to the English monsters in their Jacobean manifestations also deserve some discussion. It is certainly a curious circumstance that two such similar sheets issued in the same year should use two quite different pairs of names to describe the same beasts, a fact that perhaps argues for independent derivation from a common and presumably foreign original. For Chicheface we have *Pinchbelly* and *Thingut*; for Bigorne we have *Fillgut* and *Bulchin*. Semantically we are looking at names of nickname-type used originally to refer to very fat and very thin human beings.

---

[22] Achille Jubinal, *Mystères inédits du XVe siècle*, 2 vols. (Paris: Téchener, 1837), 1:390–91.

[23] Jean Avalon, "Bigorne et Chicheface," *Le livre et ses amis* 2 (1945), 29–32.

[24] Sheila O'Connell, "The Peel Collection in New York," *Print Quarterly* 15 (March 1998), 66 and fig. 39.

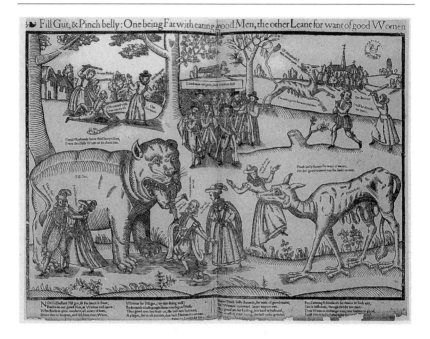

Figure 1. "Fill Gut & Pinchbelly," a woodcut with verses by the Water Poet, John Taylor. 1620. London: Society of Antiquaries of London.

Pinch-belly (not recorded to date before ca. 1650) is defined by the OED as 'one who denies himself or others sufficient food,' but the better attested contemporary term is *pinch-gut*. *Thin-gut*, meaning 'one who has a thin belly, a lean starved-looking person, a starveling,' is attested by OED only between 1602 and 1631.

Bulchin means 'bull-calf' and is a variant of *bulkin*, at which entry OED gives this perhaps suggestive etymology: "the form of the variant . . . *Bulchin* may possibly be due to the pronunciation of the Dutch suffix indicated by its later spelling *-tje(n)*. No other instance is known in English of *-chin* as a variant of *-kin*."

Fillgut is not entered in OED, but there are single instances of the clearly related *fill-belly* (1553), defined as 'glutton,' and *fill-paunch* (1659), the latter glossing the Italian *Tira-pancia*, together with *stretch-gut* and *gulch-belly*.

Figure 2. "Bulchin & Thingut" engraved by Renold Elstrack. 1620. New York: The Pierpont Morgan Library.

In fact, Taylor's compound, *Fillgut*, is attested earlier than any of these as the name of a burlesque saint in Palsgrave's 1540 translation of *Acolastus* (Latin original, 1529), where *saynte fylgutte* and *saynte panchart* render Fullonius's *sancta saturitas*. *Panchart*, variously spelled, was the contemporary French name of the carnivalesque patron saint of gluttony. As early as the late twelfth century, Gautier de Coincy alludes to St. *Pancart* in his *Miracles de Nostre Dame*[25]—which, incidentally, makes him one of the earliest known burlesque saints[26]—

[25] *Miracles de Nostre Dame*, ed. Fritz Koenig (Geneva: Droz, 1966), 1.11, v. 1604; on this saint see further Lazar Saineanu, *La Langue de Rabelais*, vol. 2 (Paris: E. de Boccard, 1923), 484, "Saints imaginaires."

[26] Phallic and other burlesque saints are discussed in my *The Other Middle Ages: A Fresh Look at Late Medieval Visual Culture* (forthcoming).

thereafter he is popular particularly towards the end of the Middle Ages. He appears as a canonized Carnival in *La dure et cruelle bataille et paix du glorieux sainct Pensard à l'encontre de Caresme*, a piece staged in 1485;[27] is mentioned together with other burlesque saints in Jean Molinet's contemporary poem, *Le Nouveau Calendrier*;[28] and, naturally, appears in the works of the creator of Gargantua: in the opening chapter of *Pantagruel* we hear of people whose bellies swelled out like great wine-tuns, and from their stock came *sainct Pansart* and Mardi Gras. Finally, Henri Estienne recalled in his anti-Catholic polemic *Apologie pour Hérodote*, published in 1566, that the *curé* of Bourg-en-Querci, in a sermon on Mardi Gras, recommended to his parishioners the three "bons saincts, S. Panssard, S. Mangeard, S. Crevard," the last two names formed on the verbs meaning "to eat" and "to burst/split."[29] Suggestively, in *Le Testament de Carmentrant*, written by Jehan d'Abundance ca. 1540, the Carnival personification is addressed as *Gros pansart*, and a few lines earlier it is implied that Caresme is a *Chicheface*.[30] Is there, perhaps, in these names a hint that the English *Fillgut/Bulchin* is related to the personification of Carnival, and *Pinchbelly/Thingut* to that of Lent? Note how in the 1636 (1660) broadside discussed below, Lent refers to Shrovetide as "Thou puff-paunch'd monster," while Shrovetide addresses Lent as "thou lean-jawde anottamie," descriptions that might just as aptly apply to Bigorne and Chicheface.[31]

---

[27] *Deux jeux de carnaval de la fin du Moyen Age. La Bataille de sainct Pensard à l'encontre de Caresme et le Testament de Carmentrant*, ed. Jean-Claude Aubailly (Geneva: Droz, 1977).

[28] *Les Faictz et Dictz de Jean Molinet*, ed. Nöel Dupire, vol. 2 (Paris: Société des anciens textes français, 1937), 540–46.

[29] Henri Estienne's *Apologie pour Hérodote* is edited by Paul Ristelhuber (Paris: Isidore Liseux, 1879). The passage in question is to be found in vol. 2, p. 263.

[30] Aubailly, *Testament*, lines 99 and 91 respectively.

[31] *Puff-paunched* is not in OED, and the present example—if the original date of publication is accepted as 1636—represents an antedating of the compound *lean-jawed*.

The English reflex of the Battle of Carnival and Lent, an image engraved on the modern consciousness by Bruegel's famous mid-sixteenth-century painting, is curiously sparsely attested in England in the Middle Ages[32] and in the Early Modern era, though once again it is the pre-eminent poet of the popular culture of the later period, the ubiquitous John Taylor, whom we have to thank for such images as we do have. In the *Stationers Register* on February 15, 1636, two pictures were entered to Matthew Simmons described as *Lent and Shrovetide with verses to them by John Taylor*.[33] They doubtless are identical with the engraved broadsides with verses still extant, which declare themselves to have been "Printed by M.S. for Thomas Jenner . . . 1660" [Wing L1056 and S3701].[34] Furthermore, in 1620 Taylor had published a book entitled *Jacke-a-Lent his beginning and entertainment: with the mad prankes of his Gentleman-Usher Shrove-Tuesday that goes before him and his Footman Hunger attending*.[35] On its title page is a woodcut depicting a skinny Jack-a-Lent, his hair growing through his hat. He rides on a herring, followed by his skeletal servant Hunger, who holds such lenten fare as onions and fish aloft, and preceded by a fat Shrove Tuesday with basting-spoon over his shoulder. Some commentators have

---

[32] The *Lenten cladde in white with redde herrings skinnes and his hors trapped with oyster shelles after him in token that sadnesse and abstinence of merth shulde followe* . . . , which was seen at a Norwich Shrovetiding riding of 1443, is discussed in Chris Humphrey, *The Politics of Carnival* (Manchester: Manchester University Press, 2001), 63–82.

[33] *A Transcript of the Registers of the Company of Stationers of London 1554–1640*, ed. Edward Arber and Charles R. Rivington (London, privately printed, 1875–94).

[34] See Frederick G. Stephens, ed. *Catalogue of prints and drawings in the British Museum. Division 1. Satires. Vol. 1. 1320–1689* (London: J. Nichols, 1870), nos. 980 and 982. The broadside "Printed by M.S." [the Matthew Simmons of the *Stationers Register* entry] is British Library, 669, f. 26 (64 X 65). Reversed copies of the two protagonists and a full transcription of the verses may be found in J. P. Malcolm, *An Historical sketch of the art of caricaturing* (London, 1813), 46–49 and pls. XXVII–XXVIII.

[35] *STC* 23765.

suggested that this cut reproduces actual contemporary London Shrove-tide processions, but in fact the figures of Jack-a-Lent and Shrovetide are copied from Bruegel's *Thin Kitchen* engraving of 1569, intriguing testimony to the familiarity with Bruegel's work in Jacobean England.[36]

As may be seen from the list below (Appendix 2) of extant Bigorne and Chicheface prints known to me (and doubtless incomplete), all the French woodcut sheets—as well as the Dutch engravings by de Meyn and Claes Jansz. Visscher, which, in any case, probably derive from the French sheets—antedate the English versions. Both English sheets represent the fully developed state of the unified composition with landscape background, so it seems likely that they derive immediately from the Dutch engravings rather than the French woodcuts. There is further support for this putative route of transmission in that, although born in London, Elstrack was himself of Dutch extraction and, pre-sumably retained family contacts with his fatherland. Moreover, P. Van der Keere, who issued the sheet dated 1621, had worked in London in the early 1590s.

Apart from Chaucer's fleeting allusion to *Chichevache* in his Envoy to The Clerk's Tale, we have a bare two centuries during which we know the paired "monsters of misogyny" flourished in English art and literature.[37] Lydgate's poem is significant for iconographers in that, while not being precisely datable, it must belong to the first half of the fifteenth century. Thus it is the earliest witness, albeit secondhand, that we have to the European tradition of the visual depiction of the mon-sters, such as "a werthy citeseyn of London" might want to have in his "halle . . . parlour or . . . chaumbre," and, furthermore, one which seems to indicate the sort of unified composition that is not extant

---

[36] Wells-Cole (*Art and Decoration*, 184) notes that the alabaster overmantel in the hall at Burton Agnes, Yorkshire, derives from Bruegel's *Wise and Foolish Virgins* engraved by Philips Galle and issued by Cock in Antwerp in the late 1550s/early 1560s.

[37] Though note that Elstrack's engraving of 1620 has come down to us only in the late seventeenth-century state as sold by Robert Pricke, which implies, at least, that there was still a market for the image even on the eve of the Age of Enlightenment.

before the late sixteenth-century type. Otherwise, the earliest evidence for the representation of the monsters is inferred from the single late fifteenth-century woodcut broadsheet of Chicheface, which must have been very like those which Coquillart saw on sale near the Palais de Justice in Paris in 1480. The early sixteenth-century paintings at Villeneuve-Lembrun, with their close textual and iconographic relationship to the paired broadsheets issued in Lyon ca. 1537, represent the double motif in its earlier sixteenth-century form, before the pan-European popularity of the late sixteenth-century type, a type which curiously is represented in Jacobean England by one woodcut and one engraved broadsheet, both issued in 1620 and rare testimony to the visual popular humor of the period.

APPENDIX 1

TEXTS OF THE ENGLISH SHEETS (1620)

1.   [Bulchin & Thingut] engraved by Elstrack

This Monster, stranger than ea're Africke bred
Like Vsurers, with mans flesh still is fed
And good men only hee deuours: your Knaue
Could in his belly neuer find a Graue:
Pharos' fatt Kine, a Plenty did foretell:
And Plenty of Good men, make him to swell.

Like to a Spanish Moile (that seldome goes
A Iourney, without Prouender at's nose)
This Monster feeds, vntel hee well ny burst.
But wherfore hee should swallow ye head first
Is 'cause ye men haue hornes, & coursest meate
Hauing neare bin in Scotland heele first eate.

Yet better feede the Monster than bee vs'd:
Like Monsters and most slauishly abus'd:
The Poetts found in Hell only three Furyes.
In a bad woeman you may find ful Iuryes.
Thus by this Moral is discouered:
What Number of good men this age hath bred.

But this leane Monster of al shapes ye wourst
Is in her Diet lickwise most accurs'd,
Since shee is limitted only to Gleane,
Good woemen, That's ye reason shees soe leane
For know such haruest is more rarely found
Then Toades or Spiders vpon Irish Ground.

Loung hath this Starueling kept ye Deuels fast;
And Hunting ore ye World that is soe Vast,
Amongst most woemen (weare they foule or faire)
Camelion like, fed only vpon aire
Till at the last, her hunger is apeas'd;
(By chance) on one good woeman he [sic] hath seas'd.

This is a Phoenix and we neuer yet
Heard man or Beast did of a Phoenix eate.
Forbeare vngentle Monster, cease to feed
Least at one meale thou doe destroy ye breed.
Thy hunger will bee equal as before
But ye like bit thou seldome wilt tast more.

2.   [Fillgut & Pinchbelly] Woodcut with verses by John Taylor

Now full bellyed Fill gut, so Fat heere in show,
Feedes on our good Men, as Women well know:
Who flocke in great numbers, all weary of liues,
Heere thus to be eaten, and rid from their Wiues

Whereas fat Fill gut, (by this doing well)
Redeemeth kinde people from bondage of Hell:
Thus good men hee feeds on, the bad men he leaues,
A plague, for those scoulds, that such Husbands receaues.

Heere Pinch belly starueth, for want of good meate,
For Women vntoward, he no way can eate:
The good are his feeding, but hard to be found,
The worst of them liuing, the best vnder ground.

For if amongst thousands he chance to finde any,
One is sufficient, though two be too many:
Then Women exchange you, your badnes to good,
Least Pinchbelly starue here for [want of —] food.

APPENDIX 2
SINGLE-SHEET WOODCUTS AND ENGRAVINGS
[PROVISIONAL HANDLIST]

SEPARATE SINGLE SHEETS

French
(a) Bigorne
1.   Lyon, ca.1537 woodcut [Paris, Coll. Rothschild, Bib. Nat]
(b) Chicheface
2.   Paris, ca.1495 (Guy Marchant) woodcut [Munich, Bayerische Staatsbibliothek]
3.   Lyon, ca.1537 woodcut [Paris, Bib. Nat., Coll. Rothschild]

SEPARATE BUT ADJACENT IMAGES ON SAME SHEET

German
4.   Augsburg, 1586 (pub.: H. Schultes the Elder), woodcut [Zurich, Stadtsbibliothek]

UNIFIED COMPOSITION WITH SUBSIDIARY SCENES IN LANDSCAPE BACKGROUND

Dutch [two plates]
5.   Amsterdam, 1611 (pub.: David de Meyn), engraving [Gotha; &? BM, London]
6.   Amsterdam, 1621 (pub. & engrav.(?): Pieter van de Keere), engraving [Amsterdam, Rijksmuseum, Prentenkabinett; Muller no. S 418 ae]

Dutch [single plate]
7.   Amsterdam, ante1612 (pub.: Claes Jansz. Visscher), engraving [Coburg, Veste XIII, 321, 348]
8.   Amsterdam, ante1658 (pub.: Cornelis Visscher), engraving [Paris, Bib. Nat., Cabinet des Estampes Tf2 p.48]
9.   Place?, ante1684 (pub.: Hugo Allarde), engraving [= later state of item 8]

German [two plates]

10. Augsburg, ca.1628 (pub.: J. Klocker), engraving [left half (Bigorne) only] [appears to be a Dutch plate retaining Dutch captions with added German text] [Stadtsbibliothek Augsburg]

German [single plate]

11. Place?, ca.1735, engraving [Paris, Bib. Nat., Cabinet des Estampes Tf4 p. 62]

French

12. Paris, ca.1600 (pub.: S. Graffart), woodcut [Paris, Bib. Nat., Coll. Hennin 1220]

13. Lyon, ca..1600 (pub.: L. Odet), woodcut [Herzog August Bibliothek, Wolfenbüttel]

14. Place?, 1598 (pub.: D. de Mathonière), woodcut

15. Place?, 1611 (pub.: N. Proue), woodcut

English

16. London, 1620 (pub.: Allde for Gosson), woodcut [London, Society of Antiquaries]

17. London, 1620 (engrav.: Renold Elstrack), engraving [unique state "sold by Robert Pricke," active 1668–98] [New York, Pierpont Morgan Library]

DEPICTING THE INSANE:
A THIRTEENTH-CENTURY CASE STUDY

DAVID A. SPRUNGER

A PAIR OF CURIOUS ILLUSTRATIONS appears in a manuscript of the *Prose Lancelot* produced in Amiens in 1286.[1] The very different pictures illustrate significant scenes in the madness and recovery of Lancelot. The first depicts the frenzy of Lancelot going insane and fleeing from Guinevere and Elaine (fig.1). The second shows Lancelot after his mad sojourn in the woods (fig. 2). Arthur's greatest knight now huddles on the ground, bald and gnarled, restrained by Elaine and her father. The narrative cycle indicates that Lancelot's physical strength has not diminished, for the madman has distinguished himself through several episodes of physical strength, but in the illustration he appears twisted and weak. How are we to understand this monstrous transformation? In depicting these scenes, the illustrator of this manuscript has gone beyond the narrative facts by tapping separate iconographic traditions of madness and insanity. Further, the artist has taken visual elements used primarily to create static portraits in medical illustration

---

[1] Bonn: Universitäts- und Landesbibliothek MS 526, fols. 256r and 404v. For manuscript description and history see Irmgard Fischer's contribution to *Lancelot en prose: Bonn, Universitätsbibliothek, Handschrift S 526*, Codices illuminati medii aevi 28 (Munich: Edition Helga Lengenfelder, 1992), 26–30.

Figure 1. Lancelot goes insane. Bonn: ULB MS 526 (Prose Lancelot), fol. 256r. Amiens, 13th century. Courtesy of Universitäts- und Landesbibliothek, Bonn.

Figure 2. Lancelot restrained by Elaine and King Pelles. Bonn: ULB MS 526 (Prose Lancelot), fol. 404v. Amiens, 13th century. Courtesy of Universitäts- und Landesbibliothek, Bonn.

and adapted those elements to fit the demands of a narrative that incorporates the passage of time.

Before considering the iconographic legacy, however, we must codify it, for there is yet no definitive schema of visual strategies used in the Middle Ages to show insanity in programs of narrative illustration.[2] Considerable progress has been made categorizing illustrations of madness in the medical tradition, but less attention has been paid to how the medical illustrations were adapted to narrative demands.

My own survey of medieval depictions of the insane ranges from Byzantium to Britain, from the sixth to the sixteenth century, and it peruses sources from the theological to the medical to the literary. Throughout this geographic and chronological distribution emerge certain consistent visual traditions for representing madness. These iconographic markers are rooted in the tradition of medical illustration. However, illustrators of romances often adapt these iconic elements to demonstrate that madness often was cyclical and that a lunatic's disease had a distinct onset, would wax, and eventually would wane.

In portraying the insane, artists of any time period have to overcome a basic contradiction. Since madness is an invisible, internal condition, the audience must recognize insanity from external signs ranging from the oral to the visual. Paola Valesio notes that during the Renaissance madness in literature was displayed through verbal cues, especially through a character's appropriation of the "language of folklore." In the Middle Ages, on the other hand, the insane were depicted through what he calls "iconic aspect"— visual instead of behavioral

---

[2] Henri H. Beek makes significant progress in his comprehensive *Waanzin in de middeleeuwen: Beeld van de gestoorde en bemoeienis met de zieke* (Hoofddorp: ICOB, 1969), but, unfortunately, Beek died before revising (or translating) the volume, so his schema has never been further refined. The scholar who has built most successfully on Beek's work is Sander L. Gilman, *Seeing the Insane*, rev. ed. (Lincoln: University of Nebraska Press, 1996). Penelope Doob works with the medical tradition and its influence on medieval English literature in *Nebuchadnezzar's Children: Conventions of Madness in Middle English Literature* (New Haven, Yale University Press, 1974).

detail.[3] The iconic details to which Valesio refers, however, are often behavioral, such as the hero's wanderings in the woods, clowning, and undisciplined fumbling with weapons.

Such markers, whatever their form, are inevitably signs of difference that attempt to define a norm of human rationality as well as aberrant madness. Thus, in his discussion of visual depictions of illness, Sander L. Gilman has argued that the visual representation of a medical patient serves to make distinct divisions between the "healthy" and the "diseased." "The construction of the image of the patient is thus always a playing out of this desire for a demarcation between ourselves and the chaos represented in culture by disease."[4] In the case of insanity, artists emphasize what is different about the insane and reassure viewers that lunatics can be identified and avoided.

Combining Valesio's emphasis on iconic detail with Gilman's idea of demarcation allows the construction of two narrative models of madness, each clearly defining the lunatic in relationship to "normal" society. In the first model, the madman seeks control over his own environment, an environment separate from the rigid social order. This desire is suggested by the emblematic club with which he keeps others at bay. The second model stresses society's control over the madman, most often by the use of chains, stocks, or fetters. As we shall see later, these models contain important hints to the progression of madness.

Although many critical studies have explored the technical medical conditions suggested by the madnesses of Merlin, Yvain, and Lancelot, the authors and illustrators of these romances were not concerned with medical accuracy. Rather, madness symbolizes the hero's inner turmoil, and the texts draw on whatever medical symptoms and treatments are

---

[3] Paola Valesio, "The Language of Madness in the Renaissance," *Yearbook of Italian Studies* 1 (1971), 199–234. For discussion of medieval models see esp. 200–04. Valesio's "language of folklore" in Renaissance lunatics is defined on 210–12.

[4] Sander L. Gilman, *Disease and Representation: Images of Illness from Madness to AIDS* (Ithaca: Cornell University Press, 1988), 4.

most convenient to developing the plot. The result is little cohesion in portraying madness with medical accuracy. When one turns instead to visual patterns found in illustrated narratives, however, there is much greater unity. Here we find artists establishing madness through physical appearance, characteristic accessories, and distinctive behavior.

First, the artist could use some features of physical appearance to identify someone as mad. The insane person's hair (or lack of it) is one of the most distinctive features used in the depictions. In some cases, the subject's hair stands erect in clumps, looking as if the mad person's head is on fire. This "flame-hair" appears in the Middle Ages to signify someone's inner wildness, a convention John Block Friedman traces to illustrations of Vices in Carolingian manuscripts of Prudentius's *Psychomachia*.[5] This characteristic appears especially in medieval iconography of demons and those possessed by demons. Roger Sherman Loomis and Laura Hibbard Loomis also note this phenomenon, referring to it as "elf hair," suggesting some sort of supernatural origin.[6] The *Motif Index of Folk-Literature* documents the hero's horripilation beyond the Middle Ages, but in its examples throughout Irish, Icelandic, Hindi, Lorean, and Missouri French literature, flame-hair need not necessarily show a demonic condition.[7] It also could manifest itself during times of intense manic energy, such as Lancelot's waxing madness.

People illustrated with flame-hair and associated in the Middle Ages with madness are often biblical madmen, for it is in such religious contexts that insane behavior is equated particularly with literal demonic possession. The gospel of Luke provides the basic elements

---

[5] John Block Friedman, *The Monstrous Races in Medieval Art and Thought* (Cambridge, Mass.: Harvard University Press, 1981), 98.

[6] Roger Sherman Loomis and Laura Hibbard Loomis, *Arthurian Legends in Medieval Art* (New York: MLA, 1938), 95.

[7] Stith Thompson, *Motif-Index of Folk-literature: A Classification of Narrative Elements in Folktales, Ballads, Myths, Fables, Mediaeval Romances, Exempla, Fabliaux, Jest-books, and Local Legends*, 6 vols. (Bloomington: Indiana University Press, 1955–58).

of Christ's encounters with demoniacs. Jesus confronts a madman who exhibits manic fury:

> a certain man who had a devil now a very long time, and he wore no clothes, neither did he abide in a house, but in the sepulchers. . . . For many times it seized him, and he was bound with chains, and kept in fetters; and breaking the bonds, he was driven by the devil into the desert. (Luke 8:27, 29)[8]

When asked his identity (an important diagnostic question for testing the state of the patient's memory), the man identifies his singular self as a plural: "Legion, for we are many."[9] Jesus exorcizes from the patient a swarm of devils and transfers them to a nearby herd of pigs, which immediately rushes over a cliff and drowns in the sea.

The single visual image that most clearly identifies this category of madmen is the tiny demon exiting from the patient's lips as seen in an illustration from the "Bernulfus Codex," an eleventh-century lectionary from the Reichenau (fig. 3).

That the demon comes from *inside* the madman emphasizes the internal nature of the condition. In the top frame, the possessed man is under physical restraint by his friends and, additionally, has his feet shackled. The chains are mentioned in the text, but they also provide a dramatic external reminder that the demoniac has been under a more powerful, previously invisible, restraint. As Christ blesses him, the demoniac's hair rises on his head and a demon flows from his mouth, turning away from Christ as if unable to bear his presence. As in many such illustrations, the man is twisted or contorted. The illustration's lower frame shows the story's outcome: the demons ride the galloping pigs to their deaths in the sea.

---

[8] Douay-Rheims translation.

[9] For extensive discussion of this question in interrogation of demons see Timothy S. Jones, "Geoffrey of Monmouth, *Fouke le Fitz Waryn*, and National Mythology," *Studies in Philology* 41 (1994), 233–49, esp. 243–45.

Figure 3. Christ expels demons into the Gerasene swine. 11th century. Utrecht: ABM MS. 3 (Arnulfus Psalter), fol 33v. 11th c. Courtesy of Catherijnconventmuseum, Utrecht.

If illustrated madmen do not model the flame-hair, they often will have some other distinctive hairstyle. Frequently the madmen are shown completely bald, as in a well-known "dixit insipiens" from Artois at the end of the thirteenth century (fig. 4). Psalms 14 and 53 begin, "Dixit insipiens in suo corde non est Deus" [The fool says in his heart, 'There is no God']. The illuminated initial *D* beginning the psalm commonly portrays a fool or a madman, and the motif is called a "dixit insipiens."[10] It is important to keep in mind that the "dixit insipiens" illustrations are not necessarily madmen.[11] Just as often one finds the court fool or jester. Although the fool may share attributes with a madman, the two are not the same in medieval thought. Yet, they share some iconographic attributes; thus a digression on the fool is not out of place.

The fool and the madman are not necessarily linked, although, as I mentioned, they frequently are connected. My own study has concentrated on those who lapse from sanity to insanity and then recover, whereas the fool is often one whose mental limitations are lifelong. Discussions of the fool have long centered on his visual elements. John

---

[10] For discussion of the *dixit insipiens* tradition, including many illustrations, see V. A. Kolve, "God-Denying Fools and the Medieval 'Religion of Love'," *Studies in the Age of Chaucer* 19 (1997), 3–59.

For an excellent introduction to the broader tradition of fools see D. J. Gifford, "Notes toward a Definition of the Medieval Fool," in *The Fool and the Trickster: Studies in Honour of Enid Welsford*, ed. Paul Williams (Cambridge: D. S. Brewer, 1979), 18–35. Other general introductions to the fool tradition include the well-illustrated A. Gazeau, *Les Bouffons*, Bibliothèque des Merveilles (Paris: Hachette et Cie, 1882); and Maurice Lever, *Sceptre et la marotte: histoire des fous de cour* (Paris: Librairie Arthème Fayard, 1983). For discussion of specific aspects of the fool see the collection of essays edited by Clifford Davidson, *Fools and Folly*, Early Drama, Art, and Music, Monograph Series 22 (Kalamazoo, Mich.: Medieval Institute Publications, 1996).

[11] Kolve refers to over two hundred examples of "dixit insipiens" illustrations ("God-Denying Fools," 8). The psalm did not need to be illustrated with a fool; other imagery was used as well. For example, the Worcester Psalter (ca. 1350) in the Rare Book Collection at the University of Illinois, Champaign-Urbana, shows a woman stabbing herself with a knife.

Figure 4. "Dixit insipiens," with bald fool. Oxford: Bodley MS Deuce 118 (Psalter), fol. 60v. Artois, late 13th century. Courtesy of the Bodleian Library, Oxford.

Doran's 1858 study of the fool suggested two recurrent visual characteristics of the fool: a bald head and the carrying of a fool's club or stick.[12] E. K. Chambers provides extensive material on the fool's costume from the fourteenth century to the early Renaissance, and he emphasizes the same two features: the head and the club.[13] Chambers does not mention the fool's baldness or tonsure; instead, he stresses the fool's hood, which differed from that of the ordinary person in its distinctive crest, bells, and ear-like appendages. The fool also often

---

[12] John Doran, *The History of Court Fools* (London: R. Bentley, 1858), 56–67.

[13] E. K. Chambers, *The Mediaeval Stage*, 2 vols. (Oxford: Clarendon Press, 1903), 1:384–89.

carries a tiny replica of the fool's own head and shoulders mounted on a short stick (a *marotte*), or sometimes he clings to a short wand, often equipped with a rattle made from dried peas and an inflated bladder. Philippe Ménard's more recent study of fool iconography continues to emphasize "la tonsure et la massue" (the haircut and the club) as the fool's basic markers.[14]

The exact identity of the round object that the fool in figure 4 clutches has not yet been established, but one finds many illustrations of fools that show their subjects holding a similar object. R. E. Neale's study of this item observes that regardless of what specific object is illustrated, all variations portray the fool with an "oral fixation":

> The focal point of the illustration is almost always his mouth, the juncture of the two roughly circular masses of head and "loaf." The exact identity of the object he holds is therefore of minor significance: specific moral suggestions of the stupidity of trying to eat a stone, of gluttony, or even of blasphemy (in thus mistreating the *panis quadratus*) are subordinate to the illustration's main function. . . .[15]

But, to return to baldness. The connection between baldness and madness, mentioned above in Doran, appears elsewhere in medieval thought. Sometimes the baldness seems to be a natural consequence of the insanity. For example, the hero Comghan runs afoul of a druid who strikes him with a magic wand, putting him under an evil spell: "At the end of the year he had wasted away, his hair fell off, his intellect decayed, and he became a bald and senseless idiot, keeping company only with the fools and mountebanks of his father's court."[16]

---

[14] Philippe Ménard, "Les Emblèmes en la folie dans la littérature et dans l'art (XII–XIIIe siècles)," in *Hommage á Jean-Charles Payen: Farai Chansoneta Novele: Essais sur la liberté créatrice au Moyen Age* (Caen: Université de Caen, 1989), 253–66.

[15] R. E. Neale, "The Fool and his Loaf," *Medium Aevum* 54 (1985), 107.

[16] From "Acts of the Idiots Comdhan [or Comghan] and Conell." Discussed in Enid Welsford, *The Fool: His Social and Literary History* (Gloucester, Mass.: Peter Smith, 1966), 101.

More often, however, baldness is connected with a positive change in the patient's condition. The madman's baldness could be consistent with medical practice, since many of the medieval medical remedies for madness called for the patient's head to be shaved in preparation for application to the scalp of an ointment or animal part, such as a fresh sheep lung or a slit-open rooster.

Baldness also has a further symbolic connection with one's restoration to grace. Giles Constable's magisterial study of beard- and hair-lore in the Middle Ages demonstrates that the shaving of one's hair could signify "a separation from the previous world" as in the tonsuring of monks. With its implications of ritual purification and renewal of spirit, a bald lunatic could signal a person who is ready to depart the world of madness for the realm of reason.[17]

Another variation on the hair style of the insane is the so-called "fool's tonsure." As mentioned earlier, the role of fool in the social structure is not held necessarily by a madman, but in some illustrations, the fools' distinctive hair styles mark their exclusion from formal society. These tonsures are always the result of barbering and never some sort of natural reaction to insanity.

One example of the fool's distinct tonsure is when Tristan feigns madness to disguise himself and be near Isold:

> Then Tristan shaved his wonderful hair; he shaved it close to his head and left a cross all bald, and he rubbed his face with magic herbs distilled in his own country, and it changed his colour and skin so that none could know him, and he made him a club from a young tree torn from a hedge-row and hung it to his neck, and went barefoot towards the castle.[18]

---

[17] Giles Constable, Introduction to beards in the Middle Ages, *Apologia de Barbis*, ed. F. B. C. Huygens, CCL 62 (Turnholt: Brepols, 1985), 47–149, esp. 56. For a survey of medieval interpretations of baldness see John Block Friedman, "Bald Jonah and the Exegesis of 4 Kings 2.23," *Traditio* 44 (1988), 125–44.

[18] "Od les forces haut se tundi: / Ben senlle fol u esturdi. / Enaprés se tundi en croiz / Tristran sout ben muër sa voiz / Od une herbete teinst sun vis, / K'il aporta de sun païs. / Il oinst sun vis de la licur, / Puis ennerci muad culur. / N'aveit hume k'al munde fust

A scene from a Parisian ivory box from the first quarter of the fourteenth century illustrates this scene (fig. 5).[19] Tristan's mock madness is represented here by two symbols. First, he sports an unusual haircut: his head has been shaved so that a cross remains on the top of his scalp and a band of hair encircles his head. Tristan is not the only fool to model such a "cross tonsure." The protagonist of the fourteenth-century romance "Robert of Sicily" (ca. 1370), for instance, also has his hair shaved in a cross to indicate his station as a fool.[20]

The club on Tristan's shoulder introduces another dimension of the iconography of madness. Clubs certainly are not unique to the insane, but they often are shown with them. As a hand-held accessory, they have associations with the marottes or fool sticks mentioned earlier. The portrayal of a madman with a stout club is of special significance, however, for it links him to another tradition, one simultaneously connecting its owner to the more natural world and to the lower social classes.[21] A weapon that did not require human manufacture, the club could be something as simple as a tree branch or, in extreme cases such as the Tristan passage quoted earlier, an entire small tree up-rooted.

/ Ki pur Tristran le cunëust / Ne ki pur Tristran l'enterçast, / Tant nel veïst u escutast. / Il ad d'une haie un pel pris / Een sun col l'ad il mis. / Vers le chastel en voit tut dreit; / Chaskun ad poür ke il vait" (lines 209–24). Text from *La Folie Tristan d'Oxford*, ed. Ernest Hoepffner, 2nd ed. (Strasbourg: University of Strasbourg, 1943); trans. from Joseph Bédier, *The Romance of Tristan and Iseult* (1945; New York: Vintage Books, 1965), 133.

[19] For background on Parisian ivory carving and reproductions of several such works from the beginning of the fourteenth century see Loomis and Loomis, *Arthurian Legends*, 55–56.

[20] "Robert of Sicily," ed. Walter French and Charles Hale, *Middle English Metrical Romances* (New York: Prentice Hall, 1930), 933–46.

[21] For a study of Tristan's club and the different ways in which he uses it in various versions of the legends see William McDonald, "The Fool-Stick: Concerning Tristan's Club in the German Eilhart Tradition," *Euphorion* 82 (1988), 127–49. See also my discussion of the clubs carried by the hairy wild men: "Wild Folk and Lunatics in Medieval Romance," in *The Medieval World of Nature: A Book of Essays*, ed. Joyce E. Salisbury (New York: Garland, 1993), 145–63.

Figure 5. Tristan feigns madness. Ivory casket. Paris, early 14th century. Courtesy of the Hermitage Museum, St. Petersburg.

Since the cyclical madmen of medieval romance all are from noble society, their symbolic descent to the world of the lower classes is of special significance. When a person whose identity has been formed with arms is shifted to a world without them, the vertical shift downward involves humiliation and separation from the chivalric society they have known their whole lives, and the club provides a constant reminder of this dislocation.

After the hair and club, characteristic behavior provides an important visual signal about a character's madness. In particular, the patient's degree of freedom or restraint is the significant visual indicator. As I mentioned, the mad person's distorted relationship is signaled in one of two ways. Either the lunatic engages in wild antics, often involving the club, or he somehow is constrained physically, like a wild animal.

Sometimes the wild madman suggests one whose madness is a waxing frenzy, and the constrained lunatic signals lethargy or someone who is receiving treatment and is closer to recovery. Such a pairing occurs in a thirteenth-century page from a pseudo-Apuleius manuscript,

Figure 6.   Madman being treated with peony. Vienna: Österreichische National-bibliothek, MS 93 (Pseudo-Appuleuis, *Herbarium*), fol. 72v. 13th century. Courtesy of Österreichische Nationalbibliothek, Vienna.

a pharmacopoeia book listing herbs and chemical compounds and explaining how to apply them to disease and injury (fig. 6).[22] The accompanying entry explains the use of herbs against madness: "for lunatics who suffer from the course of the moon: if peony herb is

---

[22] For general introduction to the herbal tradition in England see Eleanour Sinclair Rohde, *The Old English Herbals* (1922; New York: Dover, 1971); and Agnes Arber, *Herbals, Their Origin and Evolution: A Chapter in the History of Botany, 1470–1670* (1912; Cambridge: Cambridge University Press, 1938). Any exploration of medieval medical illustrations must begin with "Extant Medical Miniatures in Treatises in Manuscripts Prior to c. 1550," compiled by Loren C. MacKinney and Thomas Herndon and appended to MacKinney, *Medical Illustrations in Medieval Manuscripts* (Berkeley and Los Angeles: University of California Press, 1965), 105–85.

bound on the neck of one who is moonstruck, quickly he will rise up healed; and if he carries it with him he will suffer no ill."[23] The entry shows in simultaneous illustration the traditional fool-jester in his belled cap and piebald gown doing a handstand. Displaying total freedom, the jester provides a diagnostic aid with a quick visual reference to the madman's behavior, characterized by lack of all restraint. The companion illustration shows the recommended treatment in action. The patient is under forced bed rest: his feet are locked in stocks linked with chains to manacles on his wrists. A large sprig of peony seems to sprout from his neck.

For a further illustration of the two narrative models, freedom and constraint, we may turn to two illustrations of the pretend madness of King David. During his flight from Saul, David ventures into the court of King Achis of Geth, a hostile camp for an Israelite. Fearing recognition by Achis's men, David escapes by feigning insanity: "And he changed his countenance before them, and slipt down between their hands: and he stumbled against the doors of the gate, and his spittle ran down upon his beard" (1 Sam. 21:13). As a result, Achis dismisses him, complaining, "Have we need of madmen, that you have brought in this fellow, to play the madman in my presence?" (1 Sam. 21:15).[24]

A thirteenth-century collection of Old Testament miniatures from the Pierpont Morgan Library illustrates the scene (fig. 7), but the artist has declined to illustrate the biblical version with the dribbling beard.[25] To the left, David receives the sacred bread and Goliath's sword; to the right, King Achis sits on his throne gesturing toward a center panel in

---

[23] Pseudo-Apuleius, *Herbarium*. Quoted by MacKinney, *Medical Illustrations*, 45.

[24] For iconographic references to the David tradition, including this scene, see Engelbert Kirschbaum et al., *Lexikon der christlichen Ikonographie*, 8 vols. (Rome: Herder, 1968–76), 1:478–90; and Louis Réau, *Iconographie de l'Art Chrétien*, 3 vols. (Paris: Presses Universitaires de France, 1955–59), 2:254–80.

[25] For a facsimile of the entire manuscript with a bibliographic introduction see *Old Testament Miniatures: A Medieval Picture Book with 283 Paintings from the Creation to the Story of David*, ed. Sydney C. Cockerell (New York: George Braziller, [1969]).

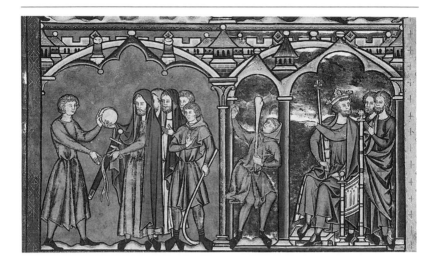

Figure 7. King David feigns madness. New York: Pierpont Morgan MS 638 (Maciejowski Bible), fol. 32r. 13th century. Courtesy of the Pierpont Morgan Library.

which David feigns insanity. The artist has portrayed David as clean shaven, perhaps emphasizing his status as boy hero, and he has represented David's madness through his freedom. David's placement in a separate frame of the illustration stresses the madman's isolation and separation, as does his curious behavior of pointing to some distant object while brandishing in his left hand a long cudgel.

This pattern of illustration was not, however, the only one used to depict this scene. A drawing in the ninth-century Stuttgart Psalter draws on the other model of madness (fig. 8). Instead of portraying David's freedom, the artist shows David being led from the court with his hands tied before him. One guard tugs at David's cloak while the other handles the leash connected to David's wrists. By showing the hero in bonds and under the control of his keepers, the artist cued viewers to the figure's madness.[26]

---

[26] For another depiction of the scene in which David's madness is signified by his being constrained see the Bible of Cîteaux, Dijon, Municipal Library, MS 14, fol. 13v,

Figure 8. King David feigns madness. Stuttgart: Württembergische Landesbibliothek MS 23 (Stuttgart Psalter), fol. 67v. 9th century. Courtesy of Württembergische Landesbibliothek, Stuttgart.

Returning to the illustrations of Lancelot from the Bonn manuscript, we now see how the artist uses the visual cues to supplement the narrative. Like the madmen of other chivalric romances, Lancelot undergoes a metaphoric fall and redemption. Lancelot finds his chivalric honor compromised. He explicitly has promised Guinevere that he will not have further contact with Elaine, and although he is tricked into it, he later finds himself in Elaine's bed. Discovered by Guinevere, Lancelot does not know how to respond. In a frenzy, he rushes from the castle and escapes to the wilderness, where he lives a wild life for some years. The first illustration (fig. 1) captures Lancelot's moment of cognitive dissonance and desperate transformation. The unidentified residents to the right have wavy hair, but Lancelot's is more extreme and rises like flames, suggesting that his madness is waxing. The club he carries indicates his exclusion from a life of civilized arms and battle. The castle and the fainting ladies behind him underscore that his freedom will separate him from the worlds of court and chivalry.

---

reproduced in Angelika Gross, *"La Folie": Wahnsinn und Narrheit im spätmittelalterlichen Text und Bild*, Beiträge zur älteren Literaturgeschichte (Heidelberg: Carl Winter, 1990).

In the cycle of chivalric madness, the lunatic eventually is brought to a primal condition from which he returns to his former position of glory. The second illustration (fig. 2) shows Lancelot at his nadir. Bald, weak, and speechless, he has become a metaphoric child, ready to be reborn and reclaim his place as Arthur's greatest knight. His body posture suggests physical weakness, which is not a trait found in the other *visual* depictions of madness, although it does have the practical purpose of allowing the powerful man to be under the control of two physically weaker people. Other narrative cycles have analogues with such weakness during recovery from madness. During his insanity, Yvain, for example, is extremely fit, but as soon as his wits return, he is so weak he can barely stand.[27]

As a further indication of the prolonged madness and his child-like condition, the bald Lancelot now demonstrates Neale's "oral fixation" by gnawing on the twisted club, the contact zone between mouth and club occurring in the visual center of the illustration. The medieval illustrator of this manuscript has supplemented the narrative with visual details from two very different traditions of madness, first presenting a frenzied madman in flight, and then, in a final illustration, showing that Lancelot's wild freedom has ended. Now under the physical restraint of Elaine and her father, he is ready at last to begin his re-integration into society.

---

[27] A similar inexplicable weakness occurs in Marie de France's lai *Bisclavret* when the protagonist is restored to human form: *Lais*, ed. Alfred Ewert (1944; Oxford: Blackwell, 1969), lines 261–314.

Magic and Metafiction in The Franklin's Tale: Chaucer's Clerk of Orléans as Double of the Franklin

Paul Battles

IN THE CLERK OF ORLÉANS, who shares little with the usual run of enchanters and necromancers populating medieval romance, Chaucer has created one of his most enigmatic characters. It is obvious that the Clerk plays a pivotal role in The Franklin's Tale. His magic allows Aurelius to fulfill the terms of Dorigen's rash promise, and in so doing sets in motion the chain of events that follow. At the same time the Clerk is a fundamentally ambiguous figure. He is the only character to whose thoughts we are never privy, and his motives remain unclear throughout. His powers nearly unleash a domestic tragedy, but they also act as ultimate catalyst for the successive displays of *gentillesse* that affect the tale's happy end. In many ways, the magician is the most difficult character to read, and much that has troubled critics about The Franklin's Tale—particularly its ending—depends on how his actions are evaluated. Given his importance to the story, the Clerk has received surprisingly little attention, though a good deal has been written about the nature of his magic,[1] most recently a penetrating iconographic analysis by V. A. Kolve.[2] Kolve, like other critics before him, draws an analogy between the Clerk of Orléans and Chaucer as makers of illusion and suggests that the tale offers a meditation on the nature and ethics of poetic art. Many details support a metafictional reading of The Franklin's Tale, but the present essay will develop this concept in a different direction, arguing that a stronger case can be made for pairing of the Clerk and the Franklin as makers of illusion. Having established this connection, the essay will then consider its larger implications for both The Franklin's Tale and the frame narrative.

The precise nature of the Clerk's magic has proven notoriously difficult to pin down. Multiple clues in the text point in very different directions, as though the Franklin had deliberately set out to muddle the issue. Three scenes in the poem involve magic: Aurelius's brother recollects students at Orléans dabbling in the magic arts, and compares them to tregetoures entertaining at feasts (1118–64);[3] the Clerk conjures up a series of illusions for Aurelius in his study, impressing the

---

[1] See W. Bryant Bachman, Jr., "'To Maken Illusioun': The Philosophy of Magic and the Magic of Philosophy in the *Franklin's Tale*," *Chaucer Review* 12 (1977), 55–67; Mary Flowers Braswell, "The Magic of Machinery: A Context for Chaucer's *Franklin's Tale*," *Mosaic* 18 (1985), 101–10; Thomas J. Hatton, "Magic and Honor in *The Franklin's Tale*," *Papers in Language and Literature* 3 (1967), 179–81; Richard Hillman, "Chaucer's Franklin's Magician and *The Tempest*: An Influence Beyond Appearances?" *Shakespeare Quarterly* 34 (1983), 426–32; Anthony J. Luengo, "Magic and Illusion in *The Franklin's Tale*," *Journal of English and Germanic Philology* 77 (1977), 1–16; Samuel Schuman, "Man, Magician, Poet, God—An Image in Medieval, Renaissance, and Modern Literature," *Cithara* 19.2 (1980), 40–54; and J. S. P. Tatlock, "Astrology and Magic in Chaucer's *Franklin's Tale*," in *Anniversary Papers by Colleagues and Pupils of George Lyman Kittredge* (1913; New York: Russell and Russell, 1967), 339–50.

[2] V. A. Kolve, "Rocky Shores and Pleasure Gardens: Poetry vs. Magic in Chaucer's *Franklin's Tale*," in *Poetics: Theory and Practice in Medieval English Literature*, ed. Piero Boitani and Anna Torti (Cambridge: D. S. Brewer, 1991), 165–95.

[3] All references to Chaucer's poetry are from Larry D. Benson, ed., *The Riverside Chaucer*, 3rd ed. (Boston: Houghton Mifflin, 1987).

squire with his skills (1189–1209); and finally the rocks are made to disappear (1261–96). The spectacles described in the first two scenes correspond to actual entertainments presented during a royal feast at Paris in 1378;[4] contemporary accounts suggest that these marvels combined elaborate stage tricks and automata to beguile the guests. This has led some critics to argue that the magic of The Franklin's Tale, too, depends on such devices, making the Clerk of Orléans a kind of medieval David Copperfield.[5] However, the third and most crucial scene, describing the rocks' disappearance, leads to an entirely different conclusion. The Clerk's elaborate astrological calculations would suggest that he either relies on astrological magic to obscure the rocks[6] or simply waits for a tide high enough to cover them.[7] The Franklin's explanation does more to obscure the issue than to clarify it:

> This subtil clerk swich routhe had of this man
> That nyght and day he spedde hym that he kan
> To wayten a tyme of his conclusioun;
> This is to seye, to maken illusioun,
> By swich an apparence or jogelrye—
> I ne kan no termes of astrologye—
> That she and every wight sholde wene and seye
> That of Britaigne the rokkes were aweye,
> Or ellis they were sonken under grounde. (1261–69)

Here the Franklin neatly summarizes the various theories outlined above, alternatively entertaining the possibility that the Clerk relies on conjurers' stage tricks (*jogelrye*), that he uses astrological magic (*astrologye*),

---

[4] Laura Hibbard Loomis, "Secular Dramatics in the Royal Palace, Paris, 1378, 1389, and Chaucer's 'Tregetoures'," *Speculum* 33 (1958), 242–55.

[5] Braswell, "The Magic of Machinery"; and Luengo, "Magic and Illusion in the *Franklin's Tale*."

[6] Tatlock, "Astrology and Magic in Chaucer's *Franklin's Tale*."

[7] Hatton, "Magic and Honor in *The Franklin's Tale*"; and Chauncey A. Wood, "Time and Tide in the *Franklin's Tale*," in *Chaucer and the Country of the Stars: Poetic Uses of Astrological Imagery* (Princeton: Princeton University Press, 1970), 245–71.

and that he waits for a high tide (*to wayten*). This equivocation is entirely in tune with the Franklin's desire to distance himself from the "supersticious cursednesse" (1272) of his pagan characters.

Yet one point remains clear: The Franklin's Tale asks us to credit the Clerk with powers of magic, consisting chiefly but not exclusively of an ability to manipulate appearances. It is a mistake to rationalize away the tale's element of the supernatural, as critics have persistently attempted to do. Stagecraft, automata, and astrology may all be part of the magician's bag of tricks, but individually none of these suffices to account for what happens in the tale. Astrological calculations cannot explain the show of illusions in the Clerk's study, while no amount of stage gimmicks could obscure a whole coastline.[8] Other details, too, cannot be explained by either theory; for example, the Clerk knows the brothers' purpose in coming to Orléans before they have mentioned it to anyone. The whole discussion threatens to divert our attention from the point at hand. It is the illusions themselves, not the process whereby they are generated, that are central to The Franklin's Tale;[9] from the beginning, the magician is associated with *illusioun* (1134, 1264, 1292), *apparence* (1140, 1157, 1265), "seeming" (1146, 1151, 1296), and deception by sight (*sighte* 1151, 1158, 1206; *sen* 1191, 1192, 1193, 1195, 1198, 1206). Moreover, insofar as they try to rationalize the magician's powers, the various theories ignore its genre, the Breton lay. Magic also plays a prominent role in Chaucer's other Breton lay, The Wife of Bath's Tale. No one would suggest that the transformation

[8] Luengo, "Magic and Illusion in *The Franklin's Tale*," combines the two theories by arguing that the Clerk's first performance relies on staging, the second on astronomical calculation. However, as Kolve has shown, even this combined theory cannot work; see Kolve, "Rocky Shores and Pleasure Gardens," at 174–87.

[9] On the importance of illusions in The Franklin's Tale see Bachman, "The Philosophy of Magic"; Carolyn Collette, "Seeing and Believing in the *Franklin's Tale*," *Chaucer Review* 26 (1992), 395–410; Luengo, "Magic and Illusion in *The Franklin's Tale*"; and Sandra J. McEntire, "Illusion and Interpretation in the *Franklin's Tale*," *Chaucer Review* 31 (1996), 145–63.

of the hag in that tale is actually accomplished with a wig and make-up. Attempts to apply such logic to The Franklin's Tale are just as misguided. Within the fictional universe of the Breton lay—a genre the Franklin surely in part invokes to justify the tale's magic—we must credit the Clerk with the ability to conjure illusions.[10]

It is this ability, moreover, which situates the Clerk of Orléans within the larger thematic framework of the tale. Throughout The Franklin's Tale one can perceive Chaucer's fascination with illusions and the processes whereby they are generated, particularly with the power of illusion to blur the boundary between reality and fantasy through the imagination.[11] Both Dorigen and Aurelius essentially fall victim to their over-active imaginations: Dorigen broods excessively over the rocky coastline in her "derke fantasye" (844), which leads her to make the rash promise in an unguarded moment, while Aurelius wallows in narcissistic fantasies of being in love with Dorigen (actually alluding to Narcissus in 951–52), making him pathetically eager to be deceived by the Clerk's illusion of himself dancing with Dorigen.[12] All this lends an insistently self-reflective, metafictional quality to The Franklin's Tale: illusion-making and the imagination are also the key elements in the process of creating the tale itself. As a number of critics have pointed out, Chaucer draws this connection most clearly in the Clerk of Orléans, whose role as magician resembles that of the poet, in that

---

[10] Robert Cook argues that the Clerk's illusions may even have been directly inspired by a Breton lay: "Chaucer's Franklin's Tale and *Sir Orfeo*," *Neuphilologische Mitteilungen* 95 (1994), 333–36.

[11] A theme he also explores in other tales, e.g., The Miller's Tale: "Lo, which a greet thyng is affeccioun! / Men may dyen of ymaginacioun, / So depe may impressioun be take" (3611–13).

[12] Compare the narrator's comment about Arveragus: "No thyng list hym to been ymaginatyf, / If any wight hadde spoke, whil he was oute, / To hire of love; he hadde of it no doute" (1094–96). *The Riverside Chaucer* glosses *ymaginatyf* as "suspicious," but the word retains the more concrete sense of "prone to imagining." Arveragus, in other words, maintains a firm grip over his imagination, in marked contrast to Aurelius and Dorigen.

both create illusions to stimulate the imagination.[13] It seems odd, in retrospect, that no one had made this point before Paul G. Ruggiers in 1965. After all, the affinity between artist and magician has long been a staple theme of Shakespeare scholarship, primarily because this idea features so prominently in *The Tempest*. Shakespeare, for his part, well may have used The Franklin's Tale as inspiration for the magic of *The Tempest*.[14] The connection between Prospero and the Clerk of Orléans was not fully explored, however, until Richard Hillman's study of 1983.[15] Since then, other critics have commented on the similarities.[16]

V. A. Kolve has proposed that Chaucer's inspiration for connecting poetry with magic may have been Geoffrey of Vinsauf,[17] whose *Poetria Nova* states that art "plays, as it were, the conjurer."[18] However, I think it more likely that the immediate impetus came not from the rhetorical tradition but, rather, from Chaucer's first-hand observation of entertainers who practiced both the arts of story-telling and conjuring—that is, minstrels.[19] The term *minstrel* (*mimus*, *histrio*,

---

[13] See Paul G. Ruggiers, *The Art of the Canterbury Tales* (Madison: University of Wisconsin Press, 1965), 235; Derek Traversi, "The *Franklin's Tale*," in *The Literary Imagination: Studies in Chaucer, Dante, and Shakespeare* (Newark: University of Delaware Press, 1982), 87–119, at 107; Schuman, "Man, Magician, Poet, God"; Hillman, "Chaucer's Franklin's Magician and *The Tempest*"; Kolve, "Rocky Shores and Pleasure Gardens," 187–88; and A. C. Spearing, "Introduction," in *The Franklin's Prologue and Tale*, 2nd rev. ed. (Cambridge: Cambridge University Press, 1994), 66–68.

[14] See R. Ann Thompson, "'Our Revels Now are Ended': An Allusion to *The Franklin's Tale*?" *Archiv* 212 (1975), 317; Schuman, "Man, Magician, Poet, God"; and Hillman, "Chaucer's Franklin's Magician and *The Tempest*."

[15] Hillman, "Chaucer's Franklin's Magician and *The Tempest*."

[16] See, for example, Derek Pearsall, *The Canterbury Tales* (1985; London: Routledge, 1993), 154; and Spearing, "Introduction," 66.

[17] "Rocky Shores and Pleasure Gardens," 188–89.

[18] *Poetria Nova of Geoffrey of Vinsauf*, trans. Margaret F. Nims (Toronto: Pontifical Institute of Mediaeval Studies, 1967), 20.

[19] In fairness, Kolve does note the importance of medieval minstrels to Chaucer's depiction of the Clerk of Orléans, but in a different context.

joculator, ministrellus, etc.), of course, embraces a medley of performers: poets, story-tellers, actors, musicians, acrobats, dancers, fools, jugglers, animal trainers, and conjurers.[20] A typical but unusually detailed description of the entertainment offered by medieval minstrels occurs in the *Lippiflorium* of Justinus, written in Germany in the thirteenth century:

> The meal being finished, the crowd of minstrels returns to its performance, each resuming his art in the desire to please the audience: one sings, pleasing the listeners by the sweetness of his voice, another performs songs of the deeds of heroes; one uses his art to make the lyre sound sweetly; one leaps and contorts his limbs with various motions. . . . One makes various images appear through the art of magic, and deceives the eyes through the dexterity of his hands; one shows the audience a young dog and a horse whom he commands to act like people; one throws a disk high in the air, catches it as it falls, and throws it back up.[21]

This passage neatly juxtaposes poetry ("songs of the deeds of heroes") and magic within the larger context of minstrels' arts, though it does not directly link the two.[22]

Interestingly, Chaucer himself establishes such a connection in *The House of Fame*, placing a whole host of magicians in the palace of

---

[20] John Southworth, *The English Medieval Minstrel* (Woodbridge, Suffolk: Boydell & Brewer, 1989). See esp. chap. 2, "Tota Joculatorum Scena."

[21] Hermann Althof, ed. and trans., *Das Lippiflorium: ein westfälisches Heldengedicht aus dem dreizehnten Jahrhundert* (Leipzig: Dieterich, 1900), lines 117–34. ("Facto fine cibis vaga turba recurrit ad artes, / Quisque suas repetens, inde placere volens. / Hic canit, auditum dulcedine vocis amicans, / Ille refert lyrico carmine gesta ducum, / Hic tangit digitis dinstinctas ordine chordas, / Hic facit arte sua dulce sonare lyram. / . . . / Hic salit et vario motu sua membra fatigat / . . . / Hic profert varias magica velut arte figuras, / Ac oculos fallit mobilitate manus. / Hic catulo vel equo populo spectacula praebet, / Quos jubet humanos gesticulare modos. / Hic forti gyro projectat in aera discum, / Quem lapsum recipit huncque remittit item.")

[22] Naturally, Chaucer would have been familiar with such entertainment. On the company of minstrels maintained by John of Gaunt see Southworth, *The English Medieval Minstrel*, 110–11.

Fame. Approaching the palace, the narrator notes that its outside is adorned with niches that contain statues depicting "alle maner of mynstralles / And gestiours that tellen tales / Both of wepinge and of game, / Of al that longeth unto Fame" (3.1197–1200). Among these the narrator identifies:

> . . . jugelours,
> Magiciens, and tregetours,
> And Pithonesses, charmeresses,
> Olde wicches, sorceresses,
> . . . .
> And clerkes eke, which konne wel
> Al this magik naturel,
> That craftely doon her ententes
> To make, in certeyn ascendentes,
> Ymages, lo, thrugh which magik
> To make a man ben hool or syk.
> . . . .
> Ther saugh I Colle tregetour
> Upon a table of sycamour
> Pleye an uncouth thyng to telle—
> Y saugh him carien a wynd-melle
> Under a walsh-note shale. (*HF*, 3.1259–62, 1265–70, 1277–81)

Colle tregetour and company are purveyors of artful illusion: servants of Fame, like the "gestiours that tellen tales" and even the great *auctors* gracing the pillars within the castle walls.

Upon closer examination, the passage cited above reveals a number of interesting parallels to The Franklin's Tale. *The House of Fame*, for example, mentions "clerkes . . . which konne wel / Al this magik naturel," which accurately describes the magician in The Franklin's Tale (compare especially the descriptions in lines 1118–34 and 1152–61). Both mention astrological magic, *tregetours*, and *jugelours* (FT: *jogelrye*). The trick performed by Colle tregetour—shrinking a windmill to the size of a walnut—resembles (in kind, if not magnitude) the feat ascribed to the Clerk of Orléans. Moreover, Colle tregetour can in all likelihood be identified with the "Colle T." mentioned by a contemporary French conversation manual[23] as an English magician "qui savoit faire beaucoup des mervailles par voie de nigromancie" residing at Orléans.[24] The point of these parallels is not to establish a link between the Clerk of Orléans and Colle tregetour but, rather, to suggest that the magician in The Franklin's Tale belongs to the same genus as those in *The House of Fame*. They are manipulators of perception, master illusionists whose powers have ambiguous origins but very real efficacy. Though no minstrel, the Clerk of Orléans too could be described as a performer and even story-teller, like the minstrel in the above-cited passage who "makes various images appear through the art of magic." The illusions he produces in his study for Aurelius, for example, have an obvious narrative quality; they portray a sequence of events unfolding in almost cinematic fashion.

If the Clerk of Orléans is connected to the process of narrating in an abstract, metaphorical sense—in that magical illusions can be likened to the fictions created by a poet—this is also true at a more obvious level: his illusions drive the plot forward to its conclusion. The Clerk enters the story at a moment when the potential for action has been frustrated; Aurelius has prayed in vain to his heathen gods for a way to cash in on Dorigen's promise. This promise represents a potential textual force, a force that, once unbound, will inexorably carry the narrative ahead; any reader will sense instinctively that the promise given must be put to the test—the laws of narrative demand as much, especially within the conventions of romance. We cannot imagine the story simply ending in Aurelius's inability to make the rocks disappear. When the Clerk enters the narrative, everything is poised for his performance; just as narratives in general cannot proceed without a narrator, so this particular narrative cannot proceed without the Clerk. Through his magical

---

[23] James F. Royster, "Chaucer's 'Colle Tregetour'," *Studies in Philology* 23 (1926), 380–84.

[24] Ibid., 382.

powers, the Clerk can activate the textual force bound up in Dorigen's promise, and the following events result entirely (if indirectly) from his action. Thus, The Franklin's Tale casts the Clerk in the role of the artist-magician not only because he has the power to create illusions but also because those illusions are integral to the production of the text.

Several critics have taken the connection between magician and poet a step further, suggesting that the Clerk of Orléans represents a portrait of the artist, that is, Chaucer. Samuel Schuman, for example, argues that "especially in the central scene of illusion-making in the Clerk's cell, [the tale] relates the imaginative efforts of the poem's magician character to those of the poem's creator,"[25] i.e., Chaucer. A. C. Spearing concurs, pointing out suggestive similarities between Chaucer and the Clerk of Orléans: both, for example, are at home in a book-lined study; they prosper through their skills and learning, rather than their birth; their income depends on producing fictions for aristo-crats; and the Clerk is the only character who utters a Christian phrase.[26] A more ambivalent relationship between Chaucer and the Clerk has been suggested by V. A. Kolve, who argues that Chaucer "means to define himself against [the magician], to set himself in contest with him."[27] Kolve, too, finds a suggested link between the Clerk of Orléans and Chaucer during the scene set in the book-lined study at Orléans. Yet, this moment of imaginative identification quickly gives way to a series of contrasts in which Chaucer uses the magician as a negative foil; thus Chaucer defines his role as a poet in *opposition* to that of clerk, who in the end proves to be a mercenary trafficker in deceitful images.[28] In short, where Schuman and Spearing see comparison, Kolve posits contrast. Still, all agree in linking Chaucer and the magician. A common thread running through these essays may help to explain this

---

[25] Schuman, "Man, Magician, Poet, God," 43.

[26] Spearing, "Introduction," 69.

[27] Kolve, "Rocky Shores and Pleasure Gardens," 187.

[28] Ibid.

move: all compare the Clerk of Orléans to Prospero. Since Prospero so clearly represents Shakespeare, it would be natural to posit the same connection between the Clerk and Chaucer.

But the equation Prospero: Shakespeare:: Clerk: Chaucer does not balance, for it overlooks the role of the tale's narrator.[29] Within the narrative framework established by *The Canterbury Tales*, it is the Franklin who is the Clerk's creator. Hence, if the magician has been created in the image of his maker, we ought to look to the Franklin as his model. Many details within the tale bear out this connection, and these are more obvious, more extensive, and more specific than any of the proposed parallels between the Clerk and Chaucer. Of course, the frame narrative is only a fiction of convenience; ultimately *both* Clerk *and* Franklin owe their existence to Chaucer. Still, we ought not simply to conflate narrator and author, especially as Chaucer goes to great lengths to create narrators with such vivid, distinctive personas. In re-orienting our focus upon the Franklin as story-teller, I propose that Chaucer directs the metafictional commentary implicit in the Clerk's magic not at himself but at the pilgrims of the frame narrative. (This perspective adds a further layer of complexity to the magician's illusions—as fiction within fiction embedded in still another fiction—and thereby makes the tale's conscious self-referentiality all the more evocative.) The dynamic between the Clerk of Orléans and Aurelius represents a not very subtly disguised rendering of the relationship between the Franklin and the Squire—as conceived by the Franklin, of course. Characteristic of this relationship, as becomes clear at the end of the tale, is its element of moral instruction: Aurelius learns urgently required lessons about love, *gentillesse*, and personal responsibility, and ultimately the agent of his education is none other than the Clerk of Orléans. Just so, the Franklin hopes to instruct the Squire. The subsequent discussion will lay out these correspondences, and their larger implications for The Franklin's Tale, in greater detail.

---

[29] An unconventional attempt to identify the Franklin with a character in his tale is made by Susan Crane, "The Franklin as Dorigen," *Chaucer Review* 24 (1990), 236–52.

The Franklin's Tale offers many parallels between its narrator and the Clerk of Orléans, both in specific detail and general circumstance. Both, for instance, are associated with food. The Franklin's portrait in the General Prologue devotes twenty-one of twenty-nine lines to describing his delight in various delicacies, and states that "It snewed in his hous of mete and drynke, / Of alle deyntees that men koude thynke" (345–46).[30] As he is compared with St. Julian, the patron saint of hospitality, the Franklin must be fond of sharing his bounty with guests. Both details find an echo in the scene at the Clerk's house, for the brothers "lakked no vitaille that myghte hem plese" (FT 1186) and eat a meal prepared by the magician's servant. Less certainly, the odd line with which the Clerk releases Aurelius from his debt, "Thou hast ypayed wel for my vitaille" (FT 1618), may owe something to the Franklin's preoccupation with food. None of these references has any bearing on the tale's action: from the standpoint of plot, they could just as well have been omitted. Their real function can lie only in characterization: they hint, in a minor but persistent chord, at a connection between the Clerk of Orléans and the Franklin. One could argue, to be sure, that the Franklin would naturally inject his own interests—i.e., food—into the tale,[31] but it is significant that he chooses the *Clerk* as the character onto whom he transfers his interests, rather than introducing them at random.

In connection with his love for food, the General Prologue also mentions the Franklin's tendency to scold his cook for not preparing a meal properly: "Wo was his cook but if his sauce were / Poynaunt and sharp, and redy al his geere" (351–52). Compare this with the brief exchange between the Clerk and his servant in The Franklin's Tale:

---

[30] Punctuation here follows Spearing's edition (*The Franklin's Prologue and Tale*).

[31] Helen Cooper notes that Chaucer often inserts "miniatures of the narrating pilgrims within the tales," citing the "food-conscious host" of The Franklin's Tale as one example (*The Oxford Guides to Chaucer: The Canterbury Tales*, 2nd ed. [Oxford: Oxford University Press, 1996], 225). See also Spearing, "Introduction," 69–70.

To hym this maister called his squier,
And seyde him thus: "Is redy oure soper?
Almoost an houre it is, I undertake,
Sith I yow bad oure soper for to make,
Whan that thise worthy men wenten with me
Into my studie, ther as my bookes be."
"Sire," quod this squier, "whan it liketh yow,
It is al redy, though ye wol right now."
"Go we thanne soupe," quod he. . . . (FT 1209–17)

As one might expect of the Franklin, judging by the portrait of the General Prologue, the Clerk adopts a brisk tone with his cook, and the implied accusation, "Why don't you have supper ready yet?" comes even before the cook has had a chance to explain that the meal has indeed been prepared. Like the details involving food, this dialogue serves no visible purpose in the plot—indeed, it seems out of place here—and I cannot imagine this to be anything other than a deliberate echo of the General Prologue.

The fact that he can afford to entertain his decidedly upper-class guests with "all kinds of dishes that might please them" suggests that the Clerk is remarkably well off. This is confirmed by his handsomely appointed home, "So wel arrayed" that "Aurelius in his lyf saugh nevere noon" (1187–88). This contrasts sharply with Boccaccio's description of Tebano, who remains a pauper despite his magic. The Clerk is a well-to-do, upper-middle-class professional who has prospered through the services he offers; one critic has memorably characterized him as a "businessman-magician."[32] This too suggests a link to the Franklin. In the General Prologue we are told that "an housholdere, and that a greet, was he" (339), and the catalogue of his offices—he has presided at court sessions, represented his county in Parliament, and served as sheriff and auditor—both provides an impressive resume of his career and also hints at his prosperity.

---

[32] Ruggiers, *The Art of the Canterbury Tales*, 228.

In keeping with their character as "businessmen," both Franklin and Clerk display what might be called, for lack of a better phrase, political acumen. Though he delights in the pleasures of food and drink, "Epicurus owene sone" (GP 336) is more than simply a jovial fellow. His praise of the Squire as story-teller, for example, is couched in the familiar double-speak of bureaucracy and politics (a clue as to how he has been able to attain such important offices):

> In feith, Squier, thow hast thee wel yquit
> And gentilly. I preise wel thy wit,
> . . . considerynge thy yowthe,
> So feelyngly thou spekest, sire, I allow the!
> As to my doom, ther is noon that is heere
> Of eloquence that shal be thy peere,
> If that thou lyve. . . . (SqT, 673–79).

Though apparently fulsome in its praise, the Franklin's encomium is in fact hedged with subtly deflating qualifiers: "considerynge thy yowthe," "noon . . . *shal be* thy peere" (not "*is* your peer"), "if that thou lyve." However politely they are phrased, these comments imply—as most critics would agree!—that the Squire has a lot to learn about telling a story. The Franklin's speech is a textbook example of rhetorical tact and illustrates that, for all his feigned ignorance of "rhetorik" and "colours," he has mastered the art of eloquence. Above all, the Franklin shows himself to be finely attuned to his audience, skillfully damning the Squire's tale with faint praise and attempting to draw him into a conversation about *gentillesse*. The Clerk of Orléans similarly reveals his skill in handling an audience when the brothers negotiate for his services. The vision he conjures for Aurelius—with its aristocratic pastimes of hunting, hawking, jousting, and dancing—has been carefully tailored to appeal to Aurelius's taste and imagination. Moreover, the Clerk demonstrates his business acumen by driving a hard bargain before taking on the job: "He made it straunge, and swoor, so God hym save, / Lasse than a thousand pound he wolde nat have, / Ne

gladly for that somme he wolde nat goon" (FT 1223–25). Sensing
Aurelius's desperation, he pressures him into agreeing to the absurdly
high fee of one thousand pounds. With little stretch of the imagination,
one could imagine the Franklin, in an analogous situation, acting precisely like the Clerk.

For all these similarities, the Franklin expressly rejects any similarities between himself and the magician. It is this, above all, which
seems to have kept critics from making a connection between the two.
The Franklin frequently voices his contempt for magic. He scowls at
the Clerk's "japes" and "wrecchednesse" (1271), which are appropriate
only for "hethen folk" (1293) who practice "supersticious cursednesse"
(1272), and he dismisses the whole business outright as "swich folye / As
in oure dayes is nat worth a flye" (1131–32). Yet all this simply rings
false. Whatever his claims to the contrary, the Franklin's story amply
illustrates his fascination with magic and illusion. Why, then, the efforts
to distance himself from the magician? Perhaps the Franklin senses that
he is treading on dangerous ground, and he therefore employs these
disclaimers to prevent too close an identification with the events of his
tale. The tale as a whole is studded with examples of such strategic
dissimulation. "I am a burel man," he says in the prologue to his tale
(716), and adds: "I lerned nevere rhethorik, certayn; / Thyng that I
speke, it moot be bare and pleyn" (719–20). He goes on to disavow any
knowledge of "colours," claiming never to have slept on Mount Par-
nassus or to have read Cicero (721–27). Of course this passage, with
its modesty-topoi and learned allusions, broadcasts the Franklin's
intimate familiarity with the tradition of which he feigns ignorance. In
a similar vein he later announces, "I ne kan no termes of astrologye"
(1266), but then launches into a lengthy and detailed passage describing the Clerk's "geeris" and "observaunces" (1273–93), using a
veritable flood of astrological jargon. With these examples in mind,
one can see that the Franklin's disdain for magic should not be taken
at face value. That is not to say, of course, that the Franklin dabbles in
necromancy; however, as his tale develops an elaborate metaphorical

connection between poetry and magic, he too could be considered a kind of "magician." Lest his audience take that connection too literally, the Franklin takes care to mask his fascination underneath a facade of disdain for pagan beliefs. Still, the various parallels between the Franklin and the Clerk of Orléans become obvious once we look for them, and the Franklin's disclaimers can only blur, but not obscure, the tracks.

The similarities between the Squire and Aurelius are even more readily apparent. Chaucer's habit of letting one pilgrim "quite" the next, usually by telling a story which depicts a character resembling the narrator of the previous tale, can be observed in The Franklin's Tale. To be sure, the Franklin's portrait of Aurelius lacks the caustic satire found in the "churlish" tales. As Helen Cooper notes, the Franklin's "tale contains, not a vicious parody of a professional rival on the pilgrimage, but a model image of a handsome, attractive, and accomplished squire."[33] Beyond the obvious similarities in profession and character—both are squires, young, amorous, and naive—the similar portraits of the pilgrim Squire in the General Prologue and of Aurelius in The Franklin's Tale suggest that the latter is created in the image of the former. Of the Squire we learn that:

> Syngynge he was, or floytynge, al the day;
> He was as fressh as is the month of May.
> . . . .
> He koude songes make and wel endite,
> Juste and eek daunce, and weel purtreye and write
> (GP 1. 91–92, 95–96)

Very similarly, the Franklin tells us of Aurelius that he:

> fressher was and jolyer of array,
> As to my doom, than is the month of May.
> He syngeth, daunceth, passynge any man
> That is, or was, sith that the world bigan. (FT 927–30)

---

[33] Cooper, *The Oxford Guides to Chaucer*, 241.

We can well imagine the Squire recognizing himself in the Franklin's portrait of Aurelius, for he inserts a strikingly similar self-portrait into his own tale. Alluding to the revel at the court of Cambyuskan, he states:

> Heere is the revel and the jolitee
> That is nat able a dul man to devyse.
> He moste han knowen love and his servyse
> And been a feestlych man as fressh as May,
> That sholde yow devysen swich array. (SqT 278–82)

From the description in the General Prologue we already know that the Squire is the right man for the job: he is both acquainted with love[34] and "fressh as May." Helen Cooper cautions that the similarities among the three portraits "may all simply reflect a formulaic repetition of qualities" typically ascribed to young squires as a class.[35] That may be so, but neither Palamon nor Arcite, nor any other analogue to the Squire except Aurelius, is ever called "fressh as May." Even if it is a formulaic phrase, it nevertheless links the two characters along generic lines. If nothing else, the appearance of a "generic" squire in a story that immediately follows a tale told by another "generic" squire surely begs for comparison between the two.

Having illuminated the connection between the Franklin and the Clerk of Orléans, as well as between the Squire and Aurelius, we can gain a better appreciation of the dynamic between the characters in the tale by reading it against the frame narrative. In doing so I would like to begin by returning to the series of illusions in the magician's study. The Clerk of Orléans shows Aurelius "forestes, parkes ful of wilde deer," and a hunt (1190–95); falconers who have slain a heron with their hawks (1196–97); and knights jousting on a plain (1198). Then comes the final, and crucial, touch:

---

[34] The other pilgrims, too, are aware of his "expertise" in matters of love. The Host requests, "Squier, com neer, if it youre wille be / And sey somwhat of love, for certes ye / Konnen theron as muche as any man" (SqT 1–3).

[35] Cooper, *Oxford Guides to Chaucer*, 225.

> And after this he dide hym swich plesaunce
> That he hym shewed his lady on a daunce,
> On which hymself he daunced, as hym thoughte.
> And whan this maister that this magyk wroughte
> Saugh it was tyme, he clapte his handes two,
> And farewel! Al oure revel was ago. (1199–1204)

Everything in this description reveals that the magician is very much master of the scene. Progressively drawing Aurelius into the spectacle, he saves the most alluring image for last, having undermined the squire's defenses in preparation for the final blow. Even the casual clapping of the hands seems calculated to impress Aurelius, who at this point must already be overawed. As a result, Aurelius agrees to pay an outrageous sum for the Clerk's services. Some critics have argued that this scene shows the magician in the worst possible light, cynically manipulating the naive squire for the sake of his personal profit.[36] Yet, in the end, the Clerk of Orléans agrees to let Aurelius renege on their bargain, an act of generosity certainly not consistent with such a reading. To put the show of illusions and the agreement into proper perspective, one must consider their larger function within the tale. In effect, the whole scene constitutes a second "rash promise": in a weak moment—brought on by a state of heightened imagination—Aurelius foolishly commits himself to a bargain that will ruin him, eventually forcing him to throw himself on the mercy of another. Aurelius thus experiences a predicament exactly parallel to Dorigen's and, so, becomes fully aware of the injustice he has very nearly perpetrated. Only by putting himself into the magician's power, then, can Aurelius ultimately redeem himself

---

[36] Kolve finds that this final illusion "marks the end of Chaucer's sympathy" with the magician, signaling "a rupture in his imaginative identification with an allied art." From this point on "things swiftly take a sinister turn as the magician/clerk transforms himself into a shrewd business man, demanding a ruinous price for making the rocks seem to disappear, and shortly after moves into something worse, a set of calculations and operations apparently competent to alter something fundamental in the created world" ("Rocky Shores and Pleasure Gardens," 189).

through an act of selflessness, and experience the generosity of others. The magician, in turn, reveals himself to be neither sinister nor selfish. Indeed, it is one of the tale's many paradoxes that Aurelius's dangerous fantasies about Dorigen are dispelled by an illusion. The show of illusions in the Clerk's study has a dual function: it indulges Aurelius's fantasy by showing him the images he wants to see, but it also creates the necessary conditions for his dis-illusioning. In a sense, the Clerk's illusions make him an agent in Aurelius's edification. Exactly the same can be said of the Franklin's relationship to the Squire. It has already been pointed out that the show of illusions creates obvious parallels between "magic" and "poetry" as arts that rely on illusion, but the tale asks us to take this metaphor one step further. Just as the Clerk of Orléans creates illusory images for Aurelius, so the Franklin creates his fiction largely for the benefit of the Squire. Moreover, both the Franklin and his mirror image, the magician, carefully tailor their illusions to the expectations and desires of their audience. Knowing that Aurelius wishes to win Dorigen, the Clerk creates an image of Aurelius dancing with her; likewise, the Franklin plays on the Squire's fascination with love, *gentillesse*, magic, and the genre of romance by telling a tale that brilliantly fuses all these elements, and of course he too shows the Squire an image of himself (Aurelius).

The Franklin's motive for doing this can be perceived from both the prologue to his tale and the function of his double within it. His intent is didactic. Of course we should not reduce the tale to a sermon, but it nevertheless contains pointed instruction on a number of issues clearly relevant to the Squire. Perhaps the most obvious of these concerns the dangers of selfish love. At each step of the way, Aurelius's infatuation with Dorigen enacts all the clichés of the courtly lover pining for the love of a lady. Although he takes himself and his persona as lover very seriously, Aurelius behaves like an actor following the wrong script, perversely determined to pull Dorigen into the same— rather tiresome—plot. Courtly love, Act II: "Now you're supposed to 'take pity' on me," one can almost hear Aurelius say. The problem, of course, is that Dorigen refuses to assume the role in which Aurelius persistently tries to cast her. When he uses her rash promise to very nearly coerce her into the role anyway, he causes nothing but anguish and misery. Only when he ceases to be obsessed with his feelings and pauses to consider those of Dorigen (and her husband)—not the feelings he projects onto her in accordance with the conventions of courtly love, but the feelings of the real, suffering Dorigen standing before him—does Aurelius himself cease to resemble a walking cliché and evolve into a character to be taken seriously. There is, of course, a lesson here for the pilgrim Squire, who throughout both the frame narrative and his own tale is associated with the same conventional attitudes about love that the Franklin critiques through the figure of Aurelius.

What redeems Aurelius in the end is *gentillesse*, the very quality that the Franklin so admires in the Squire. Much has been written about the question of *gentillesse* in The Franklin's Tale, and this is not the proper place to rehash the debate. Nevertheless, as the issue bears materially on the relationship between the frame narrative and The Franklin's Tale, some brief remarks are in order. As becomes clear from his tale, and as might be expected of him because of his station, the Squire espouses the older, aristocratic view of *gentillesse*, i.e., "virtue is commensurate with class": churls act "churlishly," while nobles behave—how else?—"nobly."[37] By contrast, the Franklin advocates *gentillesse* of character. Indeed, this might be said to be the "moral" of The Franklin's Tale, as summarized up in the tale's conclusion by the Clerk of Orléans:

---

[37] In The Squire's Tale, every character associated with *gentillesse* is also of aristocratic birth. The Squire explicitly mentions "gentillesse of blood" in line 620, an idea referred to also in line 622. Conversely, the Squire's dismissive attitude toward commoners emerges in his portrait of the crowd gaping at the magic objects: "Of sondry doutes thus they jangle and trete, / As lewed peple demeth comunly / Of thynges that been maad moore subtilly / Than they kan in hir lewednesse comprehende; / They demen gladly to the badder ende" (220–24).

Leeve brother,
Everich of yow dide gentilly til oother.
Thou art a squier, and he is a knyght;
But God forbede, for his blisful myght,
But if a clerk koude doon a gentil dede
As wel as any of yow, it is no drede! (1607–12)

This is just the kind of attitude we would expect from the Franklin. A chain of reciprocal *gentillesse* stretches from knight to squire to clerk, creating a bond between the characters that nullifies the usual barriers of social stratification; hierarchy gives way to equality (as in the marriage between Dorigen and Arveragus).

One should note, too, that the mechanism for achieving equality— money—is appropriate for the Franklin. Money buys the services of the Clerk of Orléans, which ultimately allows both Arveragus and Aurelius to display their *gentillesse*, and, more importantly, money puts Aurelius into the Clerk's power, which enables the Clerk to rival their display of "nobility." Critics have often balked at the tale's happy end, with the Clerk canceling Aurelius's debt and riding off into the sunset. Yet the Franklin has prepared us for this in advance. We know that he is wealthy; his description in the General Prologue includes, as its final and most vivid image, a purse "al of silk . . . whit as morne milk" (357–58) dangling from his belt—an iconographic detail as suggestive, in its way, as the Prioress's gold brooch. Yet he insists, in his words at the end of The Squire's Tale, that wealth must go hand in hand with virtue: "Fy on possessioun, / But if a man be vertuous withal!" (686–87). Even more telling is his criticism of his own son: I would give twenty pounds' worth of land, he says, to see my son acquire the same discrecioun as the Squire, but the son refuses to "commune with any gentil wight / Where he myghte lerne gentilesse aright" (683–85, 693–94). This illuminates the Clerk's behavior at the end of The Franklin's Tale, for his gesture of generosity also follows a display of *gentillesse*. In a unsympathetic reading, this might be said to illustrate "gentility of the pocketbook" more than "gentility of character," and to represent a self-interested attempt to redefine social hierarchy along economic lines, rather than a plea for equality. Whatever his motives, however, the Franklin clearly poses his definition of "nobility" against the more conventional one, and his reason for doing so represents another lesson for the young Squire: aristocrats have no monopoly on *gentillesse*.[38]

A third and final point on which the Franklin seeks to instruct the Squire—and one which further contributes to the insistently metafictional character of the tale—concerns a more practical issue: how to tell a story. His remarks to the Squire (discussed above) imply that the Franklin thinks he can do better. And so, of course, he can. He takes the Squire's loose, baggy monster of an interlaced romance, abstracts from it the themes of magic, illusion, love, and *gentillesse*, weaves these elements into a tightly structured Breton lay, and lends the narrative a philosophical depth entirely lacking in The Squire's Tale.[39] While this has been interpreted as a compliment to the Squire,[40] it is, like the Franklin's other compliments, not without implied criticism. He would scarcely have undertaken to transform the Squire's narrative if he had not been confident of improving upon the previous product and, in the process, teaching the young poet a thing or two about story-telling.

The various parallels between tale and frame narrative outlined above represent a particularly clear instance of the well-known "dramatic principle" of *The Canterbury Tales*, which posits a systematic correspondence between the tales and their narrators. First proposed by

---

[38] This naturally raises the vexed question of the Franklin's own social status. Unfortunately, historical data have here proven inconclusive. It seems safest, therefore, to look to the poem itself for evidence. Whether or not the Franklin has a historically legitimate claim to *gentil* status, the text places him in a different category from the other *gentils*. The Franklin travels in the company of the Sergeant of Law, not with the Knight and the Squire. Likewise, the Host's disrespectful behavior towards the Franklin stands in obvious contrast to the deference shown to the latter.

[39] See Cooper, *The Oxford Guides to Chaucer*, 227 and 241.

[40] See, for example, Marie Neville, "The Function of the *Squire's Tale* in the Canterbury Scheme," *Journal of English and Germanic Philology* 50 (1951), 167–79, at 179.

George L. Kittredge and most extensively developed by Robert M. Lumiansky,[41] the dramatic principle has been and continues to be one of the most productive critical approaches to *The Canterbury Tales*. Its validity has not, however, gone unchallenged. Objections have focused chiefly on two points: that the correspondences between tale and teller frequently do not amount to much, existing more in the imagination of the critic than in the text; and that overzealous application of the principle has led to an undue proliferation of ironic interpretations, particularly of tales whose ideology or narrative mode are not in line with modern critical sympathy (such as The Prioress's Tale and The Squire's Tale).[42] To be sure, there is truth in these charges. The dramatic principle has been invoked to justify wildly improbable readings, and clearly it can be applied more profitably to some tales than to others. Yet, in concluding this essay, I would like to show that this criticism does not apply to The Franklin's Tale.

Having outlined the correspondences between tale and teller in the previous pages, there is no need to answer the first objection in detail. The parallels really *do* exist, and they are so precise and so obvious that they cannot be said merely to reside in the fancy of the critic.[43] As for the proliferation of ironic readings of The Franklin's Tale, the problem concerns not so much the *presence* of irony—for practically no pilgrim or tale entirely escapes ironic commentary—as its *degree*. Certainly Chaucer plants clues to weaknesses in the Franklin's character: he is too preoccupied with food; too concerned with social status; and too patronizing toward the Squire. It does not follow, though, that one

---

[41] George L. Kittredge, *Chaucer and His Poetry* (Cambridge: Harvard University Press, 1915); Robert M. Lumiansky, *Of Sondry Folk: The Dramatic Principle in the "Canterbury Tales"* (Austin: University of Texas Press, 1955).

[42] See Pearsall, *The Canterbury Tales*, 40–45; and Spearing, "Introduction," 68–76.

[43] Even Pearsall, who mounts a very detailed and largely convincing attack against the dramatic principle, allows that The Franklin's Tale, at least, represents an obvious case where "the dramatic 'colouring' is quite strong and has a part in the interpretation of the tale as tale" (*The Canterbury Tales*, 44).

ought to dismiss The Franklin's Tale as the fantasies of a gluttonous, patriarchal social climber. A more balanced assessment would be that the Franklin has flaws but is not portrayed as a malicious or particularly hypocritical character (such as the Pardoner). His flaws are human and not difficult to sympathize with. After all, even fathers who are *not* social climbers tend to worry about how their sons will get on in the world. To this extent, a dramatic reading of The Franklin's Tale need not imply an ironic reading at all, and mine is not.

One final point deserves to be made. It is fitting that the dramatic principle should be so strongly developed in a tale that itself meditates on the nature of poetic fiction. Its most enigmatic character, the magician-poet-clerk of Orléans, represents not only a product of the dramatic principle but also, at the same time, a metaphorical gloss on the poetic fiction that lends him—and, for that matter, all the dramatis personae of *The Canterbury Tales*—the illusion of reality.

PORTENTOUS BIRTHS
AND THE MONSTROUS IMAGINATION
IN RENAISSANCE CULTURE

NORMAN R. SMITH

RENAISSANCE LITERATURE in every language is filled with monsters, and their study tells us much about the Renaissance mind, about shifts from medieval to modern perspectives, about theology and science, and about changes in the flow of information that took place in the sixteenth century. In the Middle Ages, monsters were strange races in Ethiopia and India. Though there is some discussion of monstrous births close at hand, medieval writers generally repeated the familiar stories from Pliny and Solinus of strange races from far away. The monstrous races still are found in Renaissance geographies and histories, but the Renaissance was less interested in the far-off monstrous races of Africa and Asia than in the monsters they could see about them—anomalous births, strange events, occurrences contrary to nature.

The portentous monster dates back at least to Babylonian-Assyrian cuneiform tablets of 2000 B.C., but more important to the Renaissance are ideas that evolved in Greece and Rome.[1] From Greece came the idea that entire races of monstrous human beings live in remote regions

---

[1] Morris Jastrow, "Babylonian-Assyrian Birth Omens and Their Cultural Significance," *Religionsgeschichtliche Versuche und Vorarbeiten* 14 (1914), 29.

of the earth. Herodotus and Ktesias of Knidos, for example, catalog the dog-headed *cynocephali* of Libya, the headless *blemmyae* whose eyes and mouths were in their chests, and the one-footed sciapods of India who hold their single giant foot umbrella-fashion above their heads when the sun is hot (fig. 1).[2]

Most Roman discussions of the monstrous deal with the darker side of the subject. For Livy, Rome had fallen on dark days of impiety and disregard of the gods; he recorded the frightening monsters and portents of Roman history to show the divine involvement in human affairs (*Historia* 43.13.1–3).

Livy inspired the shadowy late classical figure Julius Obsequens to write an entire work on the subject of Roman portents. Julius's *Prodigiorum Liber* ultimately was printed at the Aldine Press in 1508, and it became very popular in the monster-obsessed Renaissance. Only Cicero, in his *De Divinatione*, refused to believe that monsters and portents were messages from the gods or that they were valid indications of future occurrences.

Cicero borrowed his ideas from Aristotle, who discussed the monster in the *Generation of Animals* in a very scientific way. A monster, he wrote, "belongs to the class of 'things contrary to Nature'," the natural being for Aristotle simply that which usually happens.[3] But Aristotle went on to say that nothing really is contrary to nature in its entirety, but only to nature in "the generality of cases. So far as concerns the Nature which is always and is by necessity, nothing occurs contrary to that."[4] The monster, then, though it differs from the normal, nevertheless conforms to natural and understandable laws.

---

[2] *Ancient India as Described by Ktesias the Knidian*, ed. and trans. John W. McCrindle (London: Trubner, 1882).

[3] *Generation of Animals*, trans. A. L. Peck, (Cambridge, Mass.: Harvard University Press, 1979), 4.4.770b, lines 9–10: "ἔστι γὰρ τὸ τέρας τῶν παρὰ φύσιν."

[4] Ibid., 4.4.770b, lines 10–12: "παρὰ φύσιν δ᾽ οὐ πᾶσαν ἀλλὰ τὴν ὡς ἐπὶ τὸ πολύ· περὶ γὰρ τὴν ἀεὶ καὶ τὴν ἐξ ἀνάγκης οὐθὲν γίνεται παρὰ φύσιν·."

Figure 1. African and Indian Monsters. From Sebastian Munster, *Cosmographiae Universalis* (Basel, 1550), 1151. Courtesy of the Rare Book and Special Collections Library, University of Illinois at Urbana-Champaign.

St. Augustine established a definitive Christian doctrine of the monstrous that was to remain influential for over a thousand years. Augustine vigorously attacked Aristotle's teratological rationalism— indeed, he attacked the whole of Aristotelian thought with regard to the ability of God to interfere with the normal order of things. "The freakish births of animals," Augustine wrote, are "portentous events."[5] They occur because "God, Who made the visible heaven and earth, does not disdain to work visible miracles on heaven and earth, whereby He may quicken the soul, hitherto given up to visible things, To worship Him,

---

[5] "ea . . . monstrosa contingunt, queles sunt inusitati partus animalium (*Civ. Dei* 10.16). I have used George E. McCracken's translation, *City of God*, 7 vols. (Cambridge: Harvard University Press, 1957–72).

the *Invisible*."[6] Augustine's God is not constrained, like Aristotle's, to obey the laws of nature: "He is assuredly called almighty for no other reason except that He can do whatever He wishes."[7]

Augustine stopped short of suggesting that the future can be divined by the interpretation of monstrous births. In fact, he held that predicting the future involves trafficking with demons. But his warning seems to have had little effect on subsequent thinkers. Surely, if God bothers to overturn nature in order to cause these creatures, then monsters must be indications of future events—thus reasoned, for example, Isidore of Seville and Rabanus Maurus.[8]

Despite the scientific advances of the time, Renaissance teratologists were closer in spirit to Rome than to Greece, closer to Augustine than to Aristotle. Perhaps the earliest Renaissance teratological treatise is the 1503 manuscript *De signis, portentis, atque prodigiis* of Jakob Mennel, a court scholar for the Emperor Maximilian, whose chief claim to fame is that he traced the line of Habsburg to Hector of Troy.[9] Mennel chronicles extraordinary events from the time of the birth of Christ to the turn of the sixteenth century. As well as monstrous creatures such as four-footed babies and *cynocephali*, there are incidents of blood and stones raining from heaven, earthquakes, plagues of locusts, and crosses and other designs appearing on the bodies of the citizenry.

The Alsatian humanist Konradus Lykosthenes was a lecturer on grammar and dialectics at Basel and an editor of the book of Roman

---

[6] "Quapropter Deus, quifecit visibilia caelum et terram, non dedignatur facere visibilia miracula in caelo vel terra, quibus ad se invisibilem colendum excitet animam adhuc visibilibus deditam" (*Civ. Dei* 10.12; McCracken 3:308–09).

[7] "Qui certe non ob aliud vocatur omnipotens nisi quoniam quidquid vult post" (*Civ. Dei* 21.7; McCracken 7:42–43).

[8] Isidore of Seville, *Etymologiarum sive originum*, ed. W. M. Lindsay, 2 vols. (Oxford: Clarendon, 1911), 2:3; Rabanus Maurus, *De Universo*, in *Opera Omnia, Patrologia Latina cursus completus,* ed. J.-P. Migne, vols. 107–12 (Paris, 1851), book 7.

[9] Jakob Mennel, *De signis, portentis atque prodigiis*, Vienna, Österreichische National-bibliothek cod. 4417.

prodigies compiled by Julius Obsequens. Lykosthenes has an even more impressive repertoire of oddities in the largest, most profusely illustrated, and strangest of the teratological works, his *Prodigiorum ac ostentorum chronicon* (figs. 2 and 3).[10] He starts, in world-chronicler fashion, from the creation. The first prodigy is the temptation of Eve by Satan in the form of a monstrous serpent. The rainbow of Noah is a prodigy, as is the birth of the two-faced god Janus at about the same time. He includes the Plinian monsters, created at the time of Babel; the egg-laying woman of Selenetida; and a host of apparently normal animals, such as elephants, rhinos, and camels, which struck Lykosthenes as monstrous. Lykosthenes, of course, catalogs these examples from earlier works. The egg-laying woman is typical—Lykosthenes cites Herodotus and the great Renaissance cataloger Ravisius Textor.

Like Aristotle, the Renaissance teratologists believed that monsters are not purely accidental. "Nihil sine causa" is an idea repeated throughout their works. But they attach a deeper significance to "nothing without cause" than did Aristotle. "God and nature do nothing vainly," writes Mennel.[11] Lykosthenes notes that the wisest physicians have offered natural reasons for monsters: "We don't condemn natural reasons, but we know nature to be the minister of God."[12] Lykosthenes goes on to say that monsters are signs of the ire and the curse of God. In short, the monster is not a meaningless accident of conception; it is a being created for a specific purpose by God. A monster is a sign, a portent, and indeed the very word *monster* comes from the verb *monstrare*, 'to show.'

The monster also can be the sign of future events. Don Cameron Allen has noted that all men want to know the future, but "in the sixteenth century this yearning seems to have been stronger than in the Middle Ages," because, perhaps, of growing scepticism about Christian

---

[10] Konradus Lykosthenes, *Prodigiorum ac ostentorum chronicon* (Basel, 1557).

[11] Mennel, *De signis*, fol. 1v: "Deus et natura nichil frustra faciant."

[12] Lykosthenes, *Prodigiorum*, iii: "Non condemnamus naturales rationes . . . sed scimus naturem . . . Dei ministris esse. . . ."

Figure 2. Swords fall from heaven, a cow speaks, and an elephant-headed boy is born. From Konradus Lykosthenes, *Prodigiorum ac ostentorum chronicon* (Basel, 1557), 125. Courtesy of the Rare Book and Special Collections Library, University of Illinois at Urbana-Champaign.

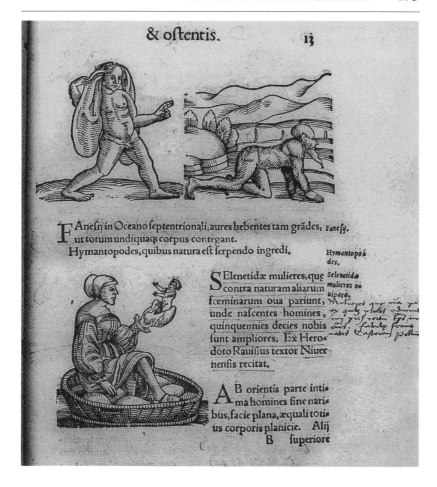

Figure 3. A giant-eared panotus, King Nebuchadnezzar, and the egg-laying woman of Selenetida. From Konradus Lykosthenes, *Prodigiorum ac ostentorum chronicon* (Basel, 1557), 13. Courtesy of the Rare Book and Special Collections Library, University of Illinois at Urbana-Champaign.

Figure 4. Elephant-, dog-, and calf-headed monsters. From Friedrich Nausea, *Friedrici Nauseae . . . Libri Mirabilium Septem* (Cologne, 1532), fol. 25r. Courtesy of the Rare Book and Special Collections Library, University of Illinois at Urbana-Champaign.

doctrine, as well as the uncertainties and misfortunes of sixteenth-century life.[13]

This is a complicated subject. The Church frowned upon judicial astrology and all forms of augury. It was not humanity's business to attempt to know that which only God could know. But the possibility of having some notion of what was fated to happen seems to have been so attractive for our teratologists that they continually toyed with the idea of knowing the future, no matter how well they might have known Church doctrine. In 1532, the theologian of Wurtemburg and eventual Bishop of Vienna, Friedrich Nausea, wrote a book on monsters and miracles called *Libri Mirabilium Septem* (fig. 4).[14] Nausea quotes Moses's command, "non augurabimini" [thou shalt not use augury; Deut. 18:10] but goes on to say that there is a difference between actively seeking a sign and merely interpreting those that come along.

---

[13] Don Cameron Allen, *The Star-Crossed Renaissance: The Quarrel about Astrology and its Influence in England* (Durham: Duke University Press, 1941; New York: Octagon, 1966), 47.

[14] Friedrich Nausea, *Friedrici Nauseae . . . Libri Mirabilium Septem* (Cologne, 1532).

Nausea attacks "insane magicians, furious necromancers, lying and deceitful astrologers, trifling geomancers, demented palm-readers . . . who predict without law or legitimacy, and without divine right."[15] Yet he suggests that the good Christian may predict future events from monsters and other prodigies, in much the same way that doctors, sailors, and farmers predict what will happen to the patient, the sea, or the crops.

Let us look at some Renaissance monsters and their meaning. In 1496 came the discovery of one of the most popular and interesting of the monsters, the reformer Melanchthon's Pabstesel, or Popeass, of Rome (fig. 5).[16] The monster had been cast up on the banks of the Tiber after a flood—not an unusual event, apparently, perhaps because of some vestige of the Roman law that required monsters to be drowned or, more probably, because the horrified farmer who found such a thing born in his barn would toss it in the river if there was one near at hand. The monster was apparently an ass with deformations that made it appear partially human. The description of the monster was transformed marvelously as its story was spread by means of broadsides. In fact, it became so popular that the brothers Tommaso and Jacopo Rodari carved a likeness of the monster in a relief in the cathedral at Como. By 1523, this representation had become known to Melanchthon and Luther. In 1523, another monster was also on everyone's mind, a calf born at Freiberg with a cowl-like growth that made it resemble a monk (fig. 6). The two reformers decided to use the two monsters in an antipapist pamphlet. Melanchthon chose the *papstesel* and Luther the *munchkalb*, and each used his monster as a means of attacking the Roman Church.

---

[15] From the dedicatory letter prefixed to Nausea's *Libri Mirabilium Septem*: ". . . magos insanientes, necromanticos furientes, astrologos fabulantes & decipientes, geomanticos nugantes, chiromanticos delirantes, . . . quum tamen recte nec legitime praenoscant."

[16] The texts of Melanchthon's and Luther's broadsides on the Pope-Ass of Rome and the Monk-Calf of Freiburg can be found in vol. 11 of *D. Martin Luthers Werke: Kritische Gesammtausgabe* (Weimar: H. Böhlaus, 1883–1900), 375–85. Lykosthenes includes both monsters in his *Prodigiorum* (505, 529).

Figure 5. The Pope-Ass of Rome. Lucas Cranach the Elder, woodcut illustration for Martin Luther and Philipp Melanchthon, *Deuttung der czwo
grewlichen Figuren, Bapstesels czu Rom und Munchkalbs zu Freijberg
ijnn Meijsszen funden* (Wittenberg, 1523). From Martin Luther, *D. Martin
Luthers Werke: Kritische Gesammtausgabe* (Weimar: H. Böhlaus,
1883–1900), vol. 11, 371. Courtesy of the Rare Book and Special Collections Library, University of Illinois at Urbana-Champaign.

Figure 6. The Monk-Calf of Freiburg. Lucas Cranach the Elder, woodcut illustration for Martin Luther and Philipp Melanchthon, *Deuttung der czwo grewlichen Figuren, Bapstesels czu Rom und Munchkalbs zu Freijberg ijnn Meijsszen funden* (Wittenberg, 1523). From Martin Luther, *D. Martin Luthers Werke: Kritische Gesammtausgabe* (Weimar: H. Böhlaus, 1883–1900), vol. 11, 373. Courtesy of the Rare Book and Special Collections Library, University of Illinois at Urbana-Champaign.

Melanchthon's *papstesel* is a truly hybrid monstrosity. The torso is that of a woman covered with scales. Although she has the head of an ass, the head of an old man peers out of her back, and she has a tail with the head of a dragon on the end of it. She has one human hand, while the other arm ends in an elephant's foot. One of her feet is the claw of a griffin; the other is the hoof of an ox. What did all this mean? John Barthlet translates Melanchthon in his antipapist tract, *The Pedegrewe of Heretiques* (London 1566): "It can not but be confessed, that it doth appertayne both onley to Rome, and also signifieth a body politique, risen in that cuntrey, to a marvellous and most horrible confusenesse."[17] The head, he concludes, is a magistrate or sovereign and, therefore, the pope, for "Nature teacheth us, that out of an Asses hed, there procedeth but Asselike instruction (that is) doctrine worldly, carnall, foolish, slouthful, wanton, and gentyle" (86r). The scales are the pope's friends and allies in the world, who defend him as scales defend the fish. The anatomical exegesis continues until, finally, Barthlet tells the reader not to fear; the monster was found dead, "and therefore must signifie an ende, conquest, and full deliverie of this worlde, and Gods sainctes therefro" (89r).

The emblematic treatment of the popeass is very similar to descriptions of another popular sixteenth-century monster, the monster of Ravenna. Shortly before Pope Julius II fought the French atRavenna in 1512, a hideous monster was born. The creature, we are told by Joannes Multivallis, had wings instead of arms, one huge bird's leg with an eye peering out of the knee, a horn in the middle of its forehead, the organs of both sexes, and the symbol of the cross and the letter upsilon upon its chest (fig. 7).[18] Multivallis interprets these characteristics in emblematic fashion: the horn is pride; the wings are

---

[17] John Barthlet, *The Pedegrewe of Heretiques* (1566; Amsterdam: Theatrum Orbis Terrarum, 1969), fol. 85v.

[18] Joannes Multivallis, *Eusebii Cesariensis Episcopi Chronicon* (Paris, 1512), fol. 175r. Lykosthenes borrows this description for his *Prodigiorum* as well (517).

Figure 7. The Ravenna Monster. From Konradus Lykosthenes, *Prodigiorum ac ostentorum chronicon* (Basel, 1557), 517. Courtesy of the Rare Book and Special Collections Library, University of Illinois at Urbana-Champaign.

lightness and inconstancy of mind; the lack of arms is the lack of good works; the eye in the knee is blindness to any reality but the earthly; the presence of both sexes is sodomy. For these vices, he concludes, Italy now is shaken by war. But the upsilon and the cross are healthy signs: they suggest that if the Italians return to the worship of Christ, they can be saved.

The Renaissance, like the Middle Ages, was fascinated by the occult, the secret reality hidden by a deceptive veil. This fascination gave rise to two very important sorts of books: the book of hieroglyphics in the fifteenth century, and the book of emblems in the sixteenth century. Each was a collection of enigmatic pictures that were given some sort of moral interpretation by the text.[19]

---

[19] See *The Hieroglyphics of Horapollo*, trans. George Boas (New York: Pantheon, 1950); and Edgar Wind, *Pagan Mysteries in the Renaissance* (New Haven: Yale University Press, 1958).

It is no accident that Maximilian, the patron of Jakob Mennel, also was passionately interested in hieroglyphics, for the interests are related. One of the most remarkable aspects of Renaissance monster lore is the pictorial representation of the monster, and the text of a monster book is often an emblematic interpretation of the picture. A glance through some hieroglyphic books reveals their similarities to the monster book. Giambattista Porta's *De humana physiognomonia*, for example, is influenced by the *Hieroglyphics* of Horapollo and the *Hieroglyphica* of Pierio Valeriano, and in it we find an ass-headed man (fig. 8).[20] He is not as sinister as the *papstesel* and merely is intended to represent the asinine fellows who never travel and thus learn nothing of the world. One can see, though, how similar are the teratological and the hieroglyphic ideas of what the bestial means when it is joined to the human.

It is just as important to view the popularity of monsters in the Renaissance in the context of the development of communications media in the period. In many ways, the Renaissance was a period of progress in technology and scholarship, a development of the critical spirit, at least in fields such as anatomy, archaeology, historiography, and text analysis. It certainly was a period of breakthroughs in communications technology, in the form of the invention of the printing press and the dissemination of cheap printed material. But Renaissance teratology, with few exceptions, does not show evidence of progress in any of these areas; indeed, it represents an extension of ideas present in the Middle Ages. The essence of Renaissance monster lore may be what Marshall McLuhan called "the hypertrophy of the unconscious," a phenomenon he associated with periods of revolution in media technology.[21] The advent of print in the sixteenth century created a great need for sensational materials to be broadcast, and this need caused ideas that formerly had been lurking only in the dark recesses

---

[20] Giambattista Porta, *De humana physiognomonia* (Hanover, 1593), 179.

[21] Marshall McLuhan, *The Gutenberg Galaxy* (Toronto: University of Toronto Press, 1962; New York: New American Library, 1969), 304.

Figure 8. The Ass-Headed Man. From Giambattista Porta, *De humana physiognomonia* (Hanover, 1593), 179. Courtesy of the Rare Book and Special Collections Library, University of Illinois at Urbana-Champaign.

of men's minds to come floating to the surface. These ideas, McLuhan argues, often seem as though they would have been more appropriate in earlier, more superstitious eras.

That such ideas are very much a part of the popular culture of the Renaissance is seen from the sheer output of teratological material. For example, the forerunner of the modern newspaper, the broadside, is largely devoted to reporting and interpreting the contemporary monstrous births. Often luridly illustrated and sensationally written, they were bought on street corners and at fairs by the barely literate masses.[22]

---

[22] See Hans Fehr, *Massenkunst im 16. Jahrhundert: Flugblätter aus der Sammlung Wickiana* (Berlin: H. Stubenrauch, 1924); and Jean-Pierre Seguin, *L'information en France avant le periodique; 517 canards imprimès entre 1529 et 1631* (Paris: Éditions G. P. Maisonneuve et Larose, 1964).

Renaissance publishing offers other examples. One of the great best-sellers of the sixteenth century was the *Histoires Prodigieuses* of Pierre Boaistuau, a sort of Renaissance Ripley's Believe-It-Or-Not containing marvelous tales on everything from the man who washed his hands in molten lead to the miraculous properties of gemstones.[23] Seventeen of the *Histoires'* forty tales are about monsters, a fact which may explain why the book was republished dozens of times, in Dutch, Spanish, and English, as well as French.

The *Histoires Prodigieuses* is a fascinating bridge between the modern and the quaint. The book, bound with additional chapters by Francois de Belleforest and Claude de Tesserant, was owned by that most modern of sixteenth-century writers, Montaigne. In his skeptical essay "Of Cripples," Montaigne mentions Belleforest's tale of the im-poster Arnaud du Tielh, who trades on his resemblance to Martin Guerre in order to take over Guerre's wife and estate. It is a theme still inter-esting enough in the late twentieth century to have been turned into two movies.[24] Montaigne was horrified by the court's death sentence for the fraud—better the court should have declared the matter beyond its understanding—a thought that forms the theme of the essay. Because humans are ignorant and error-prone, their explanations of the apparent marvels and monstrosities lead to bigotry and superstition. Indeed, there is little in the world more monstrous than our own minds. "I have seen," writes Montaigne, using himself as a synechdoche for humanity, "no more evident monstrosity and miracle in the world than myself."[25]

Montaigne immediately would recognize the late twentieth-century American landscape. As for Boaistuau, he would be hypertrophying the

---

[23] Boaistuau, Pierre, *Histoires prodigieuses et memorables, extraictes de plusieurs fameux autheurs, grecs, & Latins, sacrez et prophanes, divisees en six livres . . .* (Paris: Gabriel Buon, 1598).

[24] *Le Retour de Martin Guerre*, dir. Daniel Vigne (Fox Lorber, 1984); and *Sommersby*, dir. Jon Amiel (Warner Studios, 1993).

[25] Michael de Montaigne, *Essays* 3.11, in *The Complete Essays of Montaigne*, trans. Donald M. Frame (Stanford: Stanford University Press, 1965).

unconscious on daytime talk television. The man who wrote a chapter asking "Si les diables peuvent concepvoir" would have no trouble joining Geraldo Rivera to discuss muscular people who used to be scrawny confronting old friends or to interview the man "whose life was better in jail." In the last analysis, the monstrous is about the bizarre, and it has never gone out of style.

THE NUDE CYCLOPS
IN THE COSTUME BOOK

MARY BAINE CAMPBELL

I FIRST FOUND THIS PICTURE (fig. 1) on page 44 of a late sixteenth-century costume book, *Omnium fere gentium, nostraeque aetatis Nationum, Habitus et Effigies* (or *Recueil de la diversité des habits . . .*), on the page after "Compostella mulier" (the woman from Compestella), and, as it turned out a couple of dumbstruck minutes later, the page before "De lubecus" (the man from Lubeck).[1] My mind, long accustomed though it is through my particular research interests to pictorial representations of monsters and freaks, was boggled. I have since that time tried the picture out on a fairly wide variety of others: all have gasped or laughed before they could speak. (The Renaissance anatomy specialist followed her gasp immediately, however, with a painstakingly attentive observation on the disposition of the claws in the foot.)

Of course, the picture was not made for us, and not made by people who had much in common with us. We view this monster across a chasm. My friends and colleagues and I saw this image from a post-modern, post-scientific perspective we all share as educated,

---

[1] Desprez, François, *Recueil de la diversité des habits, qui sont de present en usage, tant as pays d'Europe, Asie, Affrique & isles sauuage* (Paris, 1562). The Latin version was published in Venice in 1563; I will be quoting from the bilingual Antwerp edition of 1572.

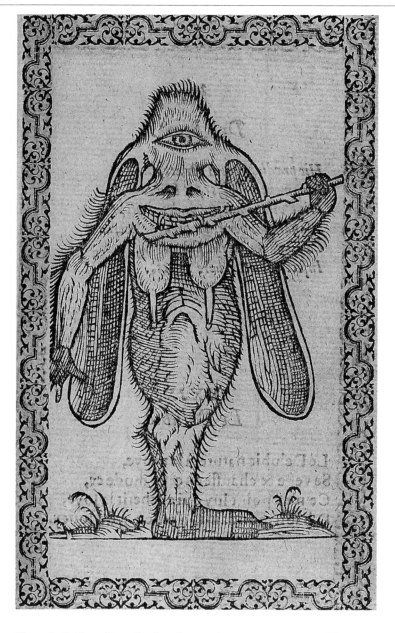

Figure 1. Cyclops, from *Omnium fere gentium, nostraeque aetatis Nationum, Habitus et Effigies*. By permission of the Houghton Library, Harvard University.

middle-class members of the late twentieth century. I saw it, in addition, from the perspective of someone immersed for almost twenty years
in medieval and Renaissance images of monstrous or exotic people and
animals.[2] That I also gasped and was boggled suggests to me that there
may, in fact, be some continuity to be traced between the original
moment of this "Cyclops'" production and reception and the moment
shared by me and my various middle-class friends. A more important
continuity is that between medieval monstrous iconography and its
Renaissance progeny, for although it changed its meanings and grew
new limbs, the core concept was not discarded.[3] But first, the gap.

Something very important does, or at any rate should, separate the
audiences of this picture: namely, the scientization of knowledge in the
intervening four centuries and, particularly, knowledge of the human
species—a knowledge once left to commentaries on Genesis and, of
course, to Poets. But that is not the same knowledge that we now leave
to anthropology and ethnology: anthropology knows that culture is a
variable and that cultures are plural; it also knows (after long knowing
otherwise) that all cultures are human, that we all share the mitochondria
of a single Eve. But more distinguishing than anthropological dogma
are the method and the aims behind it: anthropology is, unlike poetry,
an institution (in the sense that one can imagine a distinction between
amateur and professional), even a bureaucracy. It conducts, imper-
sonally, an organized, multi-party investigation into the forms of human
culture and social structure; it sends out authorized young persons

---

[2] This interest, of course, although not first sparked, was first informed and fed by the
wonders of John Block Friedman's *The Monstrous Races in Medieval Art and Thought*
(Cambridge, Mass.: Harvard University Press, 1981), one of the indispensible books
of the last two decades of work on medieval and Renaissance culture, especially in its
(for us, crucial) relation to the Other, without and within.

[3] Katharine Park and Lorraine Daston's recent book, a monumental cultural history of
Wonder and the Orders of Nature, 1150–1750 (New York: Zone Books, 1998), traces
the changing fates of wonder and the marvelous and monstrous across just this
junction, closing with the rationalization of the early Enlightenment. See esp. chap. 5,
"Monsters: A Case Study," 173–214.

possessed of a highly conventionalized method to gather knowledge of a sort called "data," givens (though they have just as often been *taken*, or bartered for). The institution is located within other institutions, from that of the particular university authorizing the field investigator, to that of the state, to that of the powerful imaginary we like to call (weirdly enough) The West. The individual researcher is lost in this Chinese box of authority and discursivity, and so is the *concept* of the individual person, the singular. What the investigator (who stands for Brandeis, the U.S. State Department, the West) wants to know—must know—is the aggregate, the forms and the *habitus* inherited by populations.

The costume books of the sixteenth century belong with the great atlases, the books by naturalists like Aldrovandi and Topsell of "Four-footed Beasts," the collections of old coins and fossils.[4] They collect and display variations on a theme, and the theme is understood to be an identity—a something that exists in more than one avatar. The something in the book from which this illustration comes is the *gens*, and the avatars are types rather than cultures. Anthropology or even a prototype is more than a century away. La Bruyère's *Caractères*, taking off from the classical work by Theophrastus and the medieval genre of "estates satire," will extend or elaborate verbally the kind of "kinds" we see here, with enormous nuance (and lots of attitude) but still no sense that the exemplum represents one function of a dynamic called a "culture."[5]

---

[4] A number of major works and essay collections on or including the subject of these collections have come out in English in the last ten years: see Krzysztof Pomian, *Collectors and Curiosities: Venice and Paris, 1500–1800* (1978), trans. Elizabeth Wiles-Portier (Cambridge: Polity Press, 1990); Joy Kenseth, ed., *The Age of the Marvelous* [with exhibition catalogue] (Hanover: Hood Museum of Art, Dartmouth College, 1991); Paula Findlen, *Possessing Nature: Museums, Collecting, and Scientific Culture in Early Modern Italy* (Berkeley and Los Angeles: University of California Press, 1994); and Park and Daston, *Wonders*, chaps. 2, 4, and 7.

[5] La Bruyère's popular, often expanded, and much translated *Caractères*, with its translation of Theophrastus (first ed. 1688), offered up a series of recognizable types (such as the Virtuoso) definable more by occupation and (to him) consequent personality than by location, gender, or kinship status, in intensely satirical portraits that sound

Still, looking backwards at this book, we can see that the types are designated mostly by place of habitation; that the subtypes distinguish genders, marital status, certain fundamental occupations or, at any rate, walks of life; that, in short, there is an analytic dimension to this genre of display. And, of course, what it displays is the object *par excellence* of cultural anthropology: the personal ornamentation and "habit" that signifies the wearer's place and function in a social structure.[6]

Most of the costumed individuals in the collection bear the label of one or another European or at least "Old World" political location. French speakers are divided into dozens of cities or provinces and types—virgin of Lyons, matron of Bruges, burgher, soldier, etc. The outer edges of the "world" as sketched in this cosmic register are very little subdivided: Brazilians (with Brazil understood as essentially a continent) come in two types, male and female. The gendered "homo" and "mulier sylvestris" have no location (other than the generic forest, *sylva*); the Monk Fish and the Bishop Fish have no location either (they belong, according to Gisbertus Germannus, to a single historical moment, in which they were presented to the King of Poland, in 1531[7]) and but

---

somewhat familiar to any reader of Chaucer's (gentler) *Canterbury Tales* or his less nuanced predecessors in the genre of "estates satire" (e.g., John Gower in his *Vox Clamantis* and *Mirour de l'omme*).

[6] Costume was a focus in many media, including map borders in atlases, ballet scenes in *opéra comédie*, and heated pamphlet discussions of fashion (with its foreign, even exotic, borrowings). See my *Wonder and Science: Representing Worlds in Early Modern Europe* (Ithaca: Cornell University Press, 1999), chap. 7, "Anthropometamorphosis," from which a few sentences of this article have been taken (along with part of a footnote from chap. 8), with the permission of Cornell University Press.

[7] Guillaume Du Bartas refers to the incident and another like it in his *Sepmaines* when listing among sea creatures parallel to land creatures "the Mytred Bishop, and the Cowled Fryer: / Whereof, examples (but a few years since) / Were shown the *Norway's*, and *Polonian* Prince" (Joshua Sylvester's translation, 1592–1609). For quotation and illustrations see T. H. White's annotated translation of a twelfth-century manuscript of the *Physiologus, The Bestiary: A Book of Beasts* (New York: G. P. Putnam's Sons, 1954), 251–53. See also Rondeletius (Guillaume Rondelet), *Libri de piscibus marinis* (Lyons, 1554).

a single gender; the Cyclops, at the outer edge of the edge, has neither location nor gender (if gender is understood as a structure of polarities). Indeed he/she/it is so singular as to have, in a sense, no identity at all: the breasts contradict the canonical male gender of the Cyclops and the Wild Man (whose branch the being wields in this deflationary case as toothpick), and there are no genitals of any kind. He/she/it is anthropology's impossible. And if clothes make the man, or at least the object of anthropology, then many of these latter characters are outside the scope of the as-yet-nonexistent science, because they are naked. Not "naked" like the "savages" found by European explorers, all of whom sported extensive adornment, usually described in some detail. But *buck* naked.[8]

In fact, these wilder specimens help to fill out a spectrum of nakedness as well as (but not isomorphic with) one of ethnicity or race. The Brazilians are pushing the European norm—they are decorated but not also hidden—as opposed to the widows, several European specimens of whom are depicted, so swathed in mourning clothes that there is no body or even real body outline to be seen (fig. 2). (The amazing implication of the mourner depicted here is that the clothes alone—there is nothing else to see—define the image's gender, as though gender were a simple and direct function of costume.) The Wild Man and Wild Woman are naked in the most ordinary sense of the word, though the Wild Woman uses her long thick hair like a mantle, and at first it is not easy to tell the difference (fig. 3). The Bishop and Monk Fish are, of course, naked in the sense that, as fish, they do not wear materials instrumentally for protection or symbolically for ornament, identification, and sexual hiding. But their own skins and odd body shapes

---

[8] Although going by usage in early modern travel reports and cosmographies one might imagine that *naked* means something besides unclothed, OED citations of *naked* go back to the year 850 and, except with reference to unsheathed swords or the condition of being unarmed, mean 'without clothing' in an absolute sense. Even metaphorical usages (for the most part limited to the sixteenth and seventeenth centuries) signify divestiture, serious lack, rather than simply "less" than I have (on).

Figure 2. Woman from Brabant, in mourning, from *Omnium fere gentium*. By permission of the Houghton Library, Harvard University.

Figure 3. Wild Woman, from *Omnium fere gentium*. By permission of the
Houghton Library, Harvard University.

contribute to an appearance indistinguishable from clothing: if clothing is a *visual* effect, then these beings are clothed (fig. 4). But unlike the naked Wild Man and Wild Woman they are not human, though they are represented as cultural—or, as "mimmix," they *represent* culture. (In contrast, the *Simia erecta*, similarly and indeed definitively not human, is wearing real clothes—see fig. 5).

The Cyclops is not wearing any foreign materials either, but he/she/it is so visually complex and morphologically disunified that the effect has something in common with the distracting *trompe l'oeil* of the Bishop Fish. It turns out that "nakedness" requires for its full effect not only a body unclothed but also a body with which one can identify one's own. Where the eye begins to sense parallels, it has only to wander a micron and find itself faced with something initially unrecognizable as body part, never mind as human body part. These stumbles on the visual path have some of the baffle-effect of clothing. And the very high readability of the monstrous iconography in the composite, given the largely decorative functions of monstrous images since the High Middle Ages, suggests in addition a kind of ornamental quality to the readable body parts themselves, though there is nothing for the parts to ornament. In this ornamental dimension the complexly naked Cyclops might be called a monstrous "nude."[9]

Of course, a costume book would have a generic impetus to expand the range of what could be considered clothing or more precisely "habit." This book pursues the matter further than any other I have

---

[9] This is hilarious to contemplate, but why? What is in the word *nude* that keeps it so immune from connotations of comedy or excess? Apparently the nude only can be a representation of Bakhtin's "official body," the whole and mesomorphic figure often imagined now in the form of Leonardo's famous sketch of anatomical proportion, the five-pointed human bounded in a circle. Perhaps it is the difficulty of psychological identification with the figure that blocks the term from seeming appropriate. On visual identifications and the need to expand our horizons beyond the official body see Kaja Silverman, *The Threshold of the Visible* (New York and London: Routledge, 1996), as well as my comments on it in *Wonder and Science*, chap. 6.

Figure 4. Monk-fish, from *Omnium fere gentium*. By permission of the Houghton Library, Harvard University.

Figure 5. Upright ape, from *Omnium fere gentium*. By permission of the Houghton Library, Harvard University.

seen, and the articulation of a many-sided "nakedness" is not only pro-
vocative (as is Montaigne after praising the wisdom of his "Canibales":
"but then, they do not wear breeches") but also theoretically suggestive. Lévi-Strauss will think like this three and one-half centuries later
with his comprehensive *Mythologiques*, differentiating manifestations
of such notions as "cooked" and their local meanings.[10]

Like this, but also not like this. This *summa* of the monstrous (appropriately additive rather than abstract in strategy) may be a joke, and
a joke that in some ways improves in hindsight, but the joke would
have packed a wallop in 1572 that it no longer generally can. The
Cyclops, which is also a Blemmy, a Sciopod, a Panotius, a Giant (huge—
somehow—and hirsute), a Satyr (the leg has a haunch), a bit of a
griffin (or at least the lion's foot of one!), a Wild Man and the "woman
with the sagging breasts" (as she is articulated in Bernadette Bucher's
analysis of de Bry's illustrations for the *Great Voyages*)—this monster
is made up of monsters which are themselves often patchworks—the
griffon has, in the time-honored formula, the body of a lion, the head
and wings of an eagle. The Satyr has the body of a man, the legs of a
goat, and sometimes the ears of an ass.[11] And so on. Though the formu-
lae may have derived pragmatically enough from attempts to describe
unfamiliar animals, they became signs of a liberatory disunity, an aggre-
gateness, theoretically possible and even authorized by God as a kind
of play—what the Renaissance came to call the *lusus naturae*.[12] This

---

[10] The four volumes of Claude Lévi-Strauss's *Mythologiques*, of which the first was *The Raw and the Cooked* (*Le cru et le cuit*).

[11] It is important to note that there were contemporary composite monsters available, offered in the very different spirit (and allegorical intention) of Reformation religious propaganda, especially during heightened periods of struggle and civil war. See Park and Daston, *Wonders*, chap. 5, which includes several illustrations of demonic com-
posites—none, however, allude to the Plinian races of medieval wonder books and *mappa mundi*.

[12] See Paula Findlen's article, "Jokes of Nature, Jokes of Art: The Playfulness of Scientific Discourse in Early Modern Europe," *Renaissance Quarterly* 43, no. 2 (1991),

aggregate of aggregates, this peculiar figure in which there is no normalizable *base*, might seem an extreme case of divine (or rather artistic) play, but its presence in a book of costume that attempts to cover at least sketchily the whole cultural world is a reminder that it still made sense to include the monstrous—if only as the imaginary that marks the outside. And the fact that all the monstrous races are bundled up into one multi-faceted exemplar hints at a developmental moment in the rationalization of what we now think of as ethnology and zoology that requires some further thinking. The sixteenth-century joke includes a very particular repudiation of medieval knowledge, a knowledge characterized by the presence of the monstrous in cosmography and by the plurality of the monstrous races.

Plurality, of course, was coming into its own by the end of the sixteenth century—it was the fact around which, for instance, *Othello* is composed, the fact expressed in cosmography and atlas, conquest and colony, and soon, with the advent of telescopic observation of the heavens, it would be a fact reflected or literalized in the visible plurality of planetary "worlds."[13] But the Cyclops here manifests a collapse of the plural into the singular—the extremely singular. Where the Middle Ages had, according to John Friedman's list, at least forty identifiable monstrous races, this costume book presents essentially one—the presence of the morphologically crazy "Cyclops" renders the Wild Man and Wild Woman saliently human rather than ambiguously monstrous—and in the singularity (in both senses) imposed on the concept "monstrous race" by this representation, the Cyclops is excluded from the structure of reality: banished to the purely festive realm of the comic, of excess and transgression, rather than to the medieval forums, less

---

292–331, for a marvelous and erudite introduction to this phenomenon. Friedman, of course, offers discussion of medieval playfulness in "natural history" in *Monstrous Races*, esp. in chap. 6, "Signs of God's Will."

[13] I have treated this topic at length in *Wonder and Science*, chaps. 4 and 5; see also Steven J. Dick, *Plurality of Worlds: The Origins of the Extraterrestrial Life Debate from Democritus to Kant* (Cambridge: Cambridge University Press, 1982).

constitutively fictional, of allegory and divine fecundity (or the Reformation's dark portentousness). Scientific investigation studies masses and populations; the seventeenth century brought us probability and statistics. The withdrawal at this point of the medieval world's monstrous but credible fecundity and diversity into a single aesthetic moment of sublime dissonance—all anarchic sweetness rolled up into one spiky ball—could almost be seen as a sacrificial offering to the emerging study of nature's *laws*, in which the monstrous becomes, eventually, teratology.

Plurality in the form of the collection had come to acquire a connotation of the analytic—a collection, although not quite a taxonomy, requires the task of sorting, requires categories and, as I have said, the key concept of an identity subject to variation.[14] Therefore the *synthetic* quality of this Cyclopean joke identifies its object as not subject to or associated with the grand tasks of classifying and sorting undertaken in the sixteenth century. It has become poetic, imaginary—in fact, sublime, if the sublime is what finally explodes the perceptual grid of reason. The monster and the monstrous race do not belong to cosmography now, though they may appear there from time to time. They represent the unknown and even the unknowable: a form of mystery the business of analysis and classification cannot properly tolerate. They therefore must be compressed into something obviously a symbol (rather than a mimesis), and laughed off the map.[15]

---

[14] On development of scientific taxonomy see Mary M. Slaughter, *Universal Languages and Scientific Taxonomy in the Seventeenth Century* (Cambridge: Cambridge University Press, 1982); and for an interesting essay on type and variation see Nathaniel Tarn, "The Heraldic Vision," *Alcheringa* 2, no. 2 (1975), 23–41.

[15] Of course, even then there were hardy souls who could see in the monster a wondrous challenge for the principles of sorting and delimiting: French physician Ambroise Paré's *Des monstres et prodiges* (Paris, 1573) gathers his specimens into mainly naturalized categories ("An Example of Monsters Who Are Created by Hereditary Diseases"); and in the nineteenth century Isidore Geoffroy Saint-Hilaire will initiate the modern science of teratology. For a contemporary view of monsters as significantly unclassifiable and mysterious see the non-scholarly but informed and accurate *Special Cases*

The equating of singularity with unknowability may help us to see why all the old monsters are summed up under the aegis of the Cyclops: the monster has the eye of a cyclops, it is true (and the iconographic club—though the club belongs as well to Giant and Wild Man), but he also has the ears of a Panotius, the face of a Blemmy, the single leg of a Sciopod, and so on. What the name does is to focus us on that eye. The almost completely redundant and tautological verses that accompany the illustrations tend to focus us on eyes as well, and on vision. They render the experience we are having as we read pretty much the topic of the verbal text, eerily dramatizing not the objects of the engraver's art but the audience: us. The Wild Woman is said to be "Au natural vous . . . icy depeinte, / Comme voyez qu'il appert a vostre oeil." The Latin text on the Cyclops begins: "Huc vertas oculos amice Lector, / Si te vera iuvat videre monstra." (The French says: "On dit encor que ce lignage dure / Avec un oeil selon ceste figure.") In a culture which believed that pregnant women could deform their embryos by looking at pictures of monsters, the concept of the gaze of the image itself had a much more widespread and vivid life than it does among the select group of late twentieth-century post-Lacanians. The Cyclopian eye, staring out at us from atop a figure so confused in its anatomical disposition that we can hardly experience it as "naked," is nonetheless the Eye, writ large, that we ourselves have been reduced to in the previous forty-three pages and, particularly, by the page we are on. A singular eye—the first-person singular you might say.

Quite apart from any modern sense we might have of the counterfactuality of this Cyclops as a type of being (with a "lineage"), we can recognize his/her/its *counter-scientificity*. This page offers an experience of the sublime or sensational, in the form of a body image both like (the large, staring, individual eye) and profoundly unlike the receiver of the text's information. It provokes an experience, rather than

---

of Rosamund Purcell, with its scores of meticulous reproductions and miraculous photographs (San Francisco: Chronicle Books, 1998).

augmenting our knowledge. Its appeal is subjective, it speaks as something pictorially unique to the eye and heart muscle of each individual, embodied viewer. Its distancing quotation of medieval knowledge allows us to regard it for a moment in the allegorical light of medieval monster-discourse.[16] Here, in the midst of a book that makes clear ahead of time the link between anthropology and fashion magazines, the objectification of the Other, we are confronted by the gaze returned from an image absolutely created by the historical European gaze. As the composite image declares a sophisticated dismissal of the old monstrous races here hyperbolized, declares their fictionality, we are simultaneously reproached and enticed by its singularity, which resembles nothing so much as our own. Cultural historians recently have been fond of demonstrating ways in which the Renaissance "invented" the "subject" we have been trying yet more recently to banish.[17] This Cyclops looks like the moment of that subject's birth—the creature that looks back, that is all eyes, that is the only one of its kind, is an amalgam, it turns out, of every medieval model of the Other. And in the moment of subsuming them, it banishes them from reality. This is an ironic picture. It makes fun of the *nouveau sujet*, mocking him with a family

---

[16] For medieval natural and unnatural history, at least as it is found in bestiaries, see (in addition to Friedman, esp. 122–25, where he discusses allegorical moralizing) Wilma George and Brunsdon Yapp, *The Naming of the Beasts: Natural History in the Medieval Bestiary* (London: Duckworth, 1991).

[17] Classic accounts from the 1980s of the emerging modern subject include Joel Fineman's *Shakespeare's Perjur'd Eye: The Invention of Poetic Subjectivity in the Sonnets* (Berkeley and Los Angeles: University of California Press, 1986); Francis Barker's *The Tremulous Private Body: Essays on Subjection* (London: Methuen, 1984); and Stephen Greenblatt's review essay, "Psychoanalysis and Renaissance Culture," in *Literary Theory/Renaissance Texts*, ed. Patricia Parker and David Quint (Baltimore: Johns Hopkins University Press, 1986), 210–24, on Natalie Zemon Davis's *Return of Martin Guerre* (Cambridge, Mass.: Harvard University Press, 1983), which fleshes out a legal case that helped to define the legal notion of identity as one's "own" (though the implications of Davis's book seem to me less clearly to point in the direction of the bourgeois subject's secure wholeness, rather to the fascinating and effortful fictionality of the construction).

portrait, a lineage ("qui encore dure") that belongs neither to the Family of Man nor to the science of the Family of Man. Would that the portrait, with its wit and reflexivity, its sophisticated reading of the projective monstrous in the context of cultural variation, had belonged to more of the founding texts of ethnology.

CONTRIBUTORS

Greta Austin is Assistant Professor of Religion at Bucknell University. She received her Ph.D. from Columbia University in 2000. Her academic research concerns the development of Latin canon law and legal reasoning in the eleventh century.

Paul Battles is Assistant Professor of English at Hanover College. He received his Ph.D. from the University of Illinois at Urbana-Champaign in 1998. His essays on Old and Middle English have appeared in *Anglo-Saxon England*, *Philological Quarterly*, and *Chaucer Review*.

Martin Camargo is Professor and Chair of English at the University of Missouri-Columbia. He has published several books and a number of articles dealing with medieval English literature and medieval rhetoric. His interest in the marvelous can be traced to the courses he took with John Block Friedman during the 1970s, while a doctoral candidate at the University of Illinois. The essay contributed to the present volume grew out of his course "Medieval Encounters with the Other," which he developed in 1994 and continues to teach regularly.

Mary Baine Campbell is Professor of English and American Literature at Brandeis University, where she teaches medieval and early modern literature, as well as poetry and creative writing. Her long-term interest in monsters and monsterization is visible in both her critical books, *The Witness and the Other World: Exotic European Travel*

303

Writing, 400–1600 (1988) and *Wonder and Science: Representing Worlds in Early Modern Europe* (1999), as well as her first book of poems, *The World, the Flesh, and Angels* (1989). John Block Friedman was important not only as a source and inspiration but also as a generous and careful reader of the medieval chapters of *The Witness and the Other World.*

Kristen M. Figg is Professor of English at Kent State University Salem, where she teaches early British literature, composition, and language studies. Her publications on Froissart include articles in *French Studies* and *Allegorica*, as well as two books, *The Short Lyric Poems of Jean Froissart: Fixed Forms and the Expression of the Courtly Ideal* (1994) and *Jean Froissart: An Anthology of Narrative and Lyric Poetry* (2001). With her husband, John Block Friedman, she is co-editor of *Trade, Travel, and Exploration in the Middle Ages: An Encyclopedia* (2000) and *The Princess with the Golden Hair: Letters of Elizabeth Waugh to Edmund Wilson, 1933–1942* (2000).

Paul Freedman is Professor of History at Yale University, where he has taught since 1997. He is the author of *The Diocese of Vic* (1993), *The Origins of Peasant Servitude in Medieval Catalonia* (1991), and *Images of the Medieval Peasant* (1999). He is currently pursuing a project concerning medieval spices, inspired by John Friedman's many works on medieval ideas and representations of the exotic.

Thomas N. Hall is Associate Professor in the Department of English at the University of Illinois at Chicago. He received his Ph.D. in 1990 from the University of Illinois at Urbana-Champaign, where he studied Middle English poetry and arcana under John Block Friedman. His articles on Old English poetry, medieval sermons and apocryphal literature have appeared in *Anglo-Saxon England, Mediaeval Studies, Medium Ævum, Notes & Queries, Review of English Studies, Scriptorium*, and *Traditio.*

Malcolm Jones is a Lecturer in Folklore and Folklife Studies in the Department of English Language and Linguistics of the University of Sheffield. His principal interests are in the non-religious iconography of the late medieval and early modern eras. His most recent endeavor, *The Other Middle Ages: A Fresh Look at Late Medieval Visual Culture*, will be published by Sutton Publishing in 2002. John Block Friedman impressed him not only with his *Monstrous Races* but also through correspondence, followed by meetings in person. Jones has long been grateful for the generosity with which Friedman dispenses his encyclopedic knowledge.

Timothy S. Jones is Assistant Professor of English at Augustana College, Sioux Falls. John Block Friedman directed his dissertation at the University of Illinois, where he earned his Ph.D. in 1994. Jones has published essays on medieval outlaws, romance, and travel literature. He currently is writing a book on medieval outlaw narratives.

Joyce Tally Lionarons is Professor of English at Ursinus College. She received her Ph.D. in 1983 from the University of Denver and is the author of *The Medieval Dragon: The Nature of the Beast in Germanic Literature* (1998) as well as articles on Old English, Old Norse, and Middle High German literature. She currently is working on a critical book on Wulfstan of York.

Andrea Rossi-Reder is currently Visiting Professor of English at Connecticut College. She has written on Chaucer's Franklin's Tale and recently published an article on the Old English *Physiologus* in the journal *Neophilologus*. She is writing a book on female martyrdom and nationhood.

Norman R. Smith is Director of Training Delivery for Automatic Data Processing. Smith earned his doctorate in Comparative Literature at the University of Illinois (1978), under John Block Friedman's direction.

Smith's publications also reflect Friedman's influence: "Portent Lore and Medieval Popular Culture," in *The Journal of Popular Culture,* and "My Ithaca Destiny," in *The Double Gun Journal.*

David Sprunger is Associate Professor of English and Discourse at Concordia College, Moorhead, Minn. He earned his Ph.D. in 1992 from the University of Illinois, where John Block Friedman directed his dissertation on "Madness in Medieval Art and Romance." Subsequent research and publications reveal his continued interest in the marvelous and the arcane. He currently is conducting a study of Chaucerian apocrypha.

Michael W. Twomey is Professor of English and chair of the English Department at Ithaca College. He was a visiting professor, courtesy of a Fulbright grant, at the University of Dresden in 1996–97. His acquaintance with John Block Friedman dates to his collaboration in R. E. Kaske's *Medieval Christian Literary Interpretation* (1988), when he sought John's bibliographical advice about Thomas of Cantimpré. The present essay commemorates their first conversation, at the Brill booth in Kalamazoo. Twomey writes chiefly about medieval encyclopedias, the *Revelations* of Pseudo-Methodius, and the *Gawain*-poet.